IMAGES
of America

BARABOO

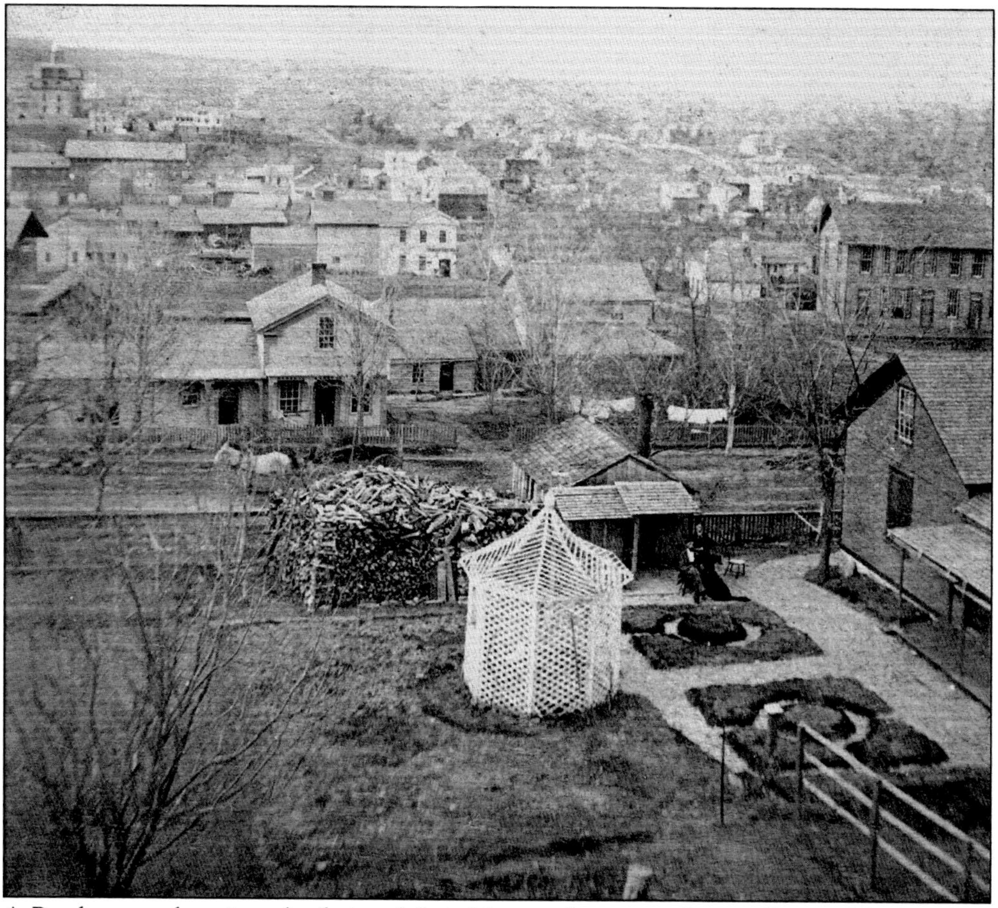

A Baraboo couple enjoys the fruits of their labor as they sit in their well-tamed backyard on Maple Street, above. They know the coming winter of 1874–75 will be more pleasantly spent with a cozy fire. In the distance to the north, Baraboo fills the valley and will double in size by 1880 now that the railroad has arrived. (Baraboo National Bank Collection.)

(*cover photo*) A view of Third Avenue, looking east, about 1918 shows one of Baraboo's earliest buildings still with wood siding and a gable front. It was built by John Taylor about 1850 on the south side of the square, and is still standing today.

IMAGES
of America

BARABOO

Sauk County Historical Society

ARCADIA
PUBLISHING

ISBN 978-0-7385-3299-8

Published by Arcadia Publishing
Charleston, South Carolina

Printed in the United States of America.

Library of Congress Catalog Card Number: 2004108746

For all general information contact Arcadia Publishing at:
Telephone 843-853-2070
Fax 843-853-0044
E-mail sales@arcadiapublishing.com
For customer service and orders:
Toll-Free 1-888-313-2665

Visit us on the Internet at www.arcadiapublishing.com

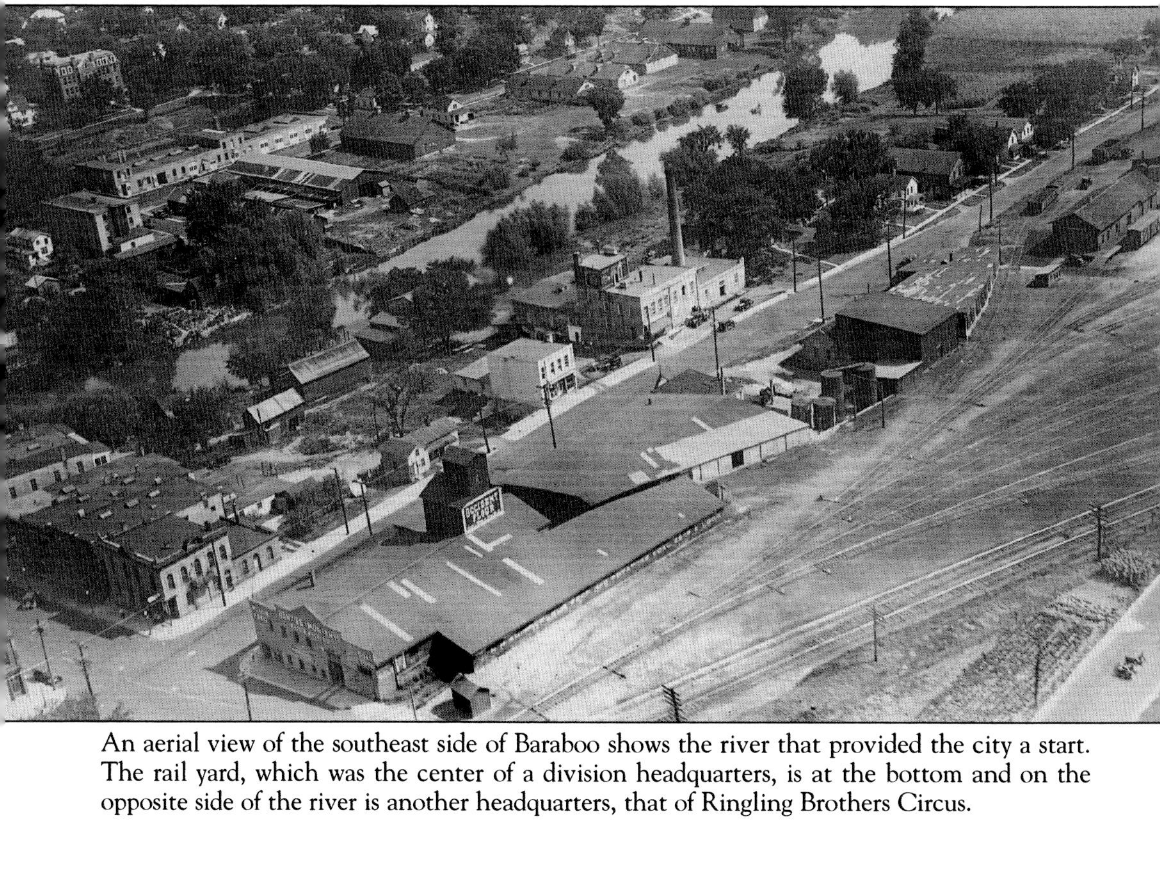

An aerial view of the southeast side of Baraboo shows the river that provided the city a start. The rail yard, which was the center of a division headquarters, is at the bottom and on the opposite side of the river is another headquarters, that of Ringling Brothers Circus.

Contents

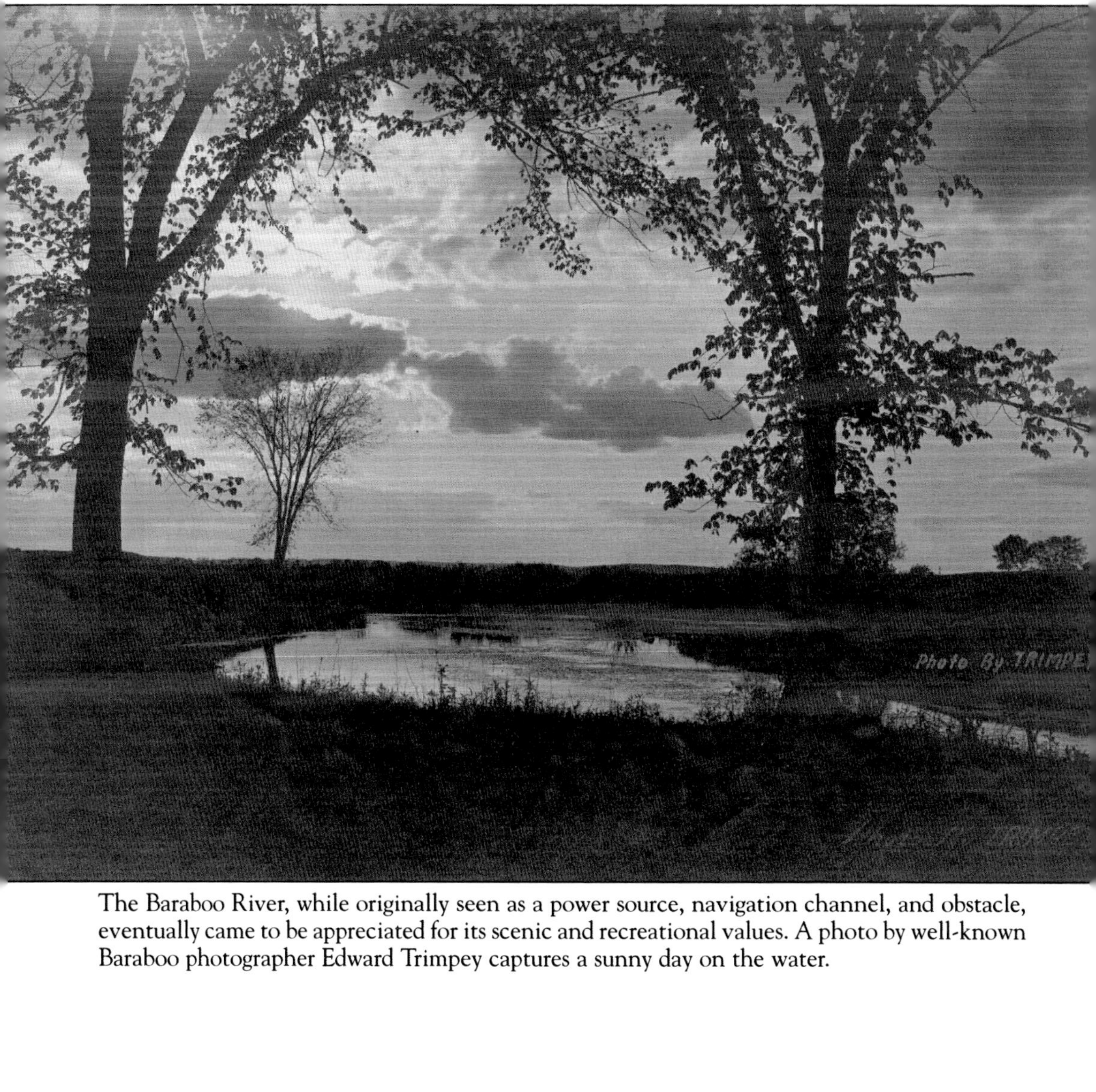

The Baraboo River, while originally seen as a power source, navigation channel, and obstacle, eventually came to be appreciated for its scenic and recreational values. A photo by well-known Baraboo photographer Edward Trimpey captures a sunny day on the water.

INTRODUCTION

One can always tell if someone is not acquainted with Baraboo when they try unsuccessfully to pronounce its name. Although the ending is not confusing, the first three letters can bring pause to the first-time enunciator. When it is pronounced correctly (BEAR-a-boo) it is unforgettable. The origin of the name has not remained so clear and has been the subject of many inquiries and numerous interpretations. What is clear, is that the river that formed the basis for the formation of the community was named long before the settlement. For over a thousand years, man has left his mark here. Early mound builders created earth works and effigy mounds in the shapes of animals near the river, and later Native Americans were drawn to these same places. To early white settlers the rapids meant that the river was dropping in elevation and could therefore be harnessed to provide water power. When settlement officially opened up in 1837, it was only a few years before permanent homes and somewhat permanent dams began to be built.

The community slowly attracted newcomers, mainly those making improvements on the river, until 1847 when two villages were platted and the county seat was located at one of them. A community quickly sprang up with businesses, hotels, homes, schools, and churches. An initial boom was fueled by the mills and industries that were created along the river and the businesses that developed to support the community. By the Civil War, the population had grown, but the economy was generally hampered by the lack of a railroad connection to larger markets. This was finally remedied in 1871 when the railroad reached the community, no small task given its location amidst hard quartzite bluffs. The effects of the railroad were of such magnitude and such lasting consequence that its arrival can be seen as a watershed moment in Baraboo's history. Without it, businesses would have stagnated and the city's growth would have remained lackluster. Nearby, Devil's Lake would also not have become as popular without the railroad. Without broad exposure to many of the state's residents it may never have become a state park. Baraboo's greatest claim-to-fame may also have never come about.

When the Ringling Brothers started their circus in 1884 they did not rely on the use of the railroad for transport, but it is doubtful their father would have moved back to Baraboo in 1875 if the railroad had not brought the prospect of greater growth. The Ringlings also may not have stayed as long as they did if the railroad had not been available so they could switch to a rail show in 1890. Their effect on the city lasted until 1918, when they moved their winter quarters away. Their departure roughly marks the end of the history which this volume attempts to cover.

While by no means exhaustive, this work hopes to partially fill a void in the published history of Baraboo, which has never had a stand alone work of any great size or scope. While much has been recorded about Baraboo's history, to be sure, it remains scattered in county histories, individual biographies, newspaper articles, and separate files. This volume is dependent on the pictures available and therefore does not cover every aspect of Baraboo's history. It is hoped that this volume will encourage more people to share their old pictures so that more of Baraboo's past may be seen as well as known. Some of Baraboo's most famous landmarks and greatest moments remain only in the imagination. Baraboo's octagon house, Capener's opera house, the visit of Mary Todd Lincoln, and the first Ringling Brothers Circus performance all remain to be seen along with many others.

Baraboo's history is as unique as its name, a fact that was not lost on even the early settlers. The Sauk County Historical Society was founded in Baraboo in 1905, only 65 years after the county was founded. Its first president and co-founder, Harry Ellsworth Cole, wrote the longest history of the county, published in 1918. His work was in no small way dependent on the work of others before him, including an 1880 history of the county and especially the works of William H. Canfield, early pioneer and historian. Canfield saw the necessity of recording history almost before it really was history. The history in this volume is dependent on all of these early writers and more from today including Joe Ward, Bob Dewel, and Mark Carlson. It is also dependent on the numerous photographers, most unknown, who captured moments in time to help us today to connect with the past. Special thanks goes to those who have shared their collections with the society and those who contributed specifically to this book. A word of praise also goes to Bill Schuette, who in recent years has digitized more than 10,000 photos in the society's collection and actively seeks out more hidden away in private collections. He has been instrumental in putting this book together and deserves much credit.

This book is dedicated to the people of Baraboo, past, present, and future. Those in the present and those in the future will hopefully use this volume as a way to remember where they have come from. Baraboo has changed much since its first settlers arrived along the river. Today, however, with the removal of the last dam in 2001, the river looks more like it did in 1839 than it has for the past 160 years. Now it is easier to imagine what Abe Wood, Eben and Rosaline Peck, and others experienced when they arrived here. The pictures in this book will hopefully help people gain a better understanding of how the community started and why it prospered.

–Paul Wolter, President
Sauk County Historical Society

The Board of Directors and members of the Sauk County Historical Society would like to acknowledge the efforts of Society President, Paul Wolter, without whose dedication this project may not have come to fruition. His expert knowledge of architecture and his acute interest in the historic structures of Baraboo have been a great asset during the research and production of this publication.

One

RIVER AND RAPIDS

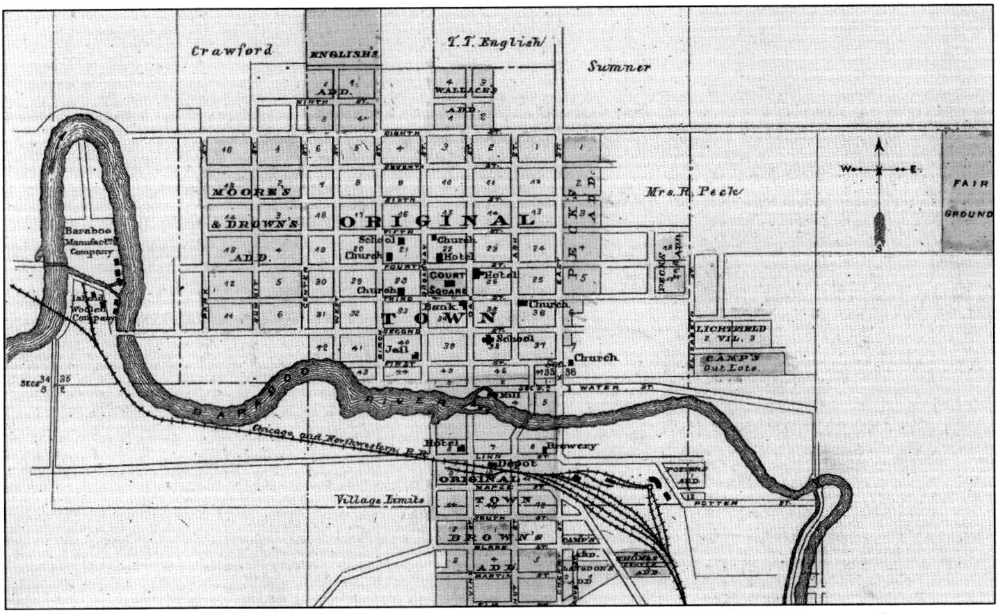

Long before white settlement, the area now known as Baraboo was also a favorite gathering spot for native peoples. Ancient mound builders constructed a variety of earthworks along the river, particularly near the two oxbow-shaped bends. These areas were the gathering spots for later Native Americans like the Ho-Chunk. Eventually, this is where white settlers came as well, although drawn for a different reason. The Baraboo River drops more than 40 feet in the distance of two and half miles as it winds its way through the area, providing the incentive of water power to those who could harness it. The name of the river still remains something of a mystery and much has been written on it, but a strong case may be made for the corruption of a similar French surname, Baribault, belonging to an early trader whose camp was at the mouth of the estuary. In 1839, the first dam was built at the upper "oxbow" bend and four more locations would follow, giving rise to factories that would produce everything from lumber to woolen goods. The river supplied an endless supply of power, but also exacted its toll when spring floods would wash away dams. The river was also an obstacle to be crossed, creating the need for bridges. Eventually, the river came to be seen as a thing of beauty as parks were built along its banks and bridges and dams were made more aesthetically pleasing as time went on.

Two villages were eventually platted along the river, above. The one to the north was originally called Adams and was platted around a public square. The one largely to the south of the river was called Baraboo. The upper "oxbow" bend in the river is seen at the left and the smaller, lower "oxbow" on the right. Three of the five dams in the area are also shown on the map from about 1872.

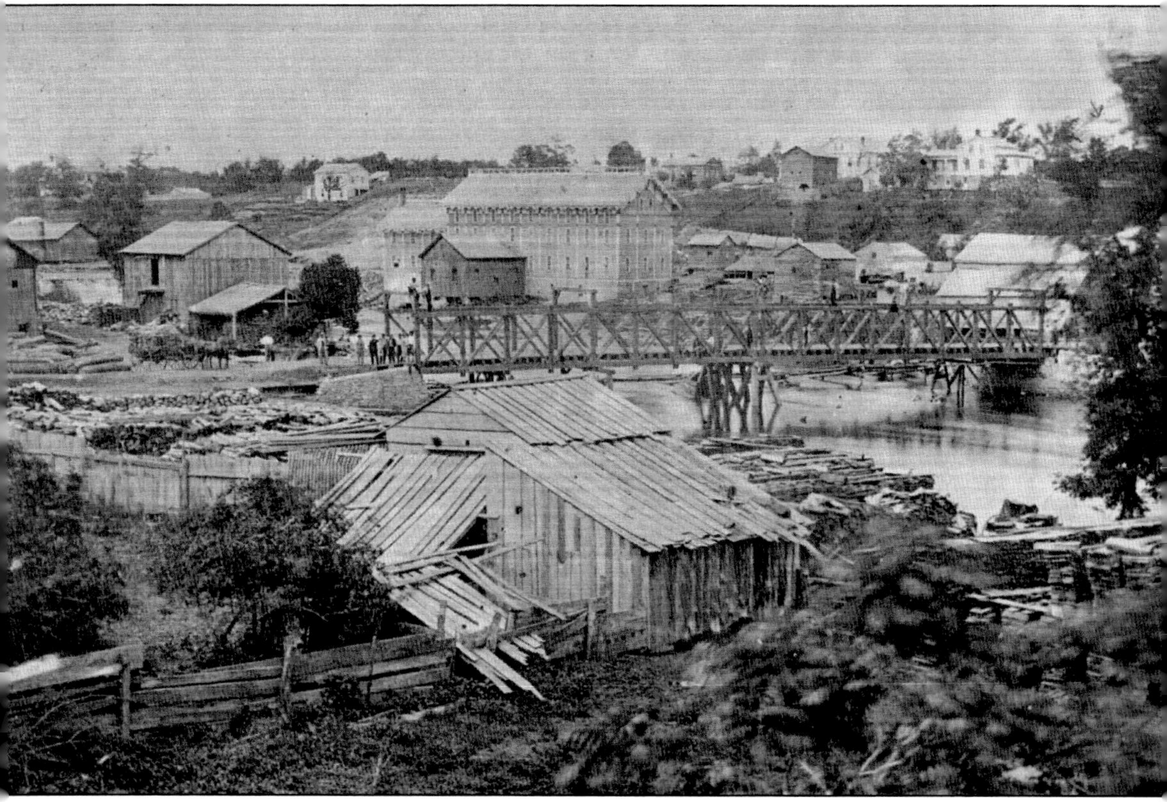

This is one of the earliest known photographs of Baraboo. Taken in 1866, it shows a view of the area around the Ash-Walnut Street bridge looking northwest. In the foreground is a lumber storage yard probably for the Pratt Sawmill, located on the south side of the Oak Street dam shown at the extreme left. The largest building in the center of the picture is the three-story Bassett Flour Mill built in 1855–57. The houses at the top of hill are on First Street and the area below was known as "under the hill." A spring flood in 1866 sent huge chunks of ice, some two feet thick, down the river, taking out all of the area bridges except one. A temporary foot bridge was quickly erected and can be seen below the new bridge, which was completed in June 1866. The foot bridge was not for the faint hearted and more than one person fell in after getting dizzy looking at the rushing water below.

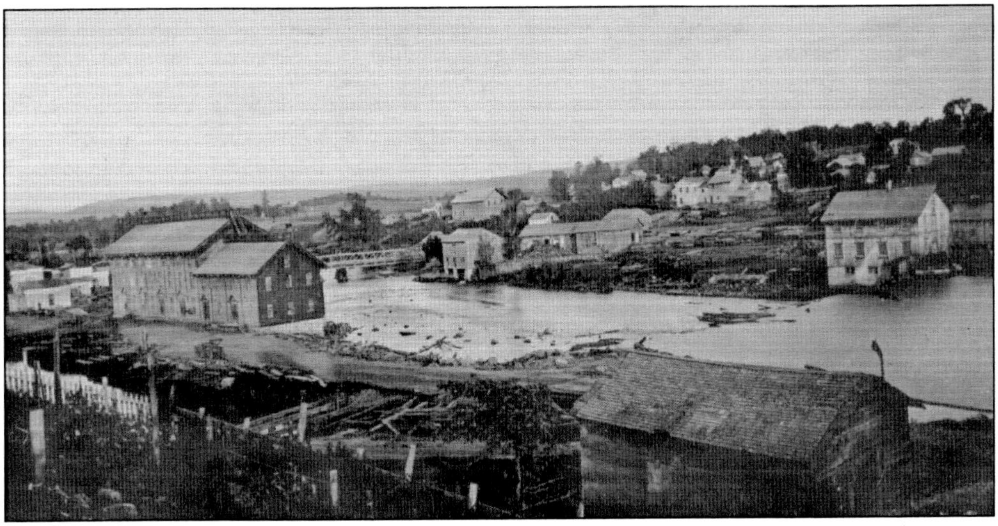

This view shows the same area as the previous photo, but looking the opposite direction, towards the southeast from the corner of First and Oak. The Bassett Mill is at the left and on the far right is the foundry of Gen. Starks. The area shown is largely the plat that George Brown had surveyed in April of 1847 and named Baraboo. In the background, above the Ash–Walnut Street bridge, is the Potter hops field.

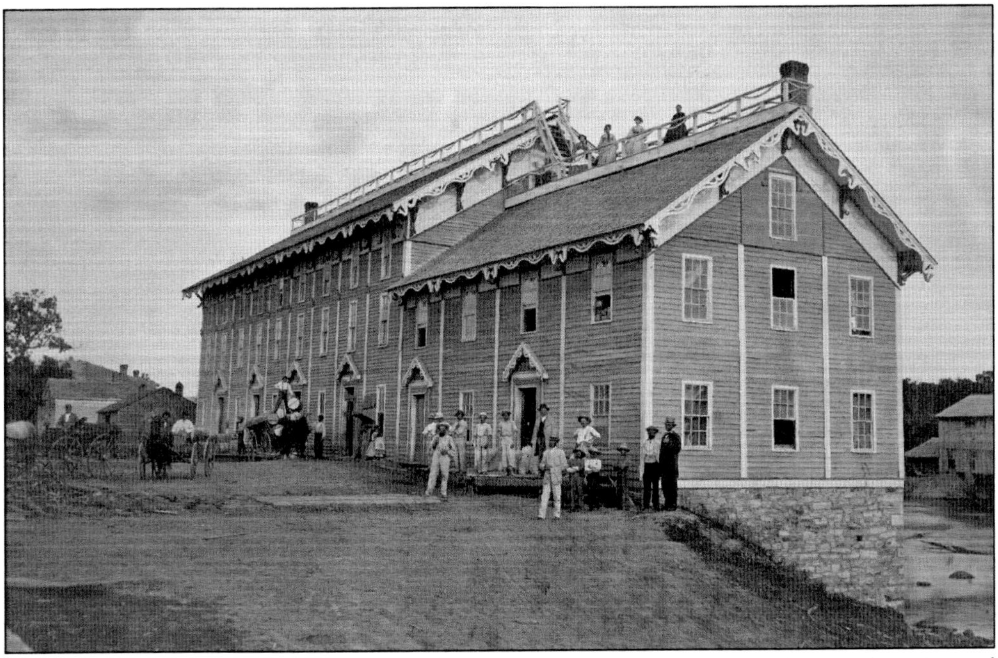

The Bassett Mill was the most impressive looking mill building ever erected in Baraboo. Started in 1855, it was twice enlarged and eventually contained six runs of stone or six grinding wheels. By 1867, the mill was producing up to 25,000 barrels of flour a year. The operation was run successfully for decades under various owners. The building burned down in a spectacular blaze at 1 a.m. on July 5, 1902, possibly caused by the fireworks launched nearby earlier that evening. Firemen could not save the structure and worked to put out fires on nearby houses caused by flying embers. Scorched papers from the mill were later found three miles away.

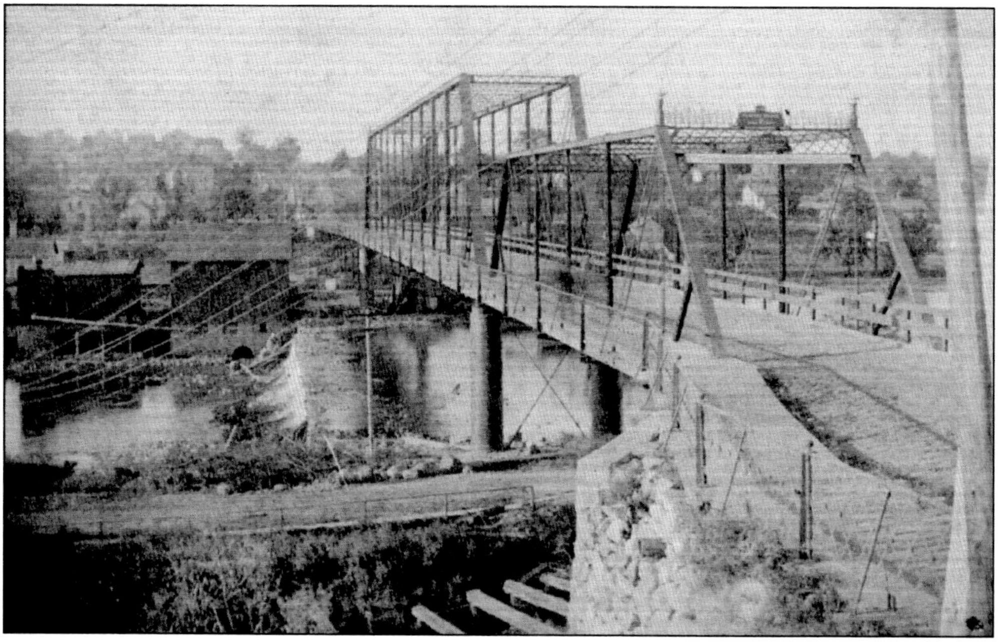

Baraboo's most spectacular bridge was built in 1890 and was appropriately called the High Bridge. It spanned the river 26 feet above the Oak Street Dam and connected the square and the depot area at the same level. It consisted of two spans, one 234 feet long and the other 120 feet. It served well for nearly 30 years and was dismantled in 1929 when the Broadway Bridge was being built.

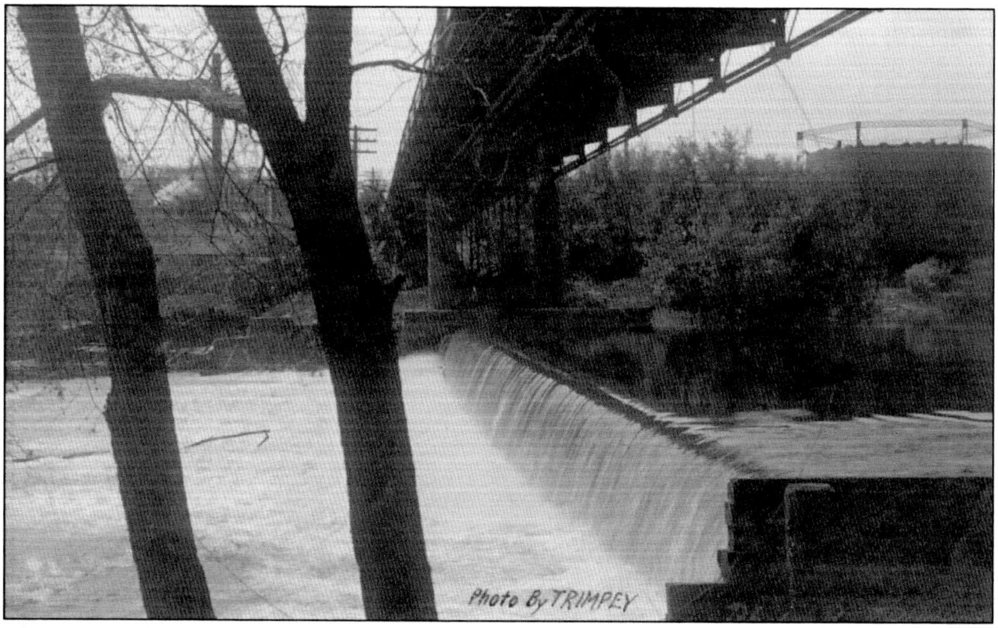

The High Bridge was built directly over the Oak Street Dam. The first dam here was built in 1844 by George and William Brown. While excavating to build a sawmill on the south side of the dam, a mammoth skeleton was found. It turned to dust upon excavation. The round storage tank to the right belonged to the Baraboo Gas Company and was built between 1904 and 1913.

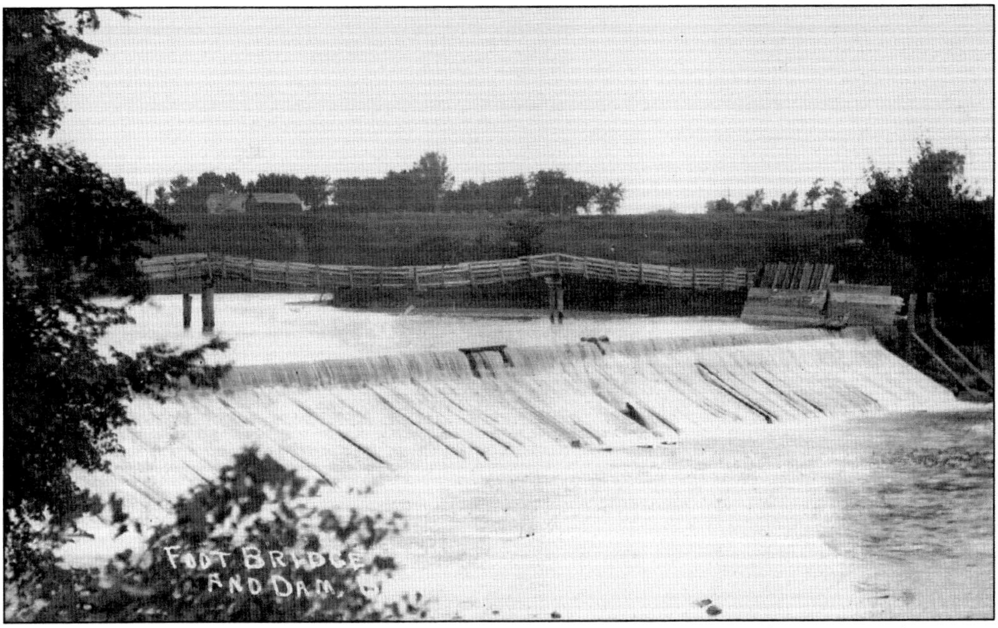

Foot bridges were built at various times to facilitate traffic to key industries. At the upper oxbow, a footbridge was built above the Island Woolen Mill Dam in 1892 to connect Lyons (today West Baraboo) with the mill. It was eventually washed away by high water on the day before Thanksgiving 1908, shortly after several people had crossed it. (Siekert Collection.)

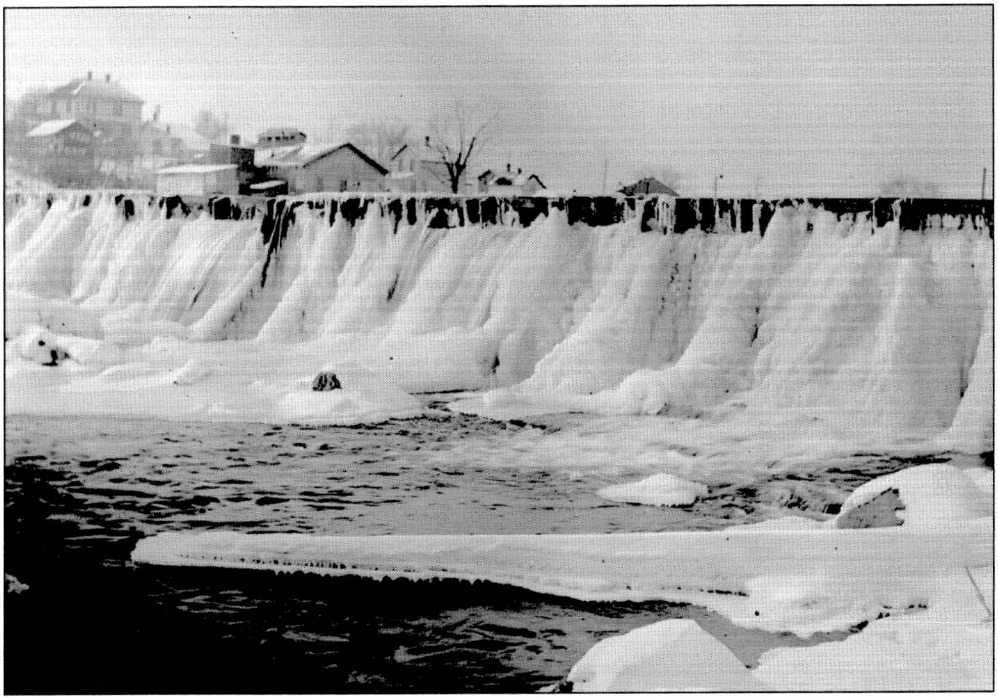

Despite the best efforts of the inhabitants of Baraboo, the dams were always at the mercy of the river. After the spring thaw, large volumes of water and ice often washed away portions of the dams. Here, the Oak Street Dam creates an interesting ice sculpture during the winter.

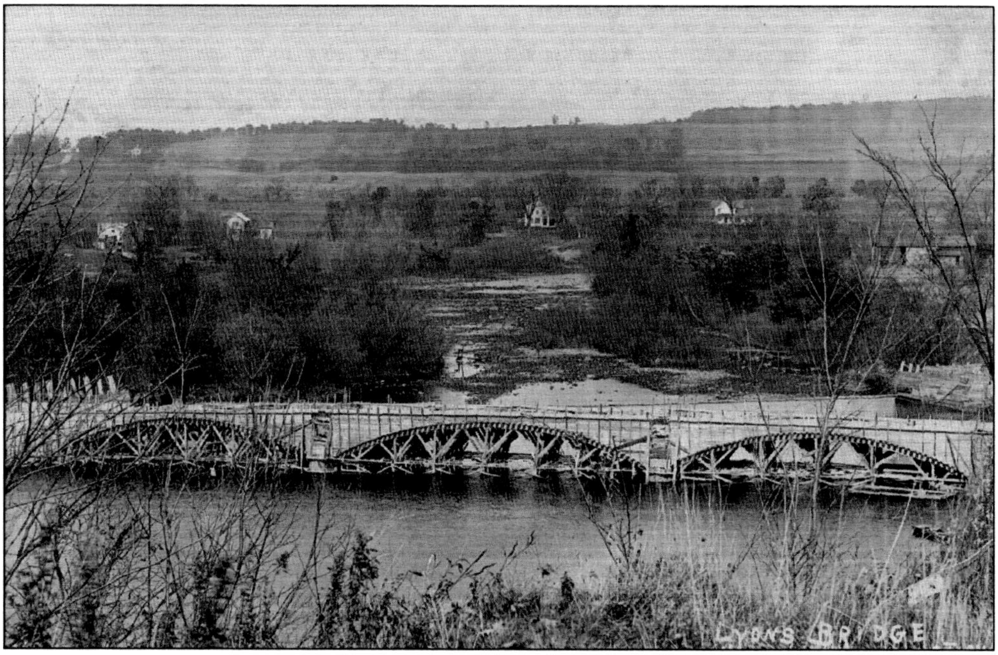
A view of the upper oxbow looking north shows the new concrete bridge between Baraboo and Lyons (today West Baraboo) being constructed in 1909. There had been no bridge here since the first one washed away in the 1860s. People were forced to use the earlier footbridge or cross on the railroad bridge. The Island Woolen Mill Dam had all but shut off the flow of the river around the oxbow. The house in the center of the photo still stands behind the Culver's restaurant on Linn Street. (Siekert Collection.)

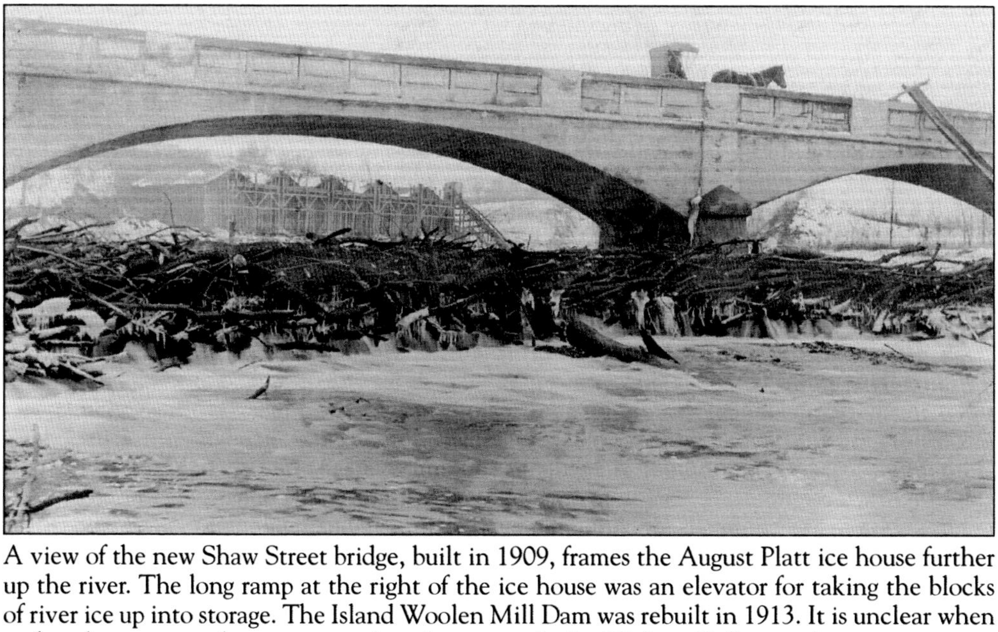
A view of the new Shaw Street bridge, built in 1909, frames the August Platt ice house further up the river. The long ramp at the right of the ice house was an elevator for taking the blocks of river ice up into storage. The Island Woolen Mill Dam was rebuilt in 1913. It is unclear when or for what purpose the temporary dam shown was built. (Siekert Collection.)

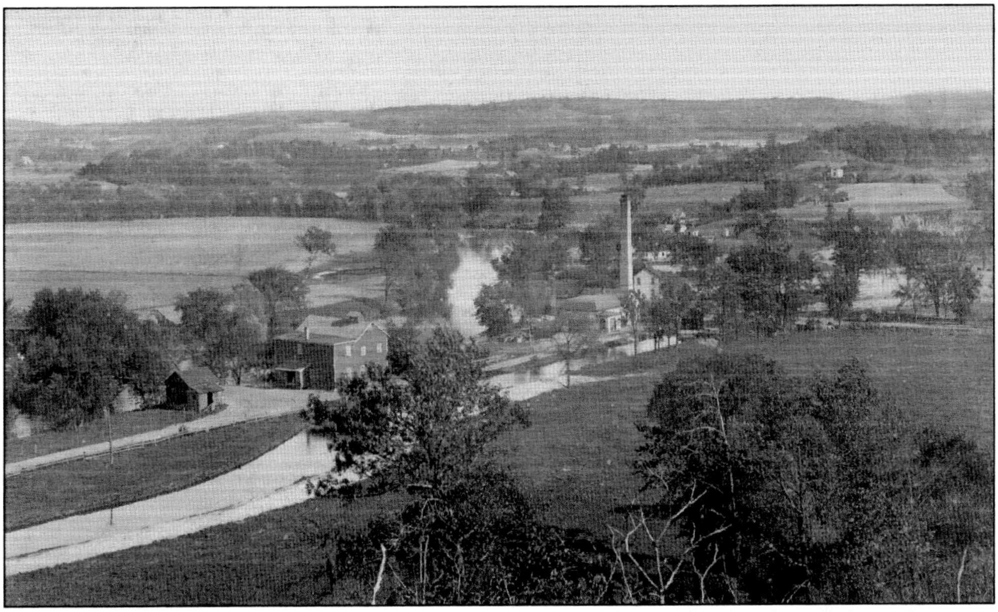

The Manchester, or Lower Water Power, was among the first to be developed along the river, taking advantage of the lower oxbow. The raceway where the water was diverted to enter the mills was the longest along the river, running about 2,000 feet. A saw mill, grist mill, and woolen mill were in use at this spot at various times starting in 1848. The Baraboo Water Works was developed in this area in the mid-1880s as a private company and was taken over by the city in 1903. (Krueger Collection.)

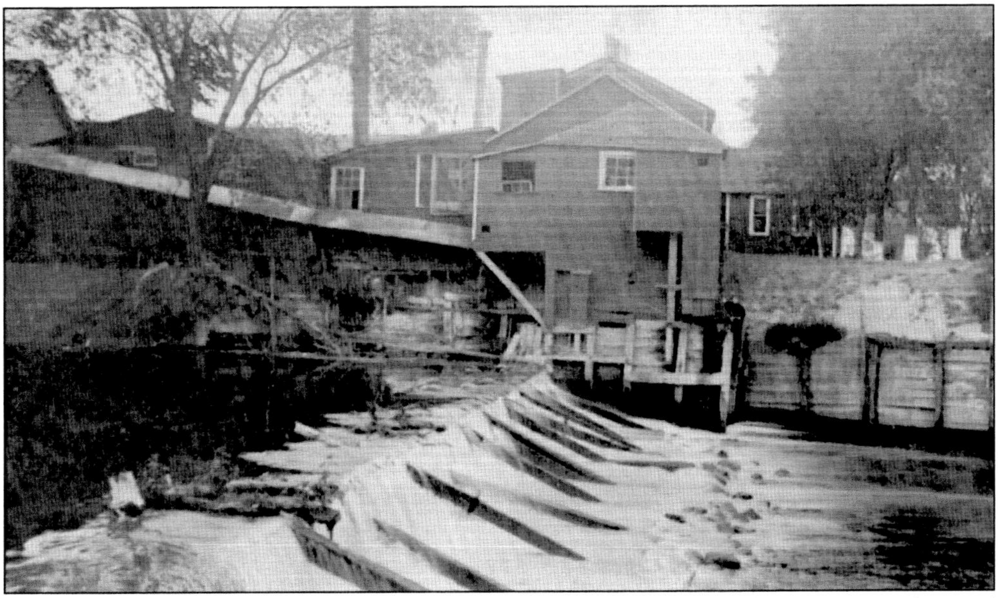

The Linen Mill, or Glenville Dam, was the last to be developed along the river at Baraboo and was the furthest downstream. It was originally a plank dam built in 1902 by George McArthur. The dam was later improved. It was the last dam to be removed from the Baraboo River, in October 2001, returning the river to its free flowing condition for the first time since 1839.

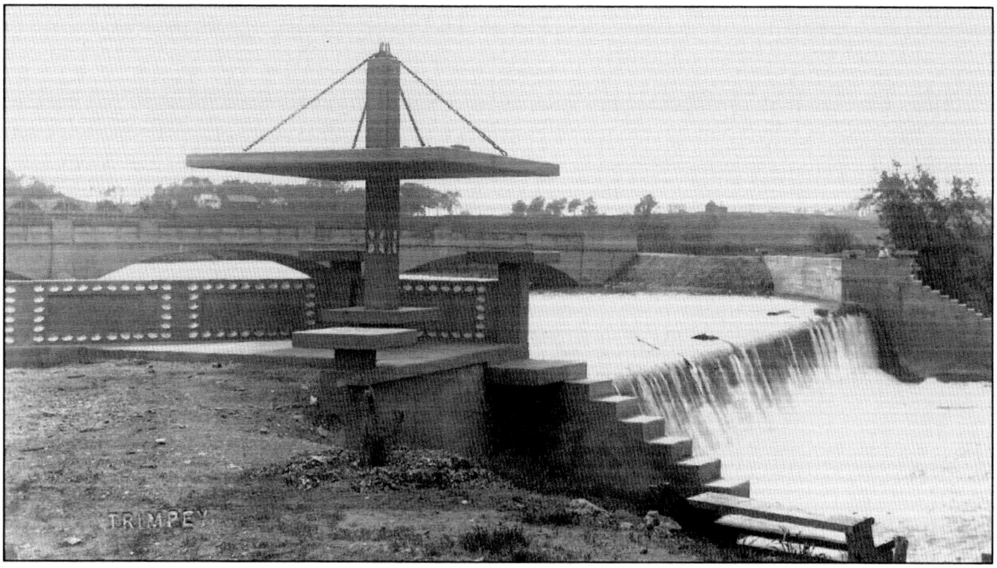

By the turn of the 20th century, attitudes regarding the river's aesthetics started to change and bridges, dams, and parks were built to take advantage of the river's natural beauty. The 1913 Island Woolen Mill dam included lookout pavilions at either end inset with mussel shells from the river. The lookouts were certainly inspired by and may have been the work of Frank Lloyd Wright, a friend of the McFetridge family that owned the mill.

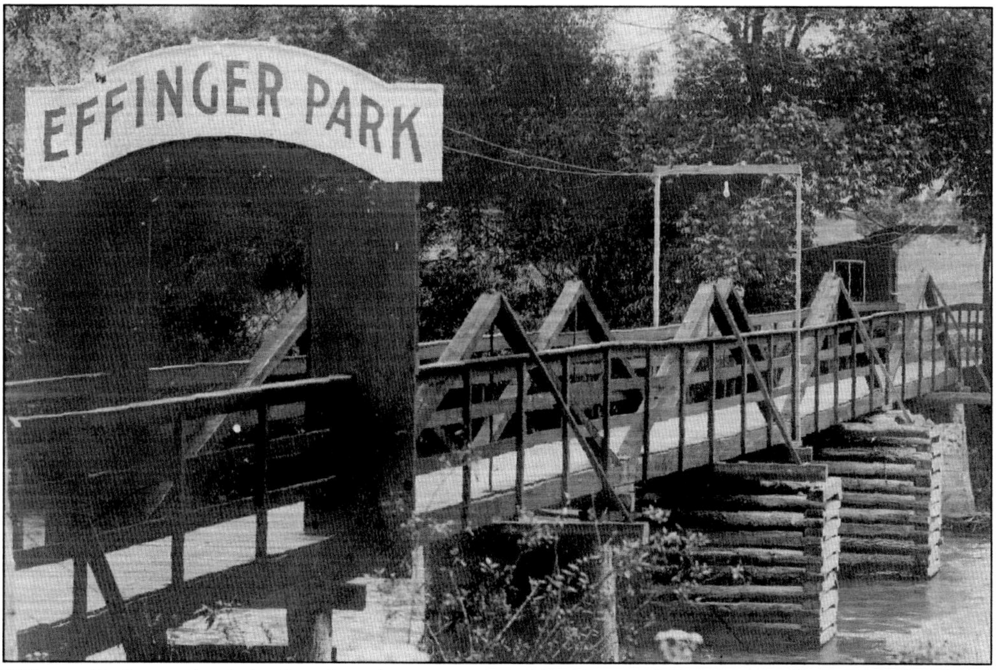

Effinger Park was built by Baraboo brewery owner Ferdinand Effinger on the east side of the river just south of the lower oxbow. It was formally opened on July 4, 1907, and could be reached by crossing the river on a special foot bridge. It took several years for the park to be developed. One of the first buildings to be placed there was the old wooden train depot purchased by Effinger in 1902, which became a dining room.

Two

Railroad Boom

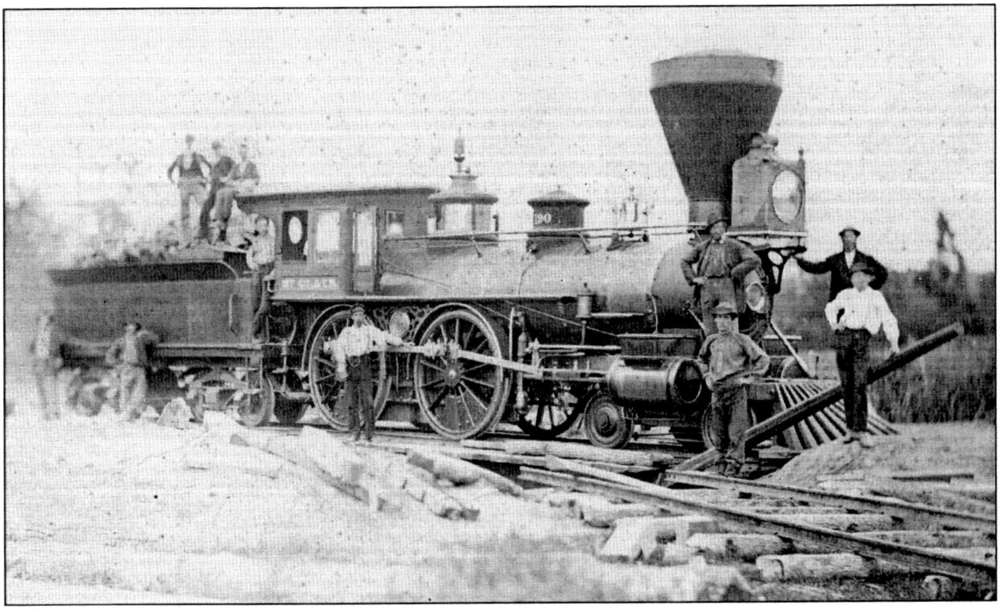

Several attempts were made to bring a railroad to Baraboo. Attempts in the 1850s were thwarted by financial panics, land-grant failures, and the crossing of the LaCrosse and Milwaukee line at Kilbourn City instead of Newport. Attempts in the 1860s were halted by the Civil War and the apparent apathy following. By July 1870, a new attempt was made and this time the timing was right. Only two weeks after the organization of the Baraboo Air Line Railroad Company, an agreement was reached with the Chicago and Northwestern Railroad to build a rail line linking Baraboo to Madison. The line was completed the following year, but not without monumental effort. In the 38-mile stretch from Madison to Baraboo, over two million cubic yards of material were moved, more than on the 242-mile stretch from Chicago to Green Bay. On September 12, 1871, the first iron horse reached Baraboo with over 10,000 people on hand. Festivities comprised two and a half hours of speeches and dedications. The train was decorated with flowers and garlands and rolled to a stop under an immense arch piled with pumpkins, strings of apples, sheaves of wheat, and stalks of corn. The effect of the railroad on Baraboo cannot be overstated. The community doubled in size in the next decade and profited greatly from being named a division headquarters for the line. A roundhouse was built along with other support buildings and eventually several hundred local employees and their families would call Baraboo home.

Although the picture above is labeled as the first train in Baraboo, its name, the St. Clair, does not match the newspaper of the day, stating that the St. Lawrence was the train of note. No doubt it was similar to the 4-4-0 American shown in the photo.

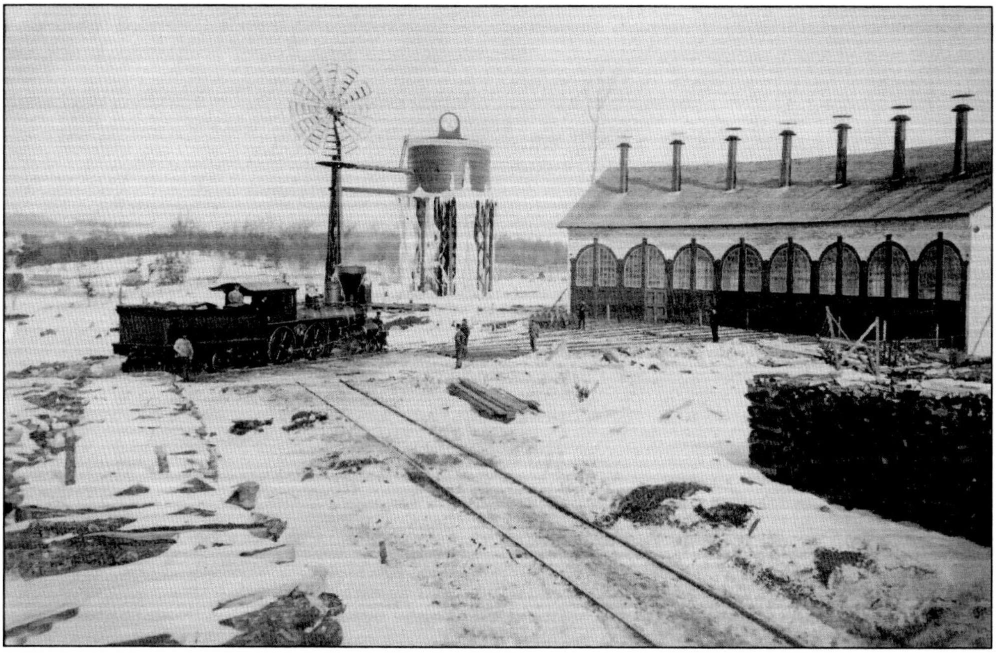

An eight-stall roundhouse with sixty-foot turntable was built in 1871 for the division headquarters of the C&NW at Baraboo. In the next several years, the building was substantially enlarged with 20 more stalls and a 225 x 80 ft. shop, including a blacksmith shop with ten fires, boiler and engine room, machine shop, and storerooms.

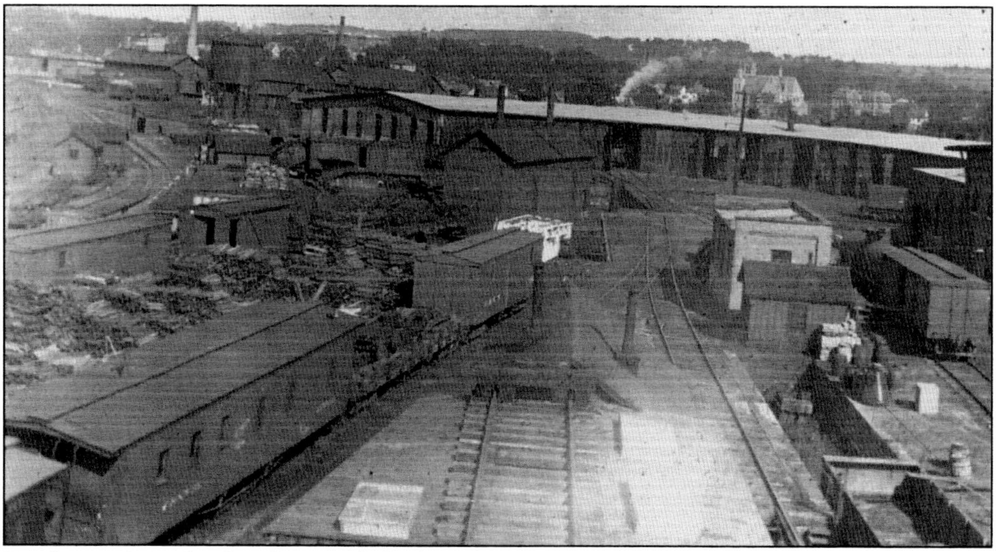

By about 1918, the Baraboo yards had grown considerably. The roundhouse now included 28 stalls and a larger turntable, and the yard is shown full of machinery, supplies, parts, and cars. In the distance, the Catholic church and school appear on the right, above the roundhouse, and near the middle the clock tower of the county courthouse emerges from above the trees. (Courtesy of Ralph Marquardt.)

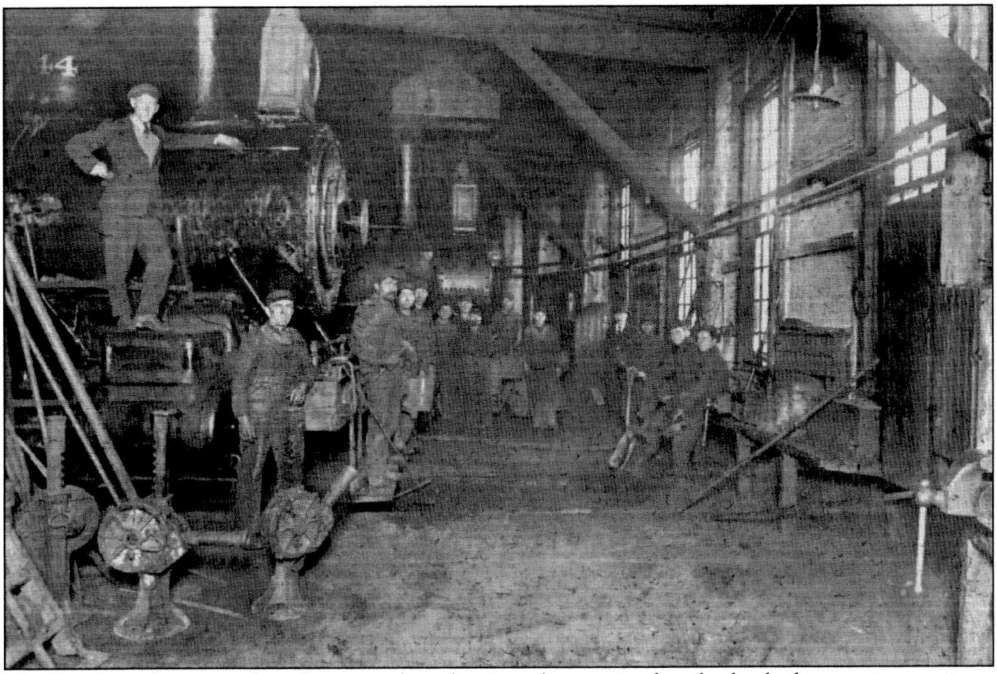

The Baraboo shops employed scores of mechanics who repaired and rebuilt the massive engines. This view inside the roundhouse shows two engines being serviced.

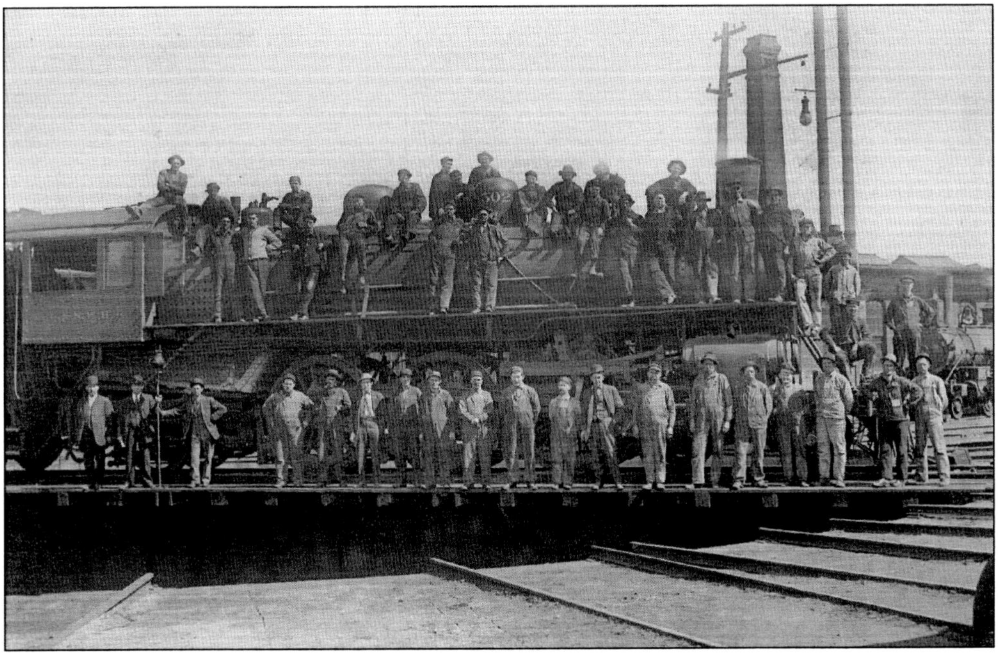

Over 45 men stood on the Baraboo turntable with an E type 4-6-2 steam passenger locomotive for this photo. The turntable was enlarged from 60 feet to 70 in 1905, and later to 80 in 1909.

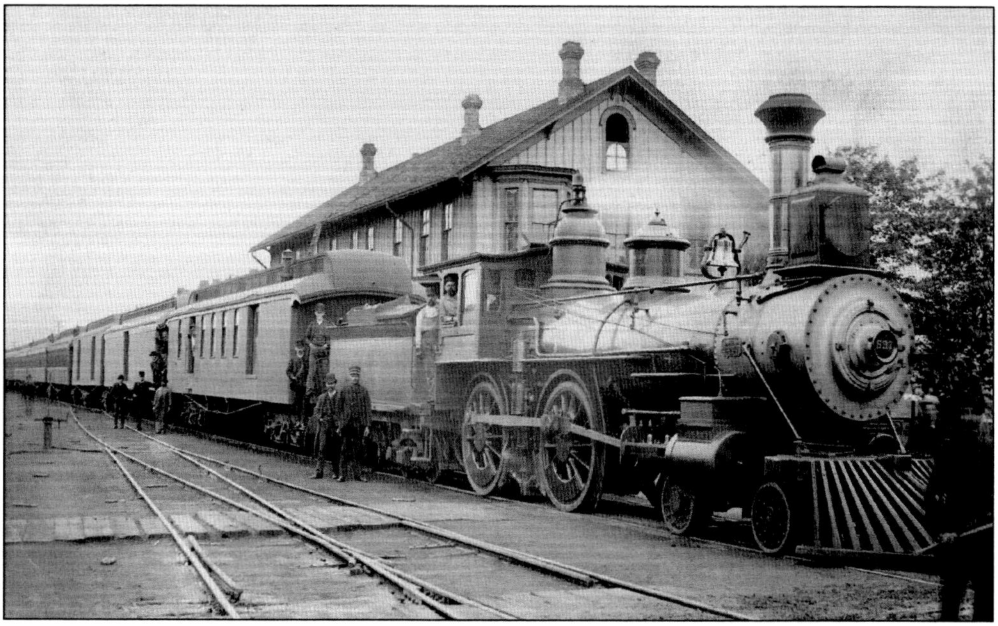

Engine 597 stands in front of the two-story railroad eating house, built in 1878 and located on the site of the future two-story brick depot just west of Walnut. The passenger depot, a one-story affair at the time, sat just behind the eating house. The first car in the train is a railway post office car where mail was picked up, sorted, and dropped off to stations along the route.

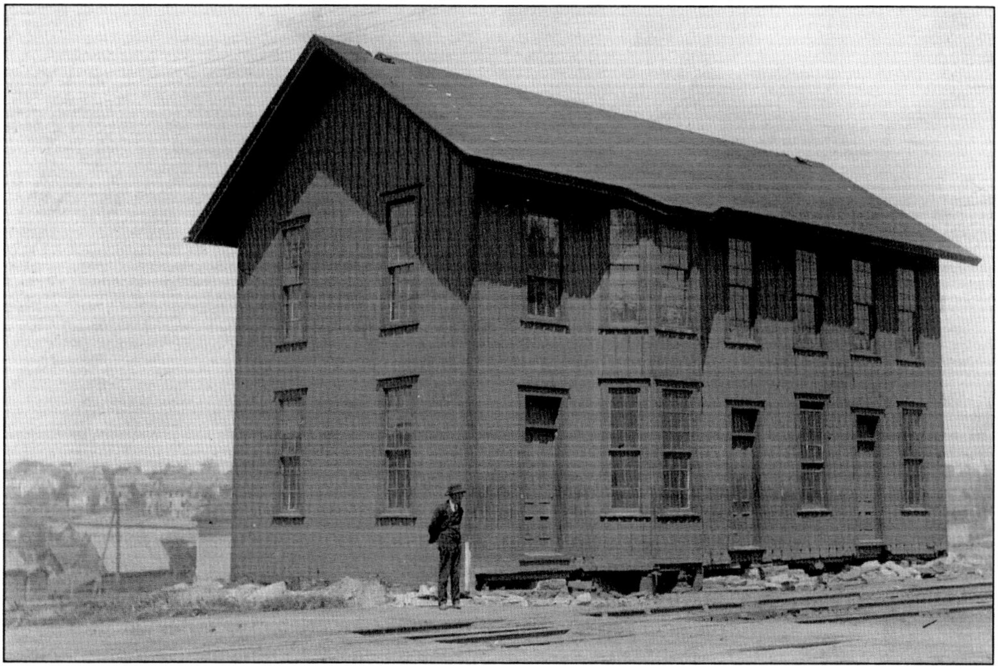

The C&NW division office building was constructed in 1874 and sat just east of Walnut, on the south side of the tracks. It was purchased by the city in 1902 and is shown about ready to be moved to an unknown location. It was made obsolete by the construction of the new depot which had offices on the second floor.

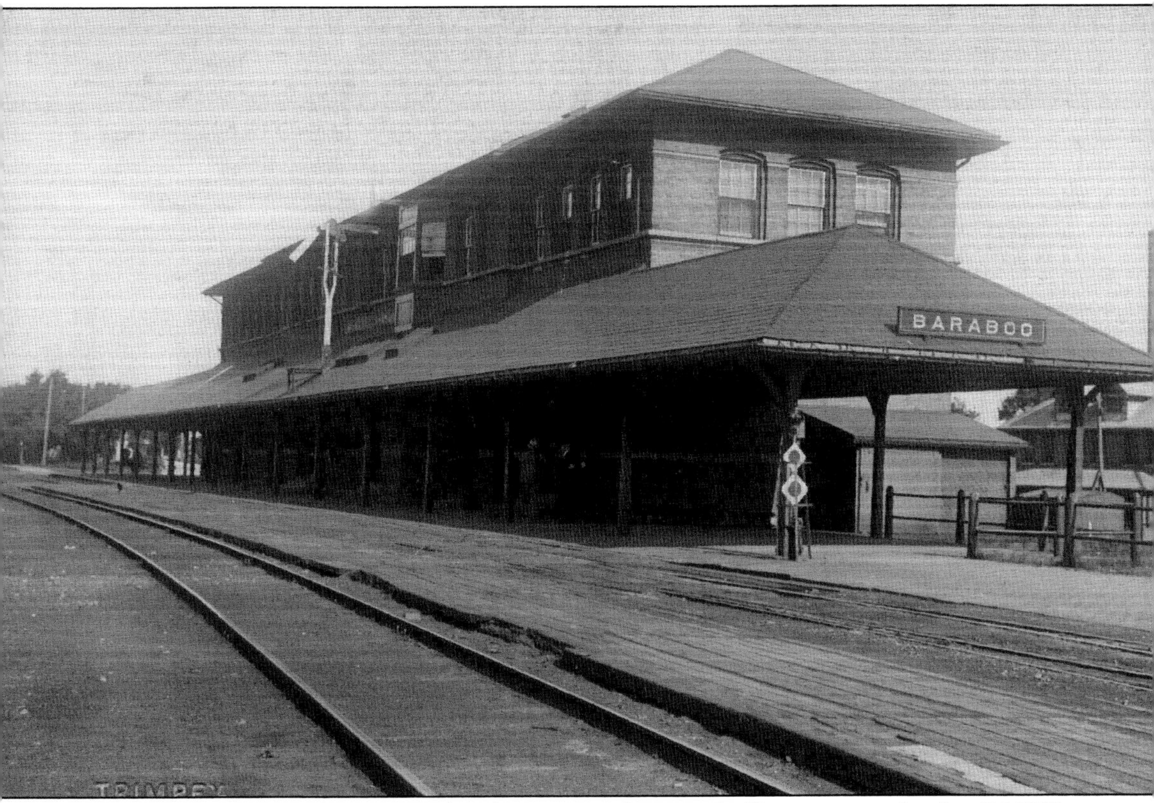

In early May 1902, work was completed on a new depot and office structure for the C&NW railroad at Baraboo. The structure consumed 400,000 bricks and 100 cords of stone and cost $45,000. Inside, the building had ticket, express, and baggage offices, waiting rooms for men and women, and a lunch room with kitchen facilities on the first floor. The second floor contained offices for everything from the division superintendent to the telegraph operators. In 1933, the division offices were moved to Madison, closing a chapter in Baraboo's history. The last passenger train service to Baraboo was discontinued in 1963. The building still stands today, although stripped of its lengthy canopy, part of which stands today at Circus World Museum.

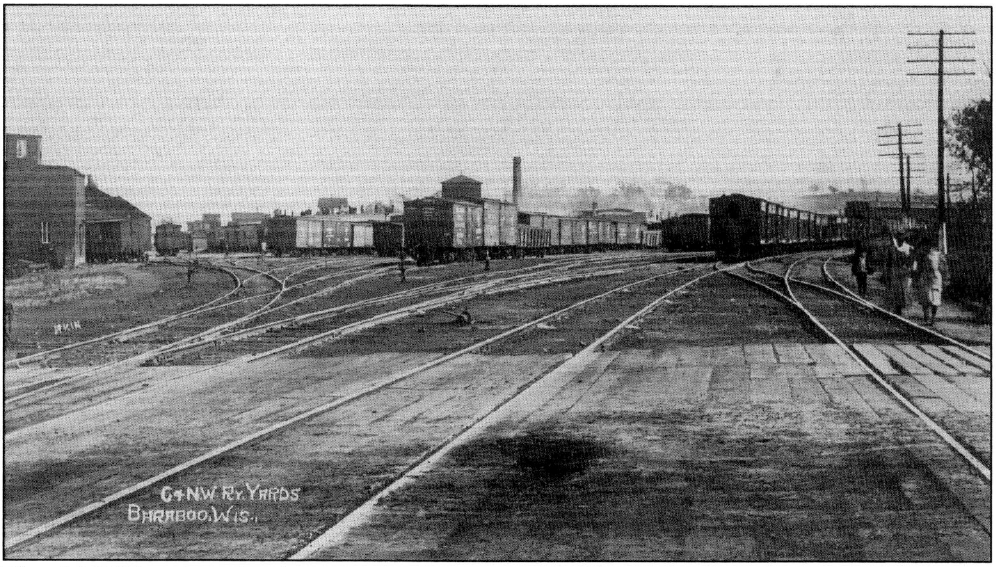

The C&NW yards at Baraboo grew to encompass roughly 20 acres. The crossing, shown here at Walnut Street looking east, included four tracks.

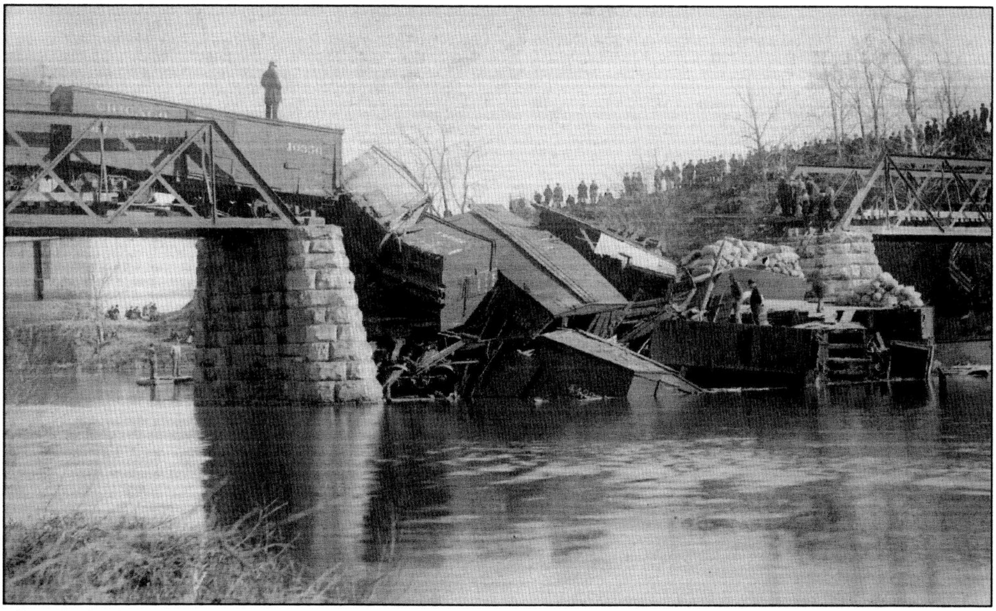

Shortly before 11 p.m. on the night of November 22, 1890, one of the worst railroad accidents in Baraboo's history occurred at the bridge between Baraboo and Lyons. After one car jumped the tracks, a chain reaction started that sent 24 cars into the river, demolishing the bridge. No one was injured in the disaster, although one of the brakemen was on the last car to remain on the bridge. A temporary bridge was built in 48 hours and much freight was salvaged from the wreck. The stone bridge abutments can still be seen at Haskins Park in West Baraboo.

Three

Square and Surroundings

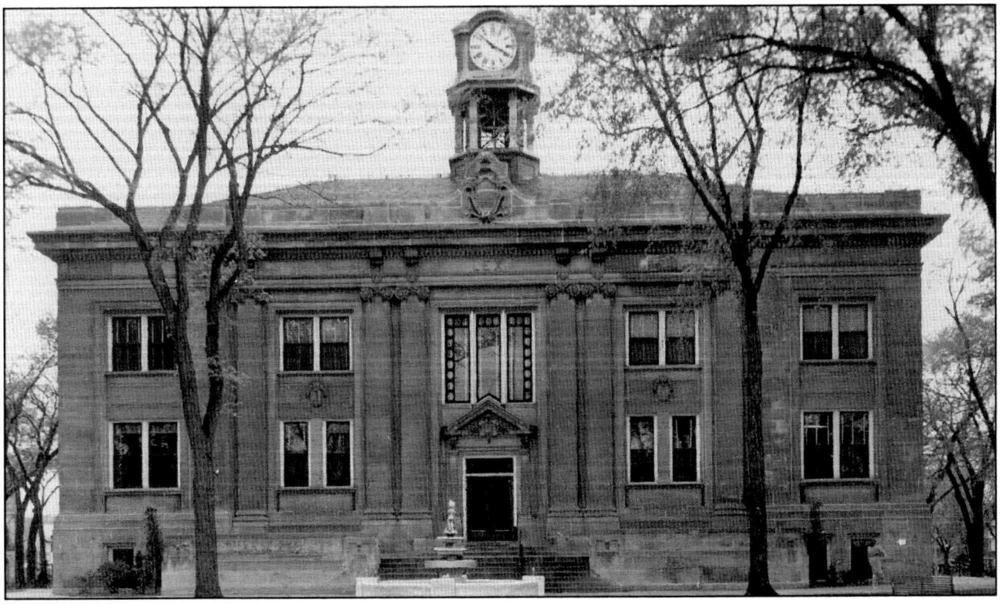

In April 1847, a plat named Adams was laid out north of the river around a public square. This was done after the fledgling county had held a referendum naming the location along the Baraboo River as the county seat and removing it from Prairie du Sac, where it was originally. The quarter section of land in the plat was purchased by county commissioner, Prescott Brigham, with his own money and deeded to the county. The name of Adams was given to the plat because of Brigham's high regard for the Adams family of presidential fame. Lots around the square were sold to raise money for the new county and with the proceeds a wooden county courthouse and jail were built on the north side of the square. A hotel was also built in 1847, along with some store buildings and houses. The square and its surrounding streets soon began to fill with mostly wooden buildings. In 1855, a new brick courthouse was commenced in the middle of the square and was finished in January of 1857. The old building went up in flames in July of 1859. Destructive fires would have great influence in shaping the look of the square. The first major conflagration in 1859 consumed seven buildings. Virtually every block in and around the square would succumb to a fire that would leave in its wake new brick buildings. Even brick buildings, though, would burn and such was the case with the brick courthouse that caught fire on the night of December 27, 1904.

A new courthouse was constructed as soon as possible on the same site and was finished in 1906. Still in use today, the building was designed by Ferry and Clas of Milwaukee. The original cupola was enlarged in 1915 to house a Seth Thomas clock with four faces and two bells, the largest weighing a ton. The tower was given as a memorial to pioneer resident J.J. Gattiker.

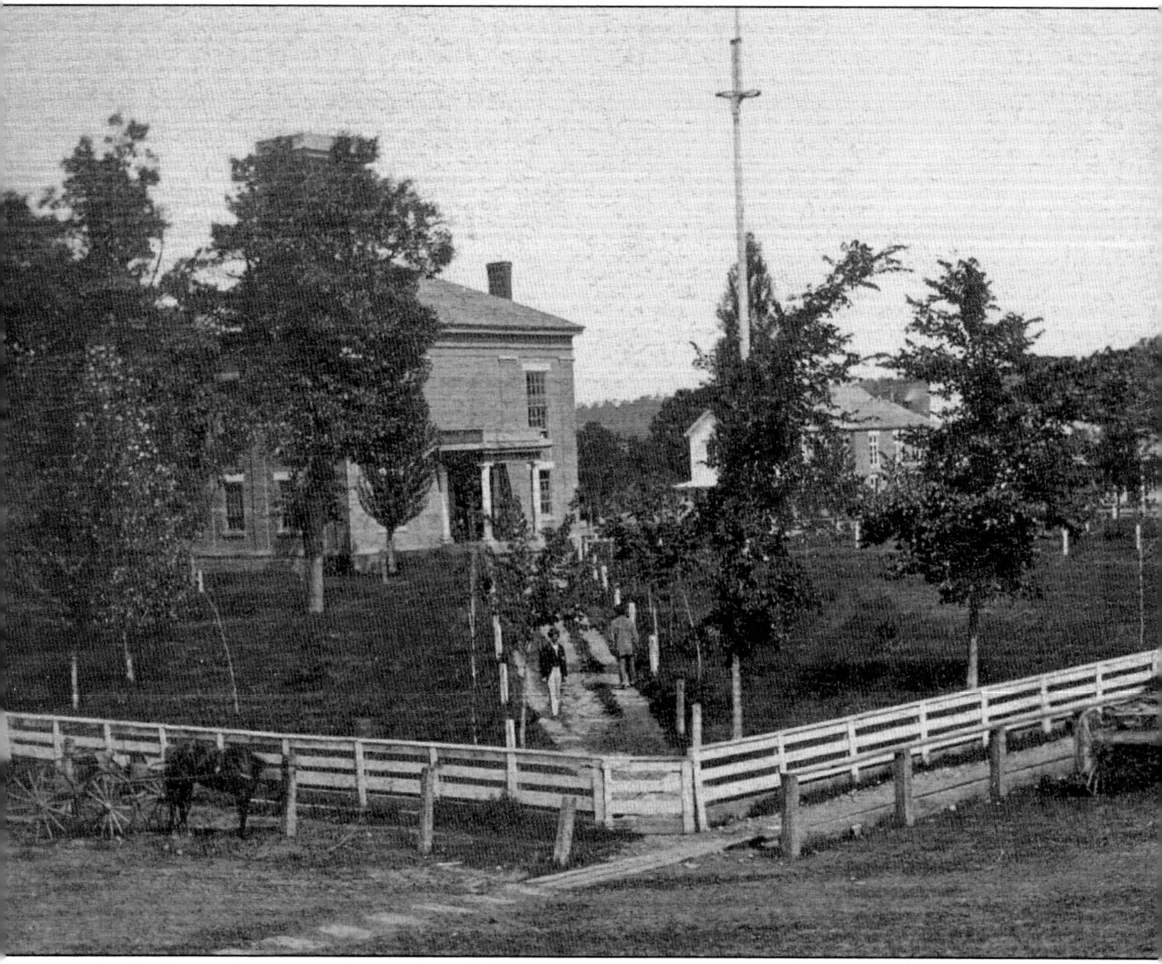

This view of the square from about 1871 comes from a stereograph card, which gave the viewer a three-dimensional image when used with the proper hand-held viewer. This is the earliest known photograph of the square and it shows a view from the corner of Third and Oak towards the northwest. In the center of the square is Baraboo's second courthouse, which was built of brick and finished in 1857. On the north side of the square, behind the flagpole, is the Wisconsin House, an early hotel that was demolished in 1912 to make way for the Al. Ringling Theatre. The two men in the photo were carefully posed to appear as if they were walking, but the horses could not remain still enough for the long exposure and appear blurred. (Baraboo National Bank Collection.)

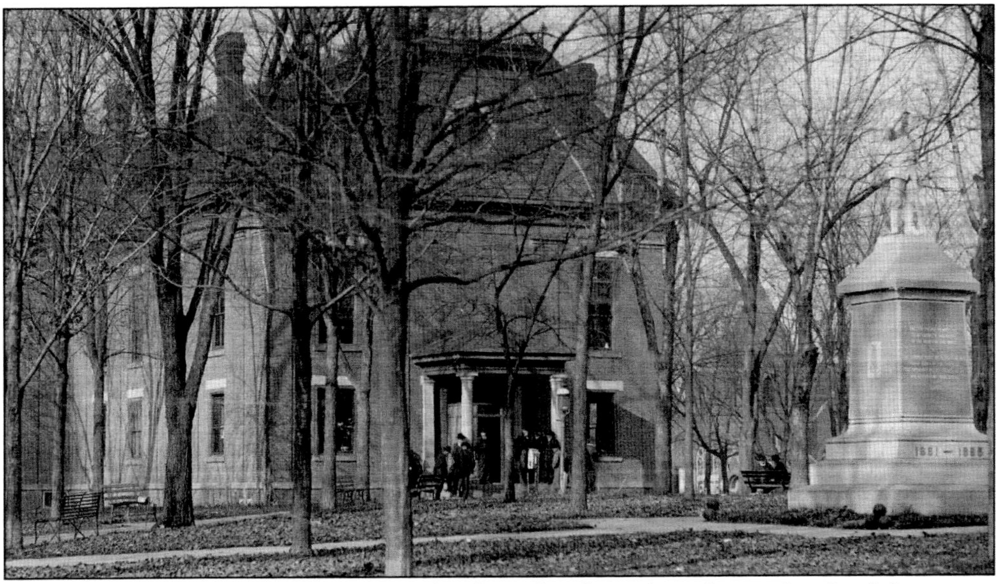

The first courthouse in Baraboo was made of wood and stood on the north side of the square. Its successor was built of brick in the center of the square during 1855 and 1856. It was enlarged in 1884 with a wing on the west end. The roof was also changed, giving the courthouse an updated Victorian look complete with metal roof cresting. The Civil War monument was added to the square in 1896. (Baraboo National Bank Collection.)

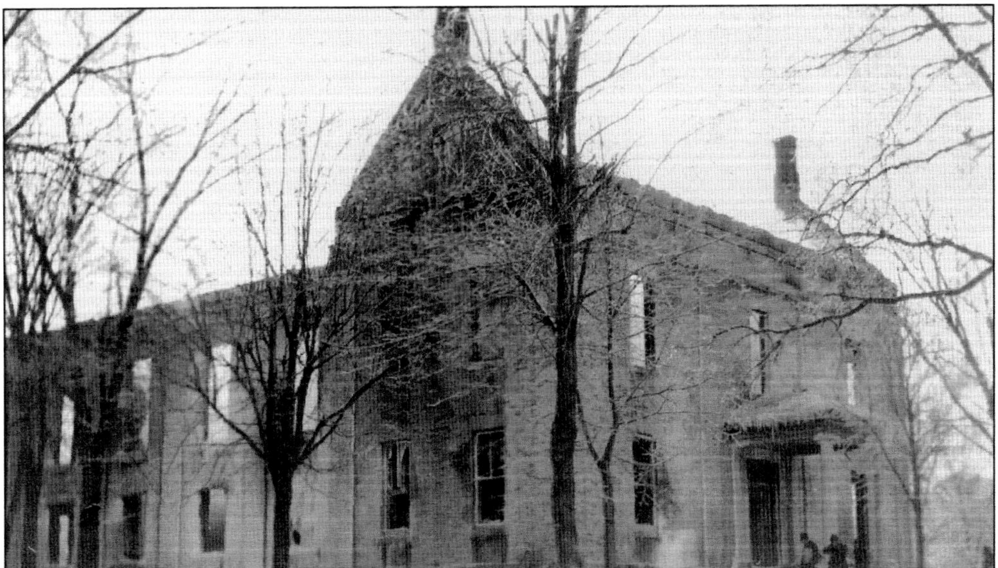

On the night of December 27, 1904, the Sauk County Courthouse was discovered to be on fire and in a few hours was completely gutted. The temperature that evening reached nearly 40 degrees below zero, which hampered fire-fighting efforts. A new courthouse was already in the works, however, as the county board had passed a resolution just the month before calling for a new $100,000 structure to be built on the site. The remains of the old building were demolished, but two of the columns still exist today on a Baraboo home on Tenth Avenue. (Siekert Collection.)

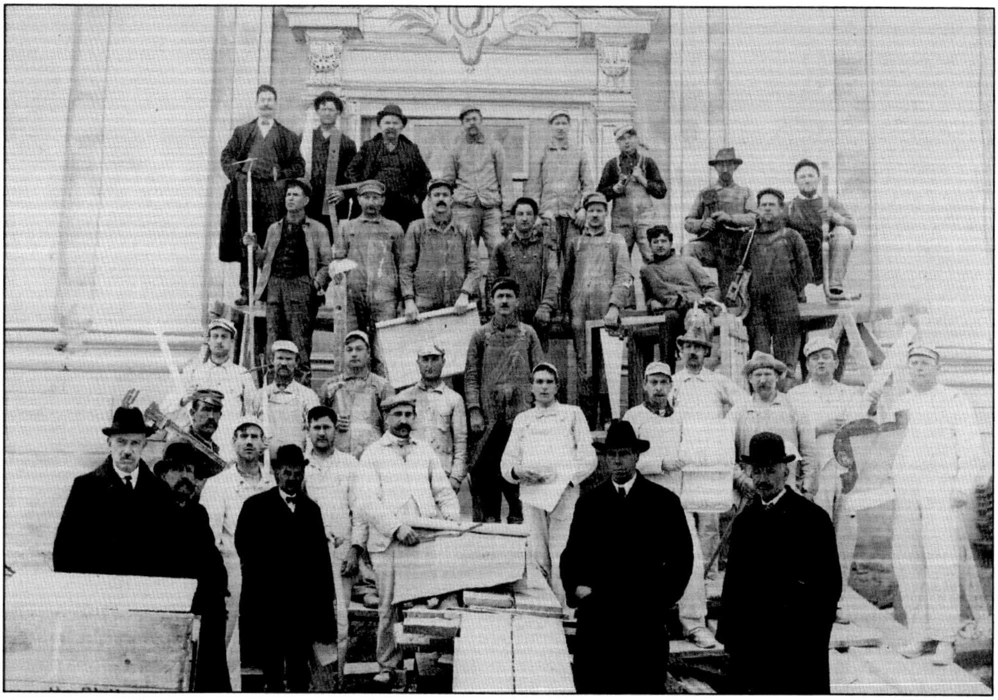

A new courthouse was commenced in 1905, after the ruins of the old brick courthouse were removed. The plans were drawn by Ferry and Clas of Milwaukee. Alfred Clas was a Sauk City native who personally supervised the construction when he visited Baraboo. The workers and supervisors posed for this photo in front of the building, many of them holding tools of their trade.

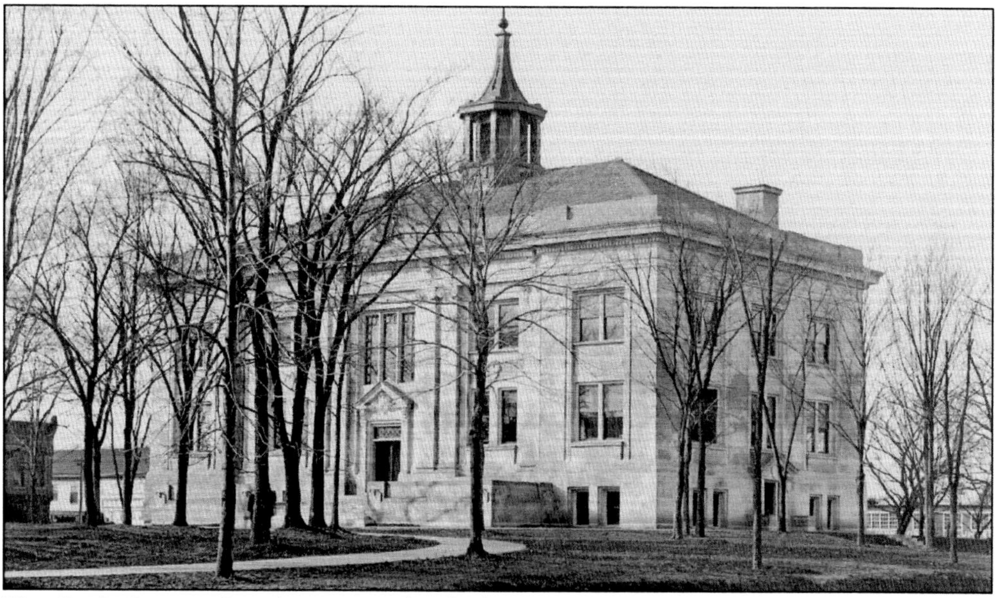

The Sauk County Courthouse was finished in August 1906. The exterior was made of Indiana limestone and the roof was covered in green terra cotta tiles. The original cupola was enlarged into a clock tower in 1915. The building was state of the art and held all the offices of county government.

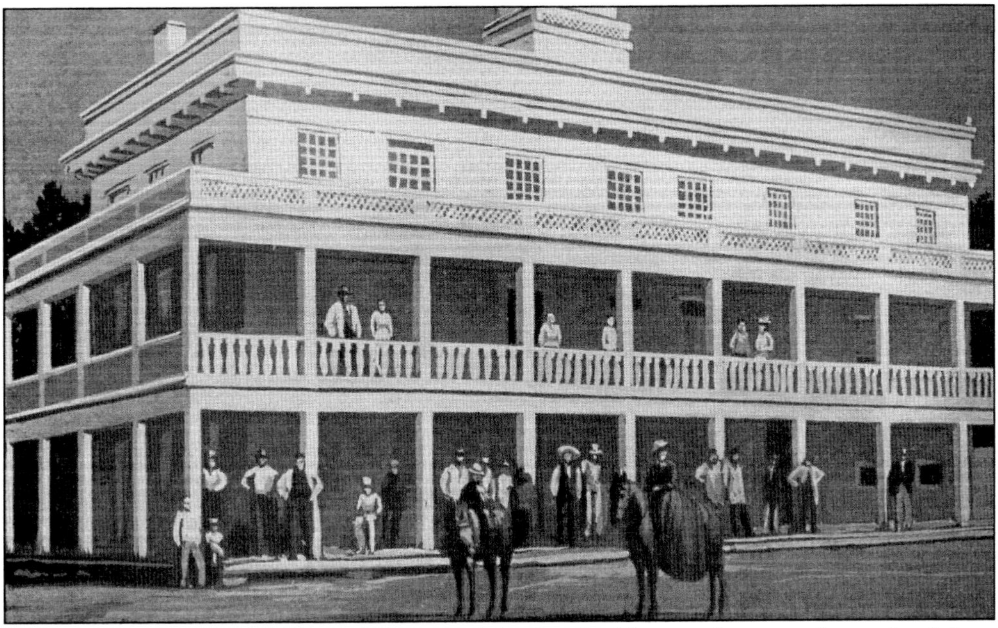

After the square was platted in 1847, one of the first buildings to be erected was the Adams House, a one-story hotel at the southeast corner of Fourth and Oak. It was later named the Western Hotel and was twice enlarged, reaching three stories with a cupola. During its day, it was the finest hotel in Baraboo and was visited by Mary Todd Lincoln in the summer of 1872. It was destroyed in a terrific fire on November 6, 1878.

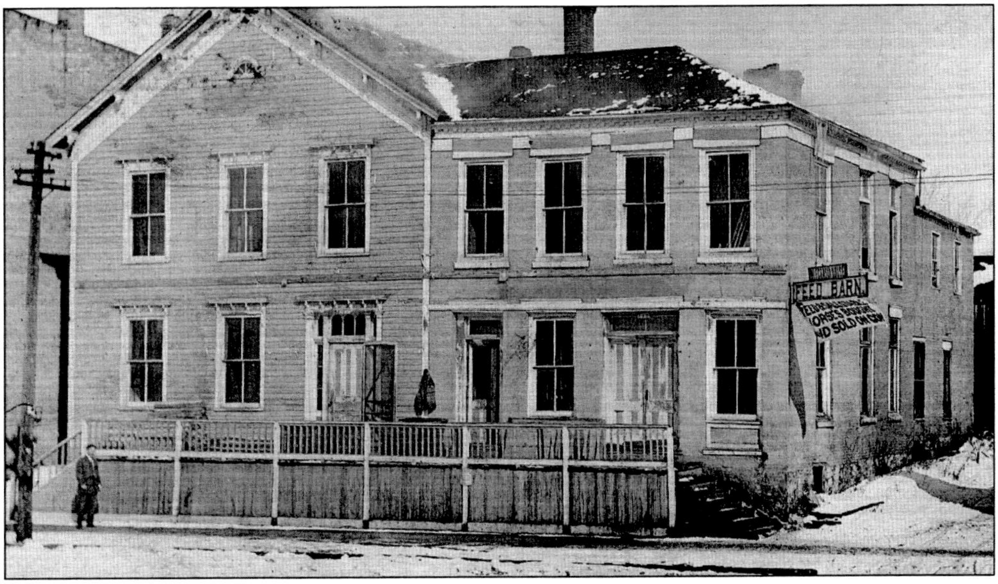

On the north side of the square stood the Wisconsin House, an early tavern and hotel. The brick portion was built in 1850 and was one of the first brick buildings in Baraboo. It was then known as the Brick Tavern and was the starting point of the Baraboo Whiskey War. In 1854, a group of angry women entered the establishment and soon forcibly drained it of its evil spirits. They were later arrested and fined $150. The building was demolished in 1912 to make way for the Al. Ringling Theatre.

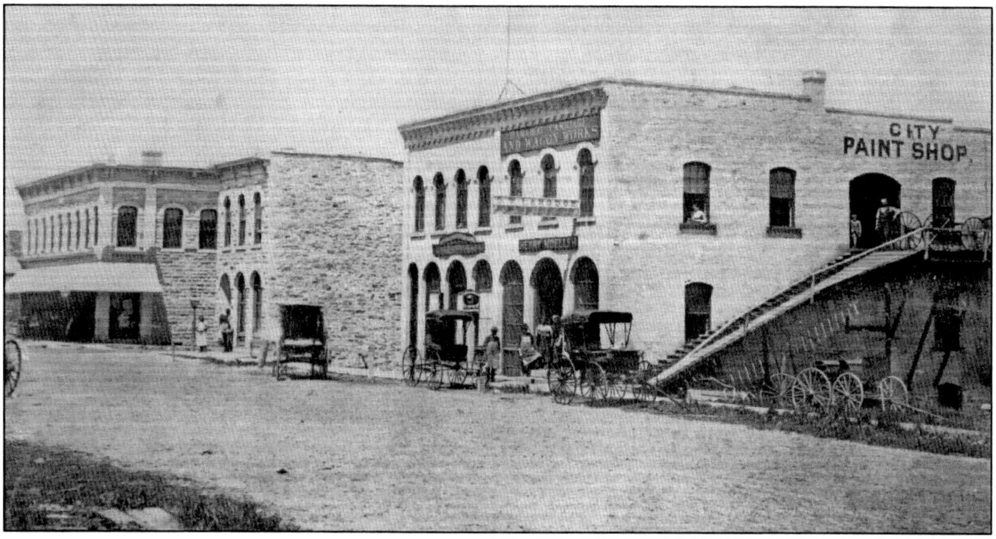

A view of Fourth Street looking towards Oak about 1880 shows the Baraboo Carriage and Wagon Works, operated by Henry Moeller, an uncle to the Ringling Brothers. The finishing rooms on the second floor were connected to the street with a long ramp. In the background is the Sumner House, built in 1877–78, later to become the Warren Hotel. Opposite that is the Gust Brothers Meat Market, today the Cornerstone Gallery.

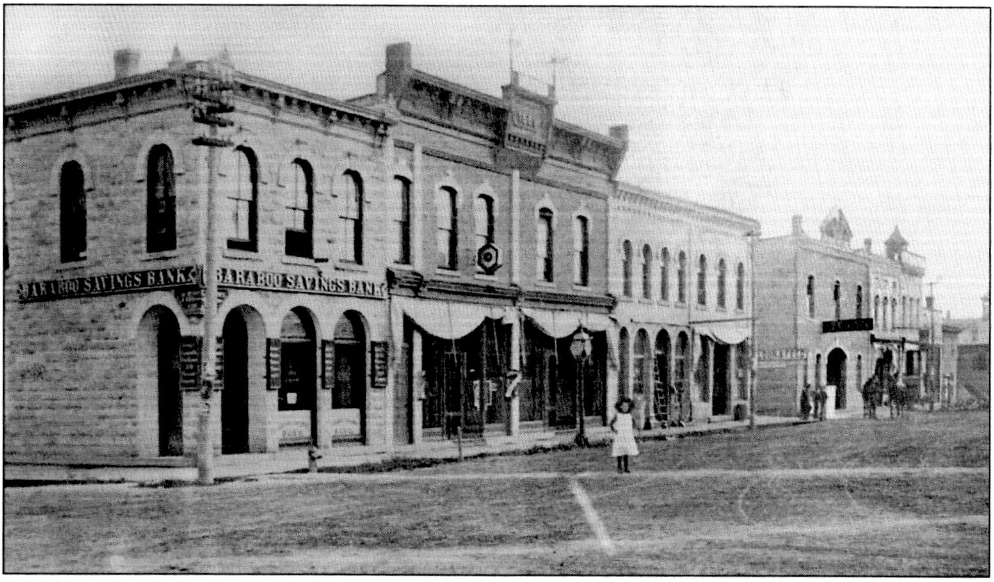

By 1890, Fourth Street had filled in considerably. Gust Brothers Meat Market had become the Baraboo Savings Bank and the space between it and the Moeller carriage works was filled by the Ewing building in 1886, which housed a saloon and large hall on the second floor. At the end of the street is city hall.

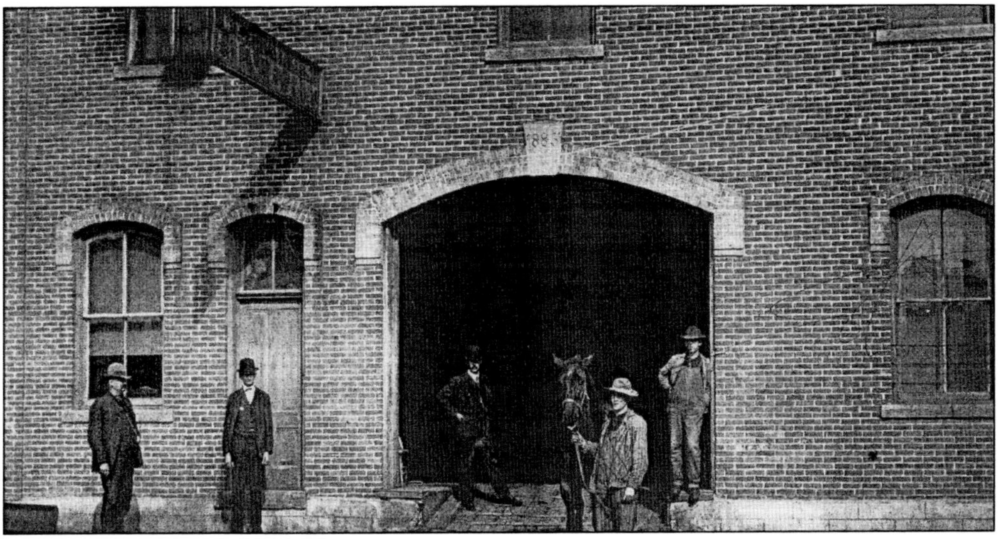

A new livery building was built at 117 Fourth Street in 1885 by Jasper Ewing. The original design of the building had an office and bedroom on the first floor along with a carriage repository and harness room. The horses were stabled in a partial basement. The second floor had hay and grain storage and a 120-barrel water tank. In the mid-1920s, the building was divided into two store fronts and a new front was put on the building. The left half has held the Alpine Café since 1930.

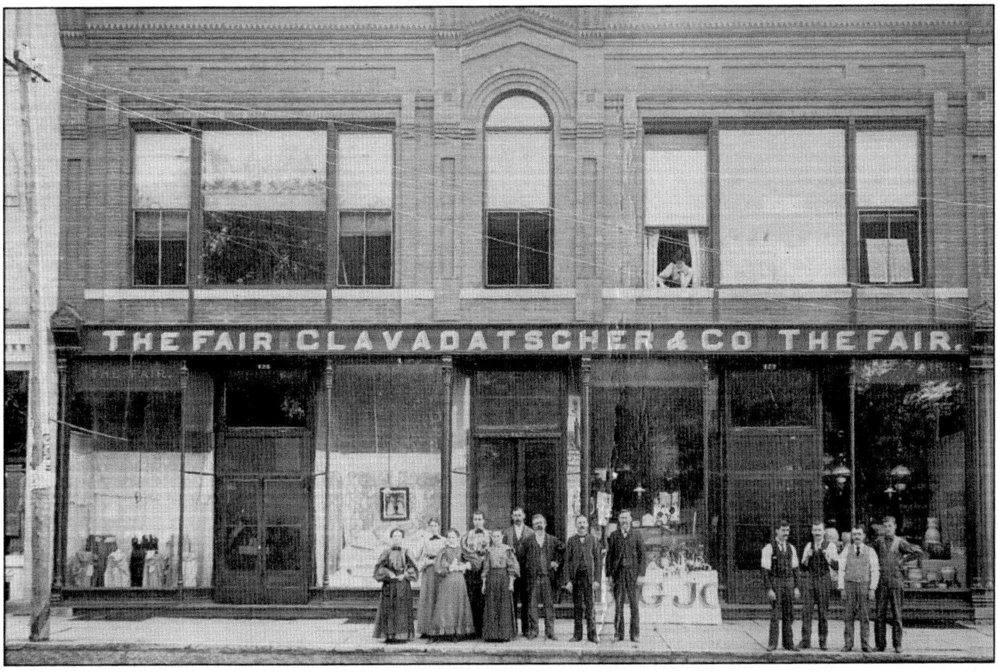

In May 1888, Tobias Clavadatscher broke ground on Third Avenue to house his growing dry goods business, known as "The Fair." Occupying both sides of this double store front, the firm became one of the largest stores in the county. This view from the 1890s shows the store staff in front of tastefully done window displays. The building was later divided into two store fronts, but was reunited by Ploetz Furniture.

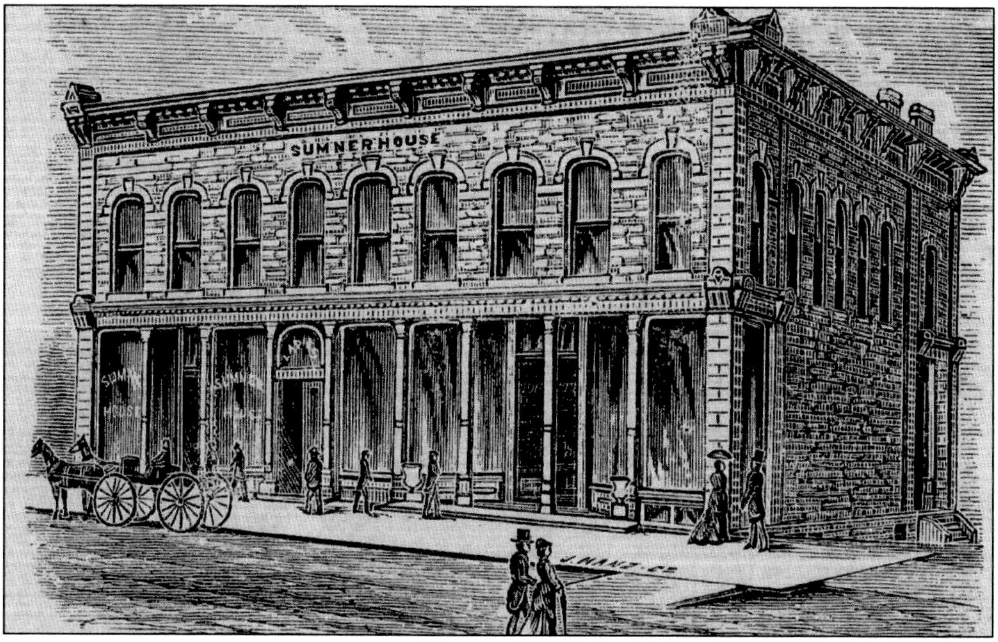

The hotel scene in Baraboo became much improved in 1878 when Charles Sumner finished a new stone building on the northwest corner of Fourth and Oak, housing his mercantile and 14 hotel rooms. The building was finished just in time to see the older three-story Western Hotel burn down nearby. (Courtesy of Joe Ward.)

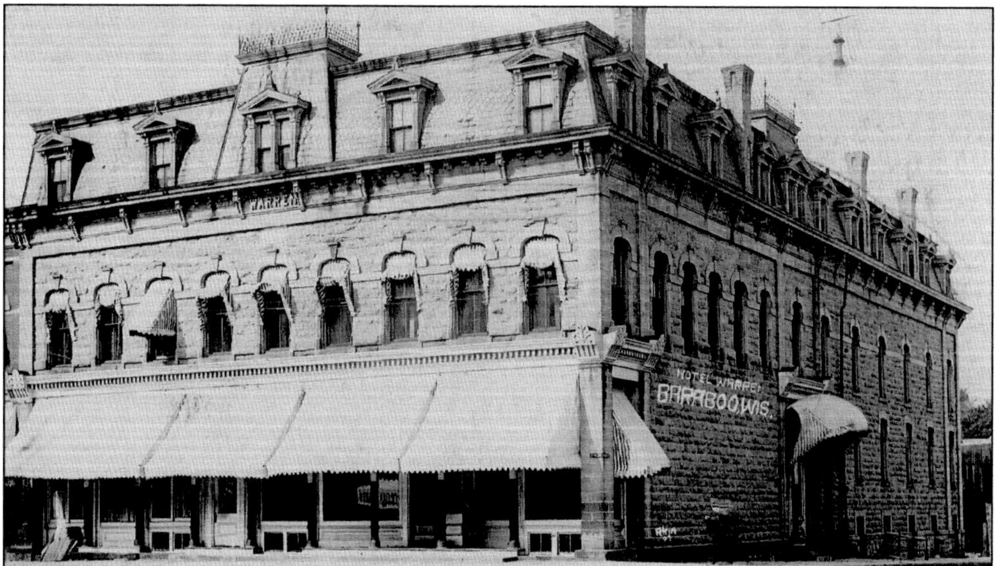

In 1884, the Sumner House was substantially enlarged by its new owner, Mayor Thompson M. Warren. A 34 x 70 ft. addition was added to the north and the whole covered with a Mansard roof, creating a third story. The new enlarged building contained 55 sleeping rooms, parlors, dining rooms, and all the modern conveniences—including a three-story water closet connected to each floor with covered walks. The Warren served Baraboo for several decades, getting periodically remodeled. In 1964, it was damaged by fire and was eventually torn down.

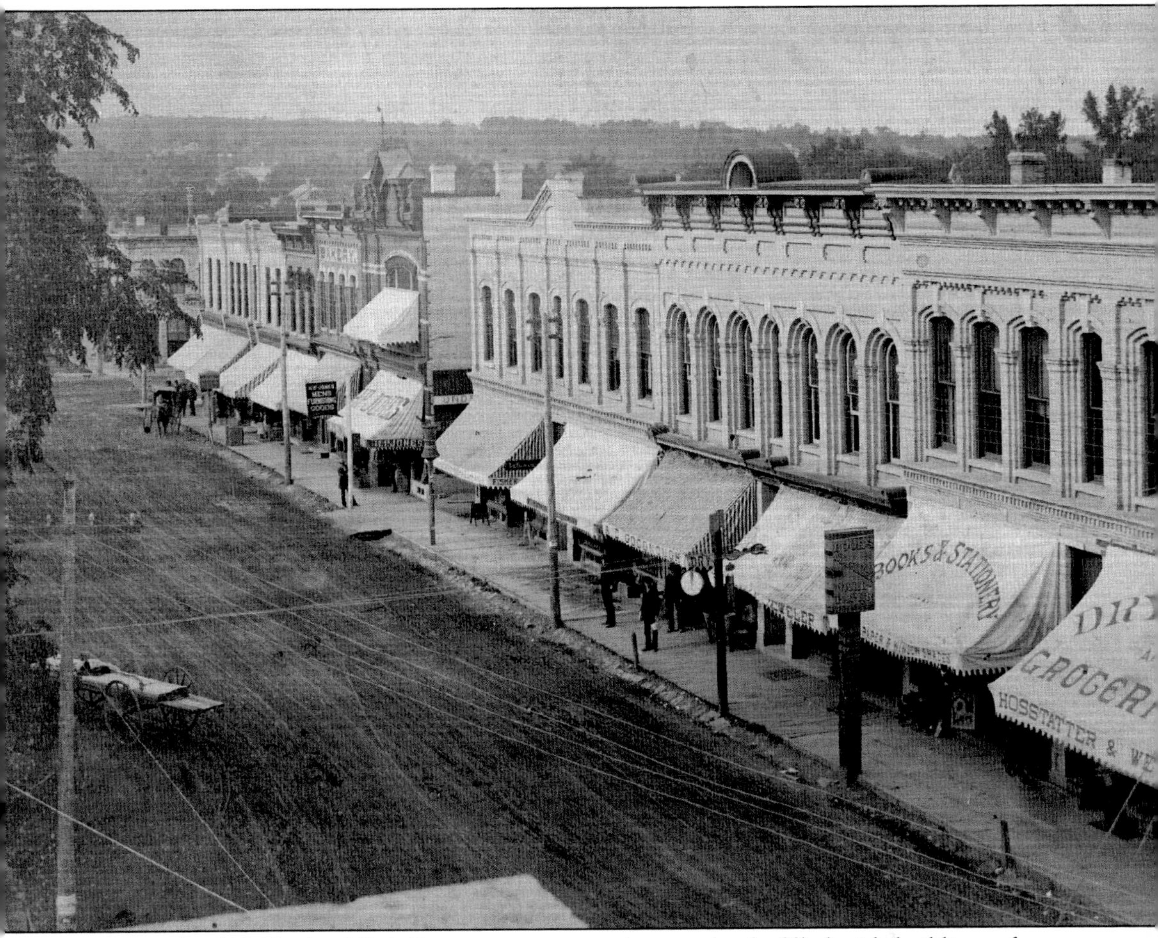

In 1886, the 500 block of Oak Street was once again completely filled with buildings after a disastrous fire in November 1878 nearly wiped out the entire block. The new brick buildings were designed largely in the Italianate style, with arched windows and decorative cornices supported by elaborate brackets. Everything needed for daily living could be had on this block, including groceries, books, jewelry, toiletries, baked goods, and clothing. The merchants placed large advertising items in front of their stores, including a giant book, watch, pair of glasses, and an oversized mortar and pestle to catch the eye of patrons. The tallest building in the middle of the block was built in 1884 as a companion to the Warren Hotel. The second floor contained an Opera Hall as an added attraction for hotel guests. It proved too small however, and briefly became a roller skating rink.

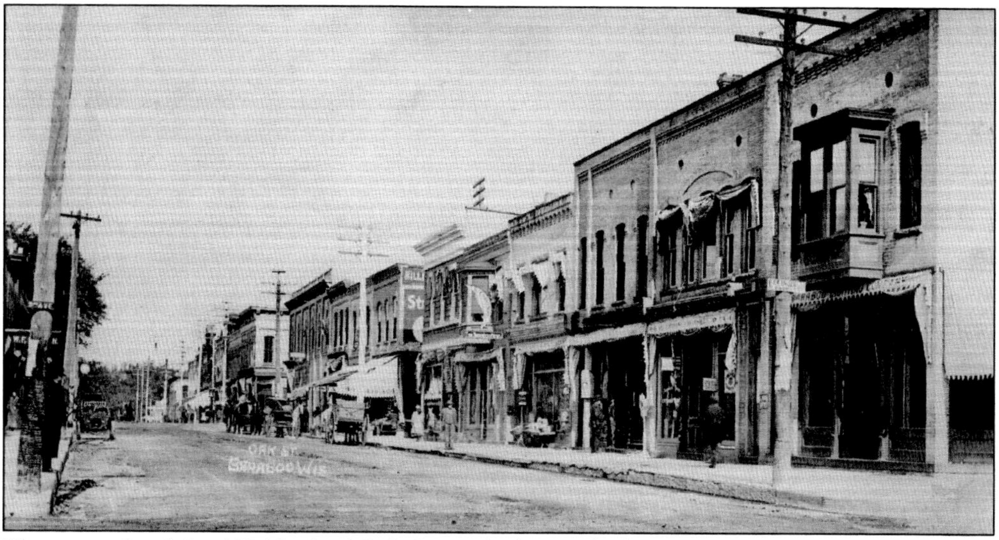

The east side of the 400 block of Oak Street looks much the same today as it did about 1910 when this photo was taken. All of the buildings in this picture remain today. On the corner in the foreground is the Baraboo Lighting Company and on the opposite end is the Corner Drug Store. In 1884, the Ringling brothers rented an earlier building on this block to work on the bleachers and big top for their first circus. (Holt Collection.)

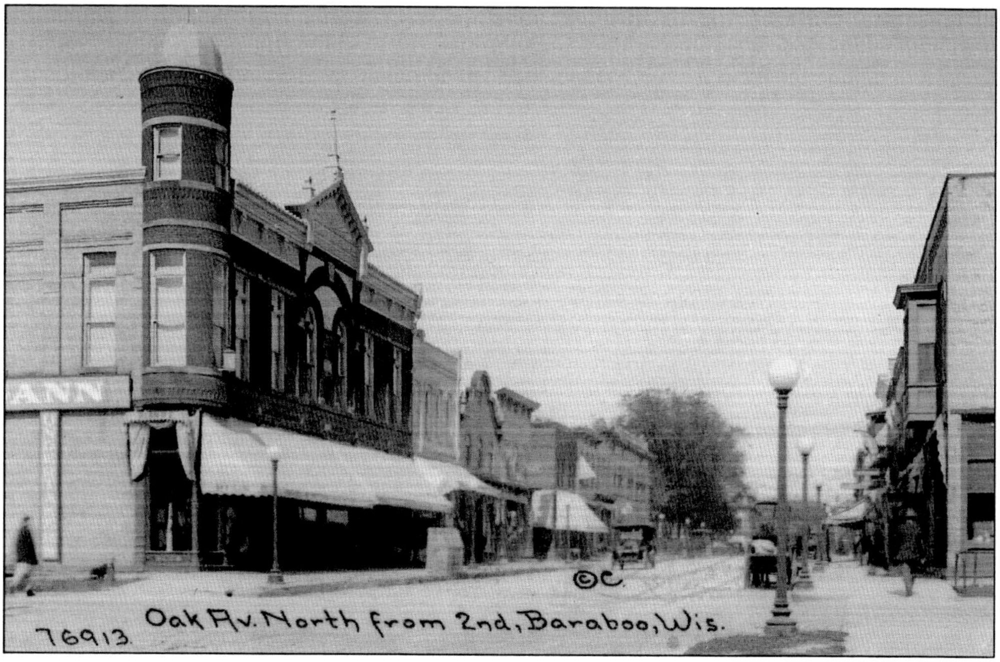

The west side of the 400 block of Oak Street has changed dramatically since this photo was taken in about 1920. Only two of the buildings on this side of the block remain today and they are heavily altered. The impressive building on the corner was built as the Masonic Lodge in 1891–92, with a second-story hall and two stores on the first floor. The Erswell, Melzl and McGann Furniture and Undertaking business was located here for many years. (Holt Collection.)

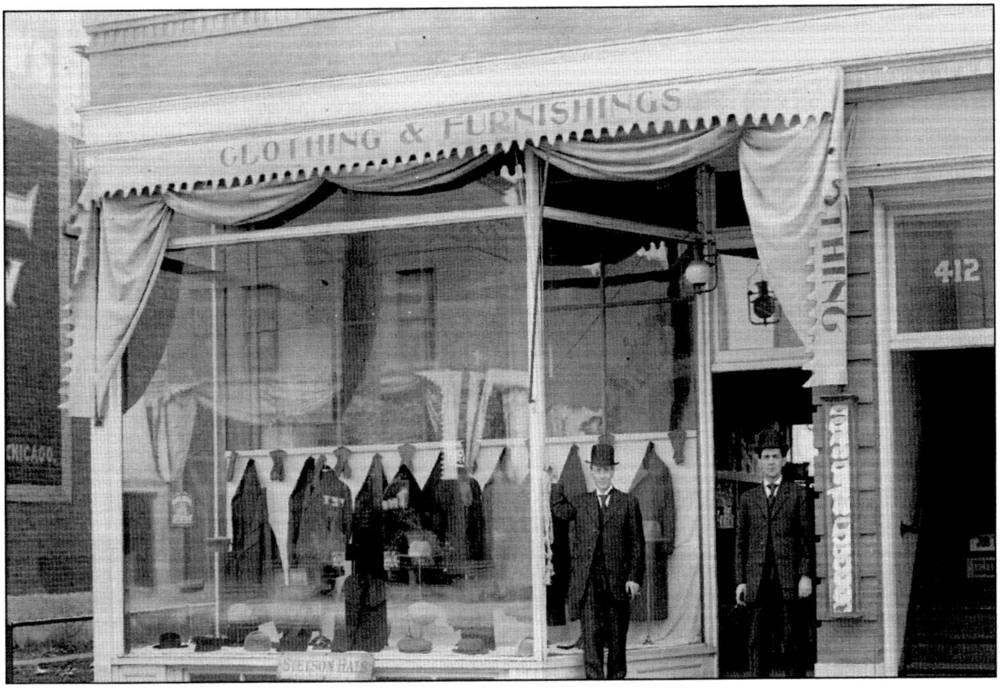

Two dapper gentlemen, most likely Mr. Curry and Mr. Burt, enjoy a cigar while standing in front of their clothing store at 412 Oak Street about 1912. The immense single pane plate glass window displays the finest in men's haberdashery, including Stetson hats. Inside, the store is filled to the brim with merchandise.

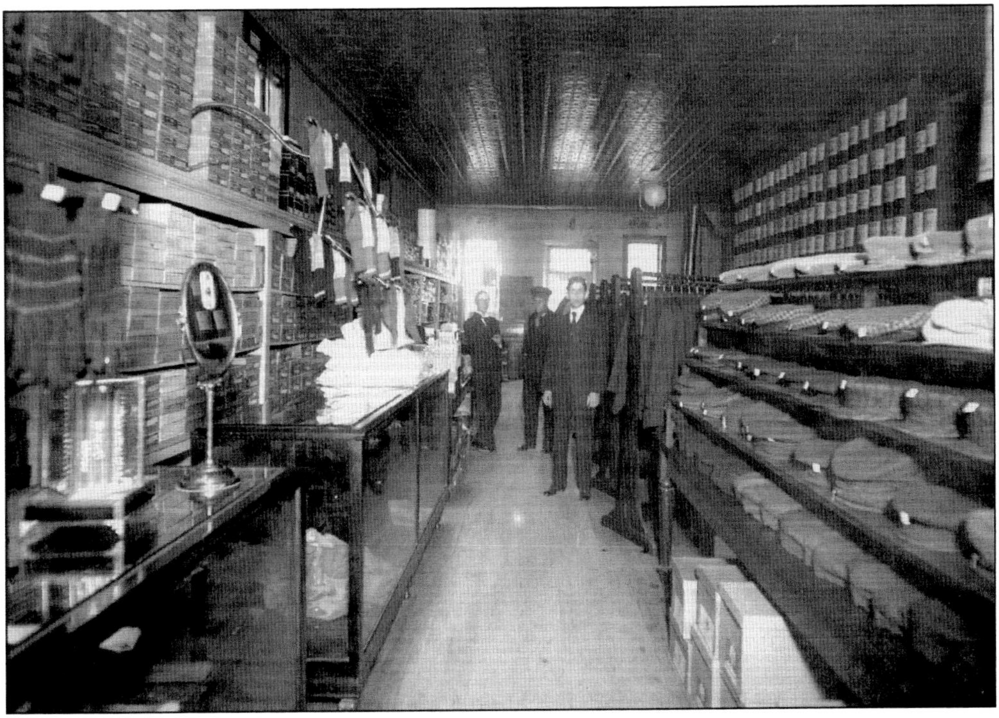

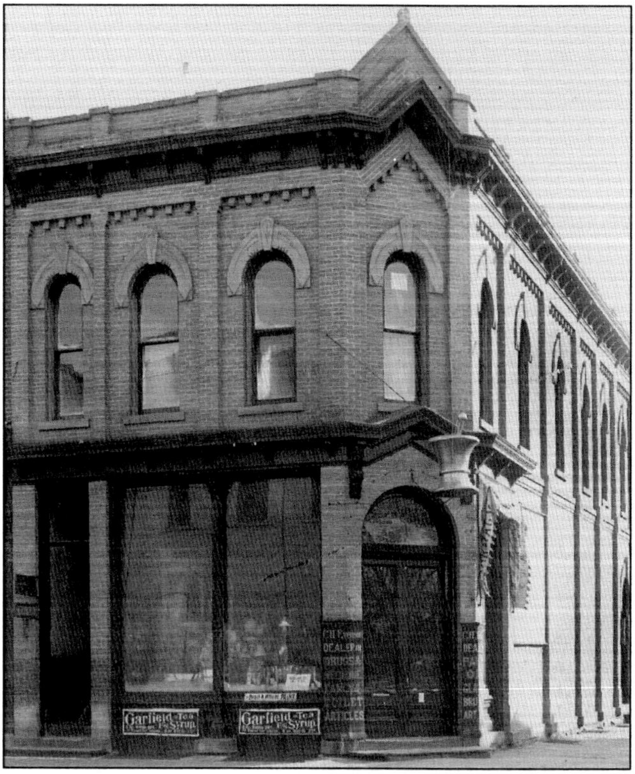

In 1855, Dr. B.F. Mills established a drug store at the southeast corner of Oak and Third. The Corner Drug Store, under various owners, would eventually stay at this corner for over 140 years. In 1880, a new building was erected after a fire consumed the original. By 1895, Charles H. Evenson was the proprietor of the Corner Drug Store, which was advertising Garfield Tea Fig Syrup. Inside, the store sold everything from medicine to lamps to board games.

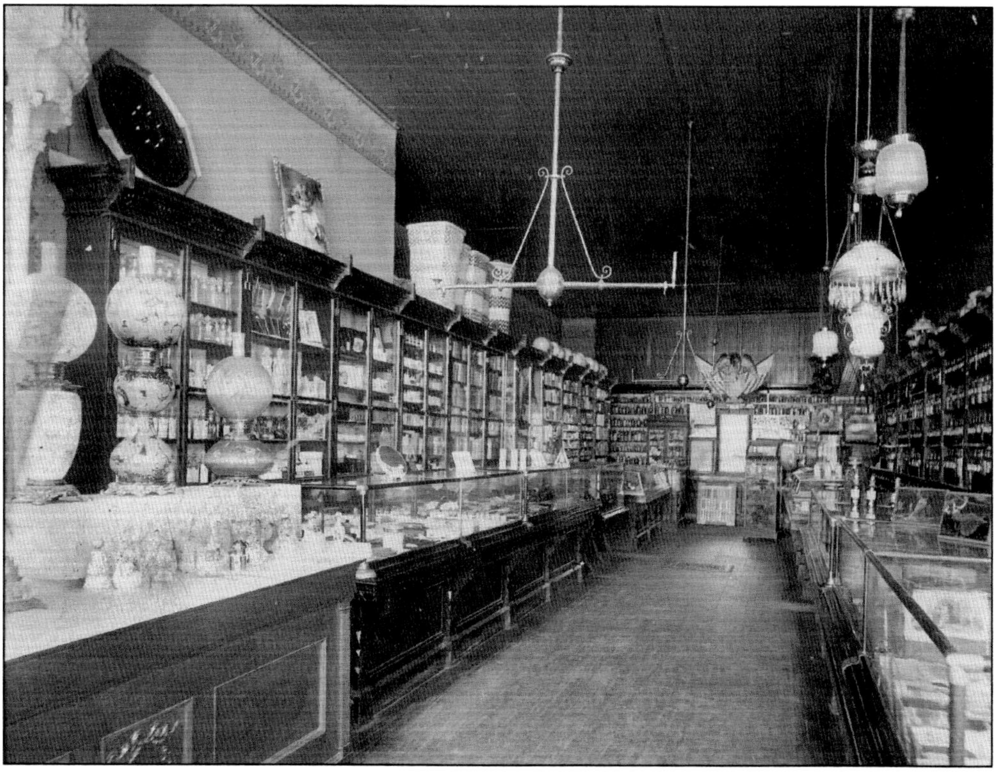

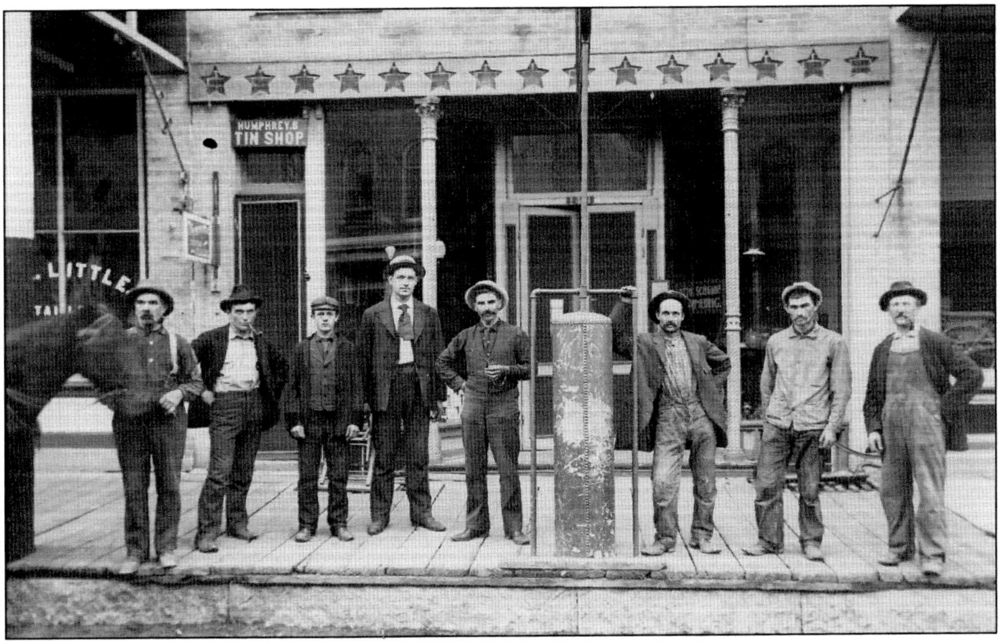

In 1894, Otto Schadde set up his plumbing business and became one of the area's most prominent members of the profession. In the mid-1890s, Schadde was located at 143 Third Street and posed out front with his employees. Schadde is fifth from the left. Schadde became a favorite of Al. Ringling and installed plumbing both at his house and theatre. Inside, the store featured a handsome showroom with water closets, bathtubs, and sinks on display. Schadde Plumbing and Heating is still in business over one hundred years later. (Courtesy of Schadde Plumbing.)

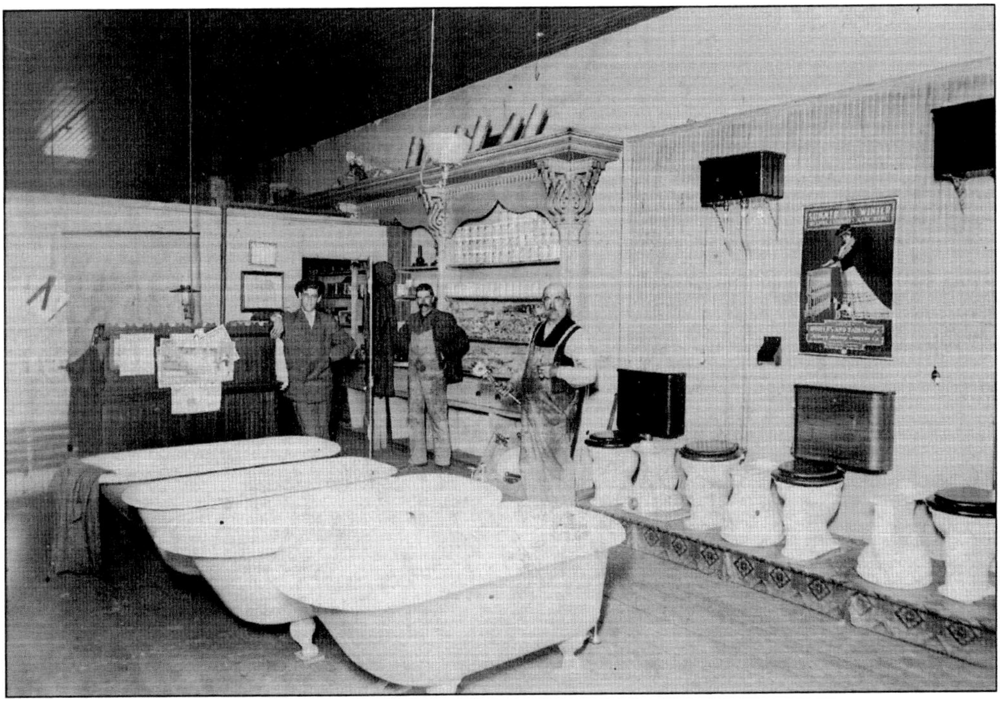

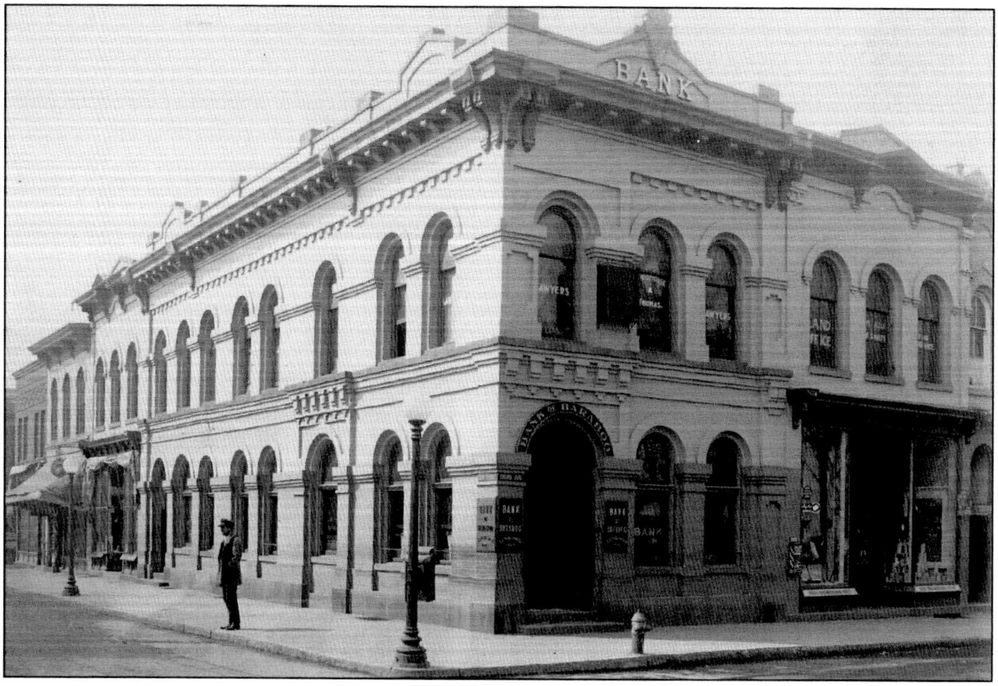

The Baraboo National Bank, under various names, was originally founded in 1857 and was located on the south side of the square. After being burned out of their rented headquarters, plans were immediately made for a new building at the southwest corner of Oak and Third. The building was designed by prominent Milwaukee architect, E. Townsend Mix and was finished in December 1867. The building was periodically redecorated and in 1905 the interior was completely remodeled under the supervision of architect Alfred Clas. On March 29, 1906, the lobby was photographed showing the new teller cages and all the conveniences a patron needed, including check writing stands and spittoon. (Baraboo National Bank Collection.)

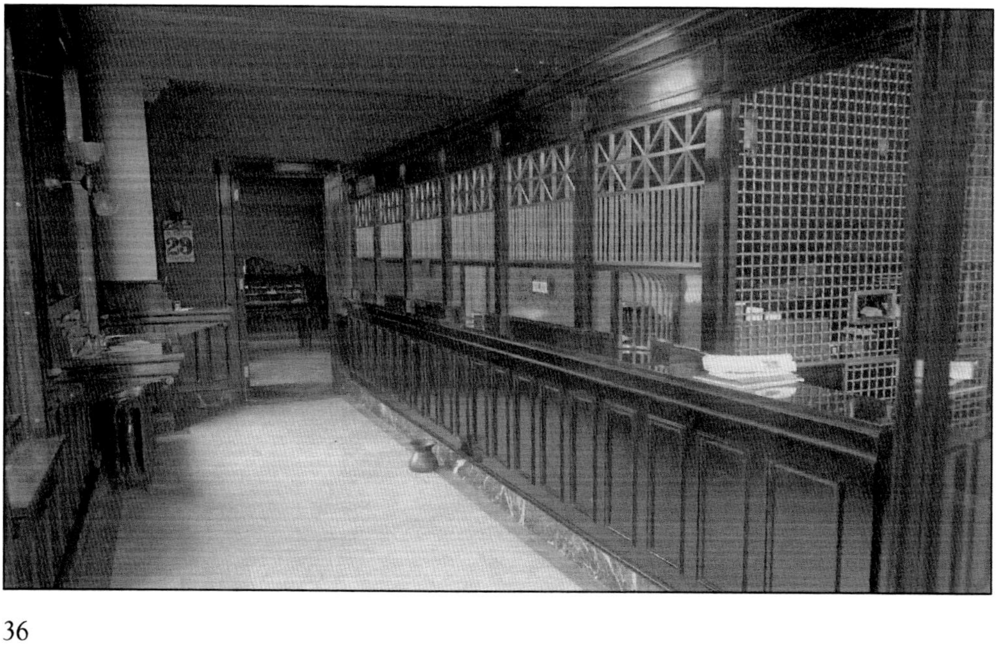

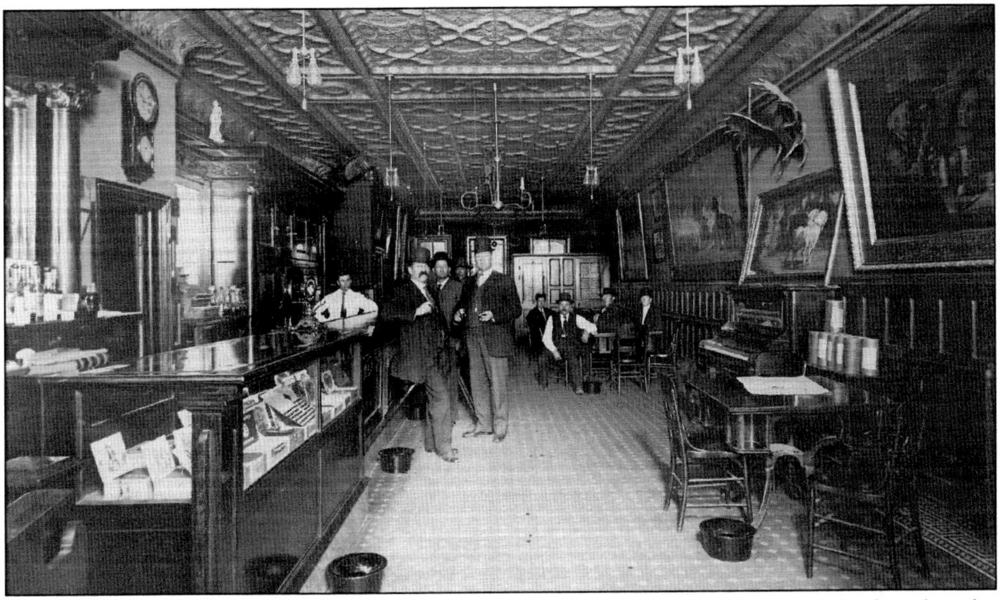

In the 1890s, Fred J. Luther offered one of the nicest drinking establishments to be found in the city. Located at 126 Third Street, the interior featured tiled floors, elaborate woodwork, and a pressed metal ceiling. An assortment of fine cigars was available and entertainment could be had using the player piano. The place was kept neat and tidy with the judicious placement of several spittoons. (Fletcher Collection.)

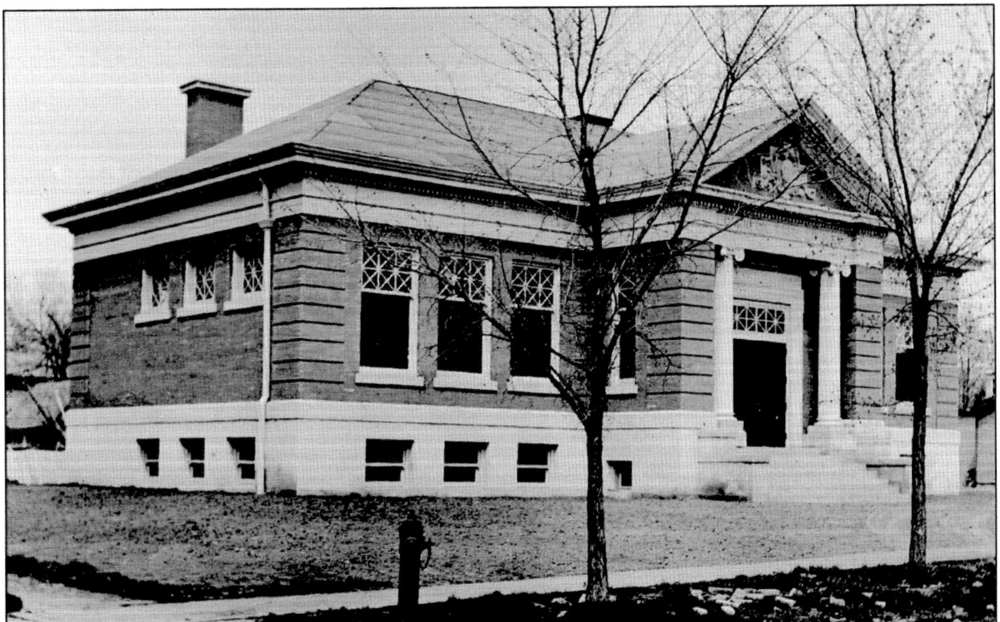

For those wishing to drink from the fountain of knowledge, the Baraboo Public Library was a haven. The handsome building was finished in 1903 and served as the permanent home for the library, which was started in 1895. The building was designed by Claude and Starck of Madison. Louis W. Claude was born at Devil's Lake in 1868. The firm went on to design more than 40 more public libraries.

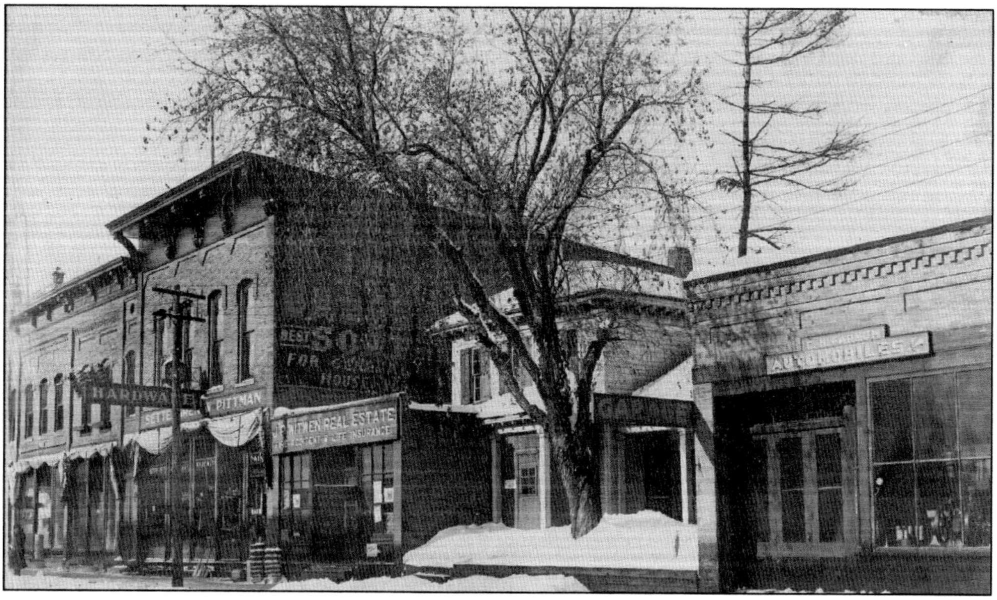

At the turn of the 20th century, the north side of Third Street still contained hints of early Baraboo in the way of a house and a tree. C.H. Farnum's automobile shop and garage heralded a new age to come on one side, while Settergren and Pittmans Hardware Store was well stocked to supply any need on the other. This valuable piece of real estate was put to better use in 1910, when the Risley brothers built a brand new clothing store on the site. The three-story business brought big city design to Baraboo, with the use of a three-story front window display and skylights for natural lighting inside a main sales floor, uninterrupted by posts. The store was known for fine fashion and the annual spring fashion show complete with orchestra was always well attended.

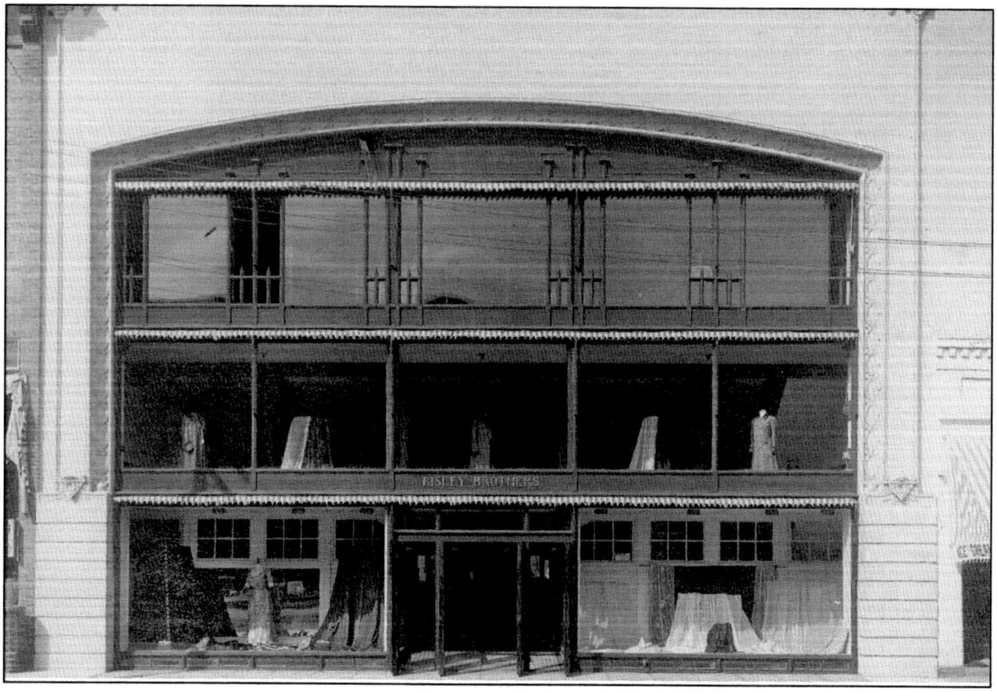

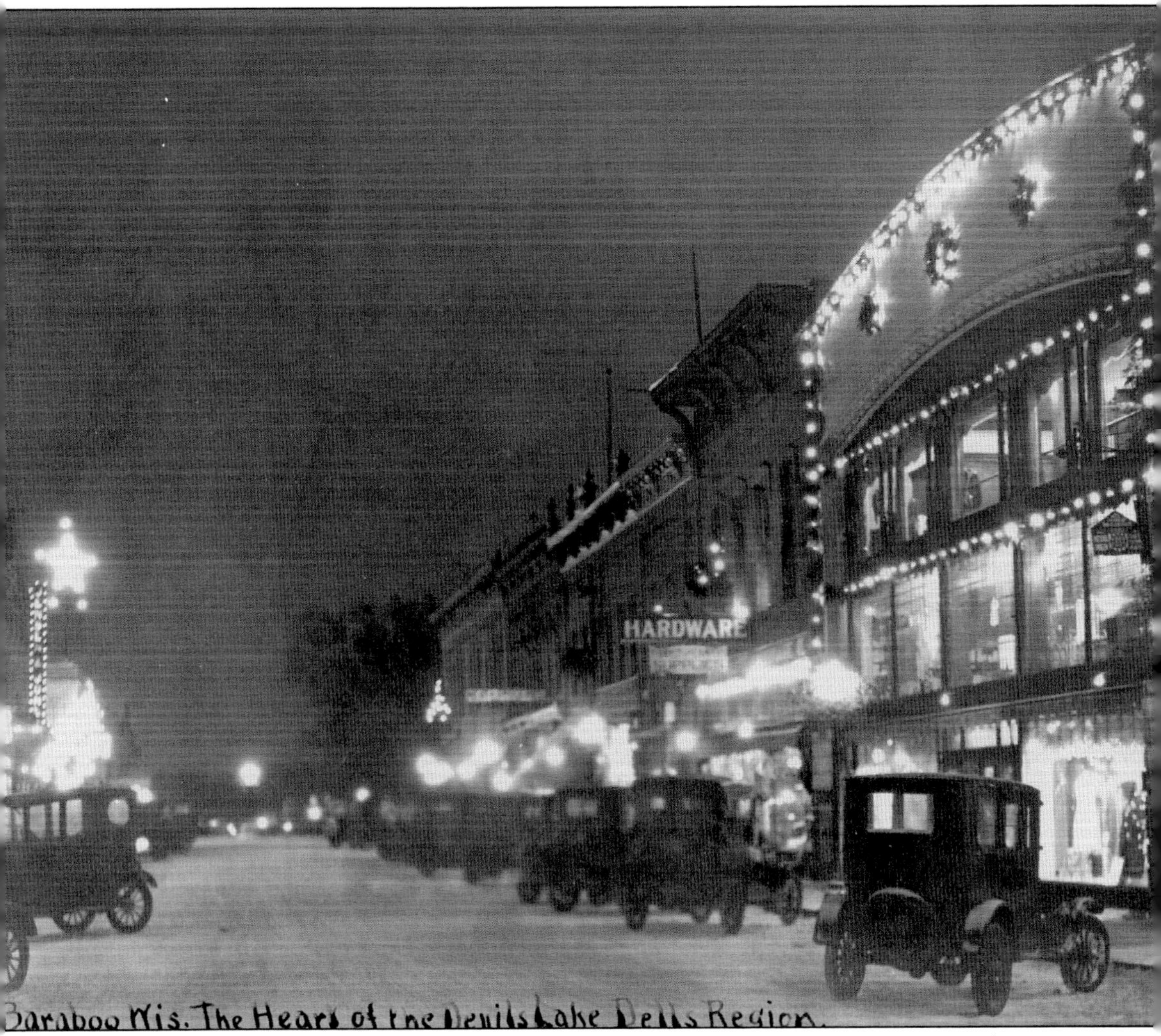

The new age of the automobile was in full swing when this Christmastime picture was taken on Third Street in the 1920s. On the right, Risley Brothers Clothing Store is handsomely decorated to attract holiday shoppers. The automobile brought many changes to Baraboo, not the least of which was more tourists. The Marriott Brothers Hardware Store offers "Tourist and Campers Supplies." (Baraboo National Bank Collection.)

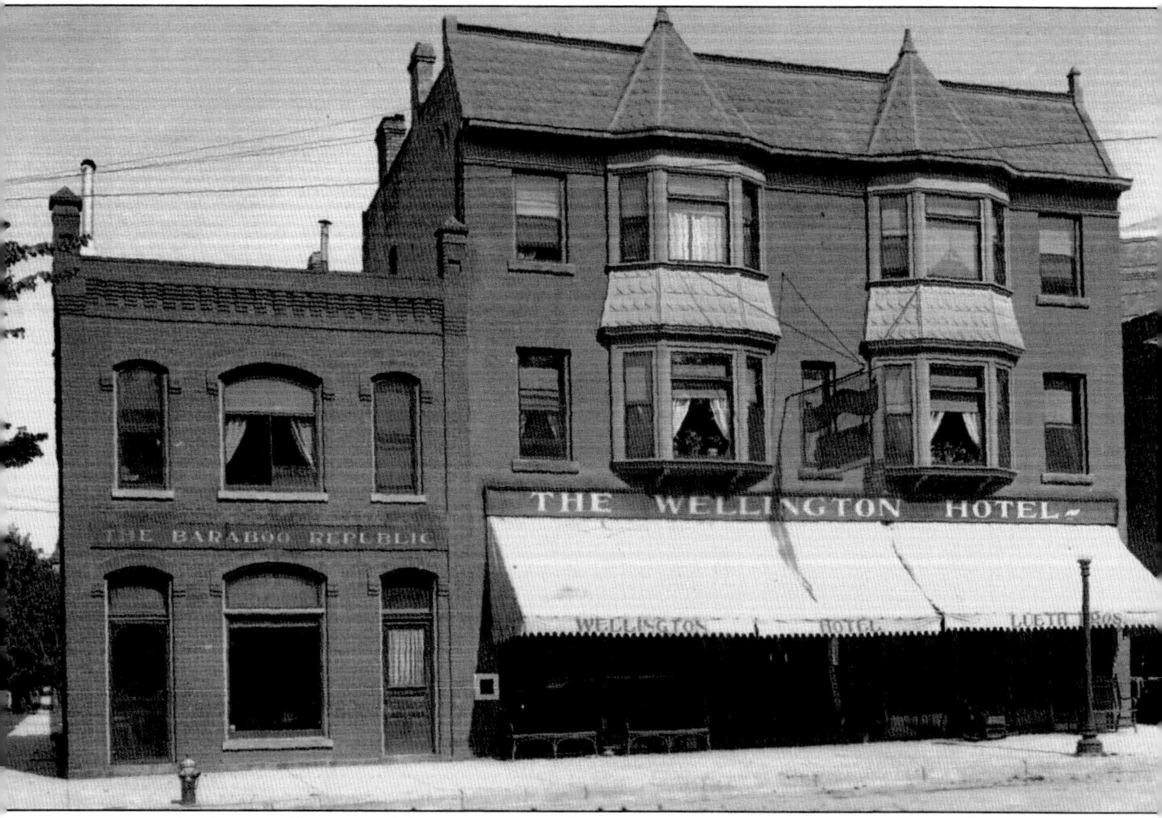

In 1895, the Baraboo Republic Newspaper bought the last remaining vacant corner on the square and constructed a new building for their operation at the northeast corner of Broadway and Fourth. The building cost $3,000 and housed the newspaper offices for the next 35 years. Four years later, work commenced on the last hotel to be built downtown. The three-story structure was started in 1899 and was christened by its owner, Ed. Lueth, the Wellington Hotel. The building is a rare example of Queen Anne architecture, a style that was more commonly used for houses due to its asymmetrical tendencies. Here, however, it has been tamed into a symmetrical composition with two bay windows and fish-scale shingles. The building was enlarged in 1908, adding a larger kitchen and baggage elevator. The newspaper next door called it, "one of the good hotels of the state." (Holt Collection.)

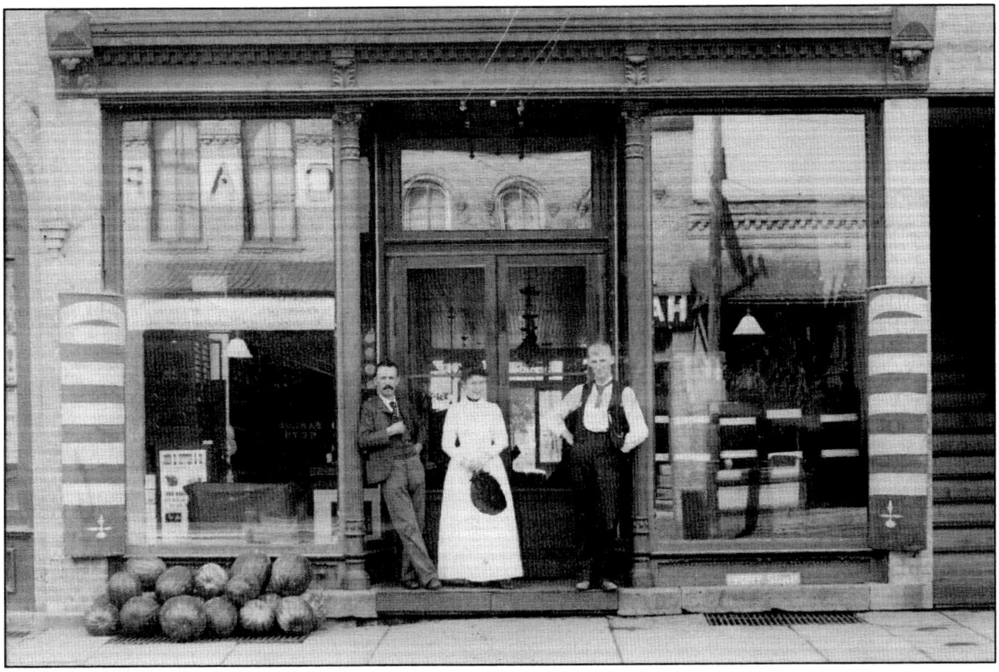

This building, at 142 Third Street, has had its assorted share of businesses, like many downtown locations. Originally built in 1878 by the International Order of Odd Fellows with a lodge on the second floor, the building contained various dry goods and grocery businesses on the first floor. In 1907, the first floor was remodeled to house a vaudeville and moving picture theatre by Lew Aronson, a former side show manager. It was called the Bijou Theatre and offered the latest subjects played on state-of-the art equipment. A few years later, the name was changed to the Gem Theatre, as it appeared in this 1914 photo. The theatre ran until 1923 when it was bought out by the Al. Ringling Theatre. (Holt Collection.)

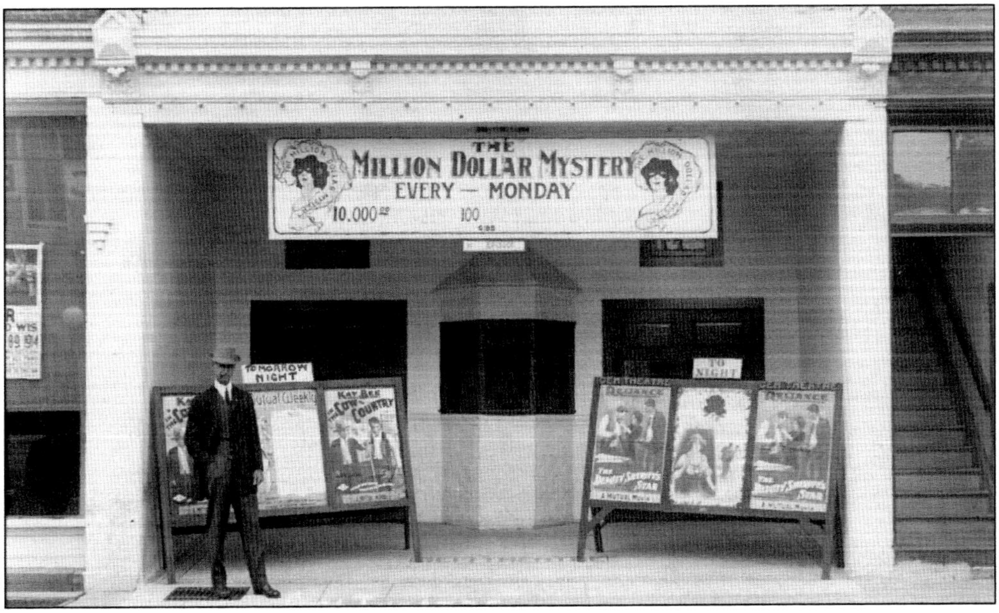

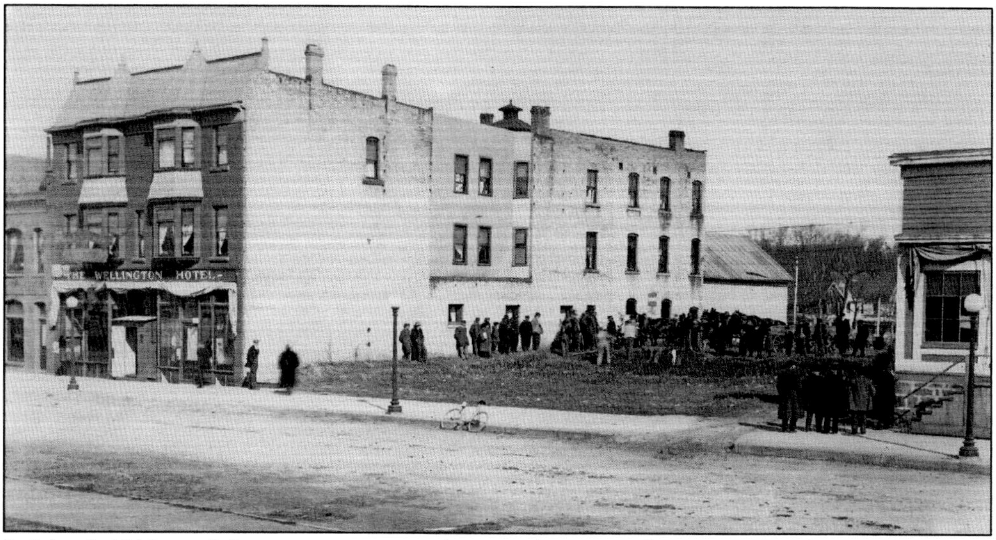

In March 1915, work began on a spectacular new theatre in downtown Baraboo on the site of the old Wisconsin House on the north side of the square. The old hotel had been torn down after Al. Ringling purchased it with plans to build a theatre, to fill the void left when Baraboo's former opera house burned down. The opera house had been at the northwest corner of Fifth and Oak and was originally an 1880s roller skating rink. Though the Wisconsin House was torn down in 1912, it was three more years before groundbreaking began, for reasons unknown. During the summers of 1913 and 1914, the ground was rented out, a large big top was erected, and silent films were played on the site of the future theatre.

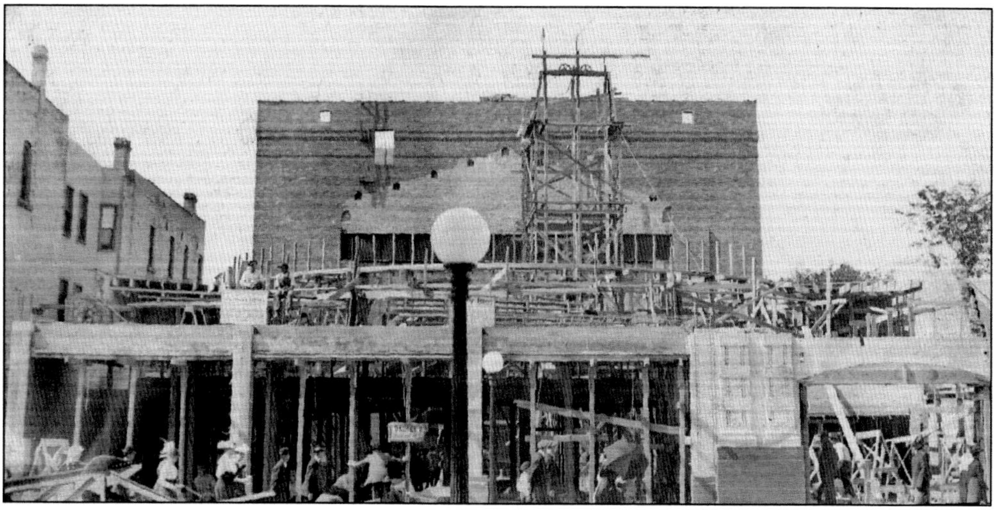

Work progressed quickly on the new theatre and by June 24, 1915, the fly loft and the elliptical shape of the auditorium could be seen behind the first story of the façade. This same day was Al. Ringling Appreciation Day, when thousands gathered in front of Al. Ringling's residence as a show of support and gratitude. Ringling's health was failing at the time. The theatre contained 59 train-car loads of brick and the largest girder over the auditorium weighed 12 tons. (Holt Collection.)

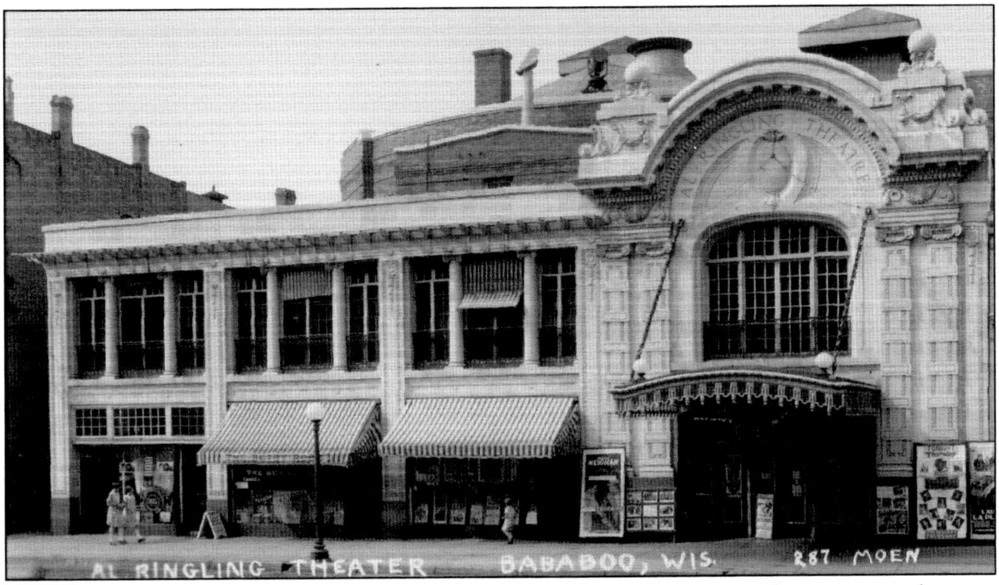

The Al. Ringling Theatre was designed by George W. and Cornelius Rapp, who went on to become nationally known theatre architects. The brothers were able to lavish large amounts of decoration on the project with the Ringling's seemingly limitless budget. The originally façade consisted of three stores, with private offices above and the theatre entrance protected by the original glass and iron canopy. Al. Ringling lived to see his theatre finished and made it to opening night on November 17, 1915, for a performance of Lady Luxury, a light comedy. Silent films started at the theatre two weeks later—Al. Ringling died on January 1, 1916. (Holt Collection.)

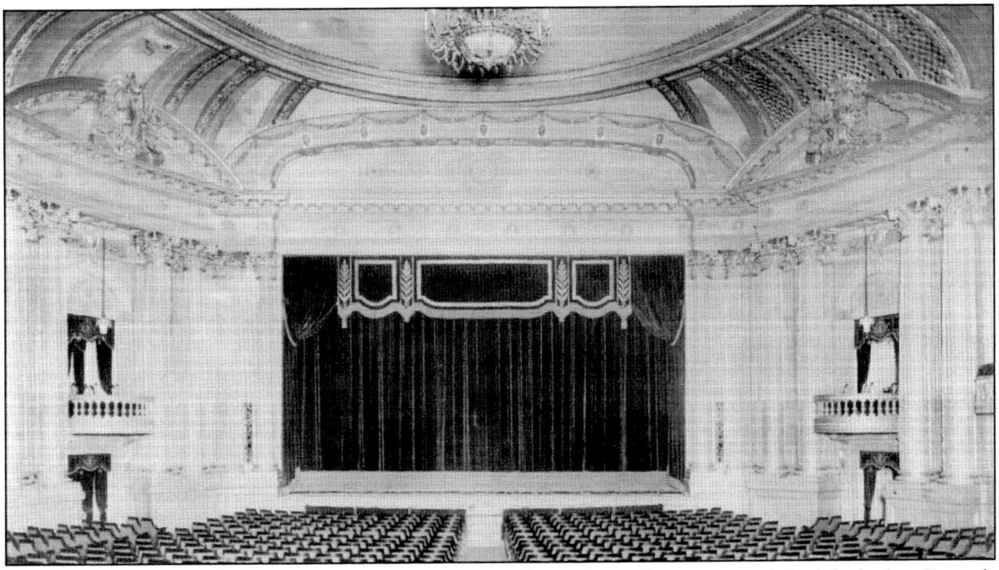

The interior of the theatre was even more astonishing than the exterior. Modeled after French theatres, including that at the Palace of Versailles, the new theatre originally had 874 seats, including the 17 boxes. Hand-painted murals adorned the ceiling above the boxes, and clouds were painted around the chandelier. The theatre was built for live shows and silent films. Eleven dressing rooms under the stage were used by traveling shows and modern projection equipment was used for the silent films.

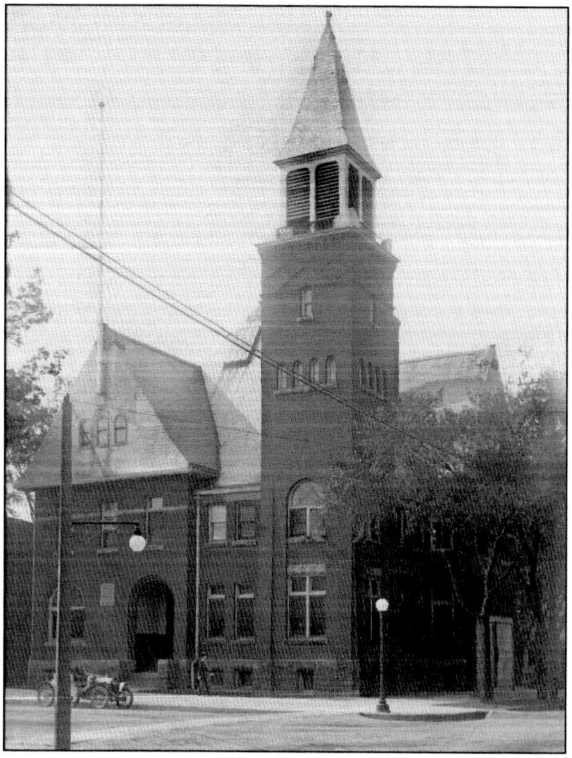

Although Baraboo was the county seat, city government was also important and in 1892 the city fathers decided to show this with the construction of a new city hall. Architects Conover and Porter of Madison drew up the plans for the building, which housed all city offices as well as the fire department. The building was demolished in the 1960s and replaced with the current Baraboo Municipal Building.

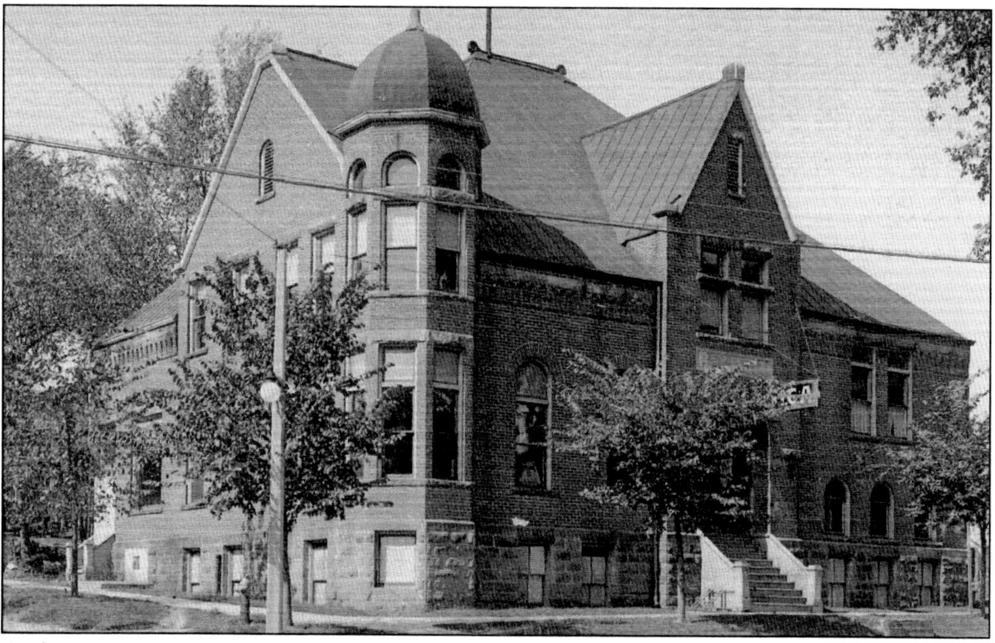

Architects Conover and Porter also designed the Baraboo YMCA building, constructed in 1890 and located at the northwest corner of Second and Ash. The building cost $15,000 and contained a game room, library, parlors, lecture room, gymnasium, and two bowling alleys in the basement. The Sauk County Historical Society held its first public meeting at the YMCA on November 23, 1905. The building was demolished in 1936 and the site is now a parking lot.

In 1857, a new jail was needed for Sauk County, as its current jail, on the north side of the square, was so insecure one of its inmates simply dug his way out and escaped. This was remedied when a new stone hexagonal jail was constructed at the northwest corner of Broadway and First. It was 24 feet on each side and contained cells as well as accommodations for the sheriff and his family. In 1884, just north of the jail, the Ringling Brothers held their first circus performance.

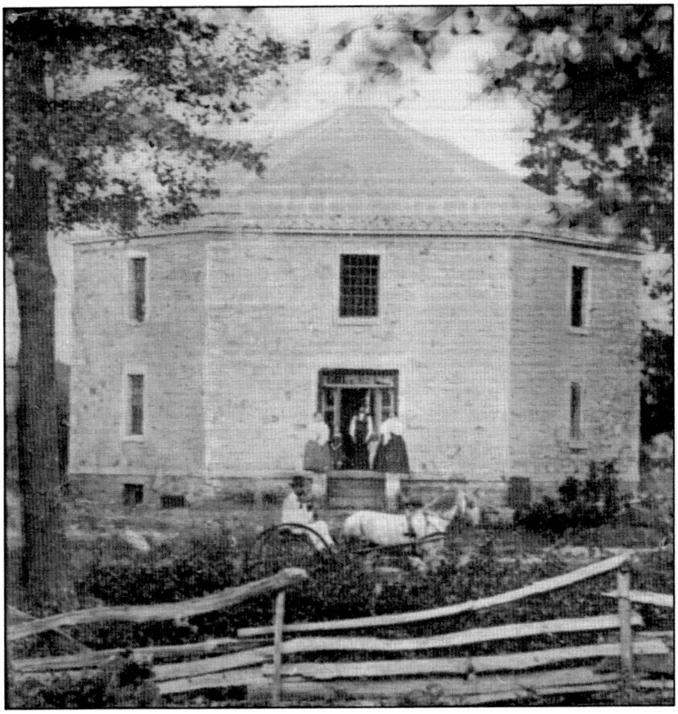

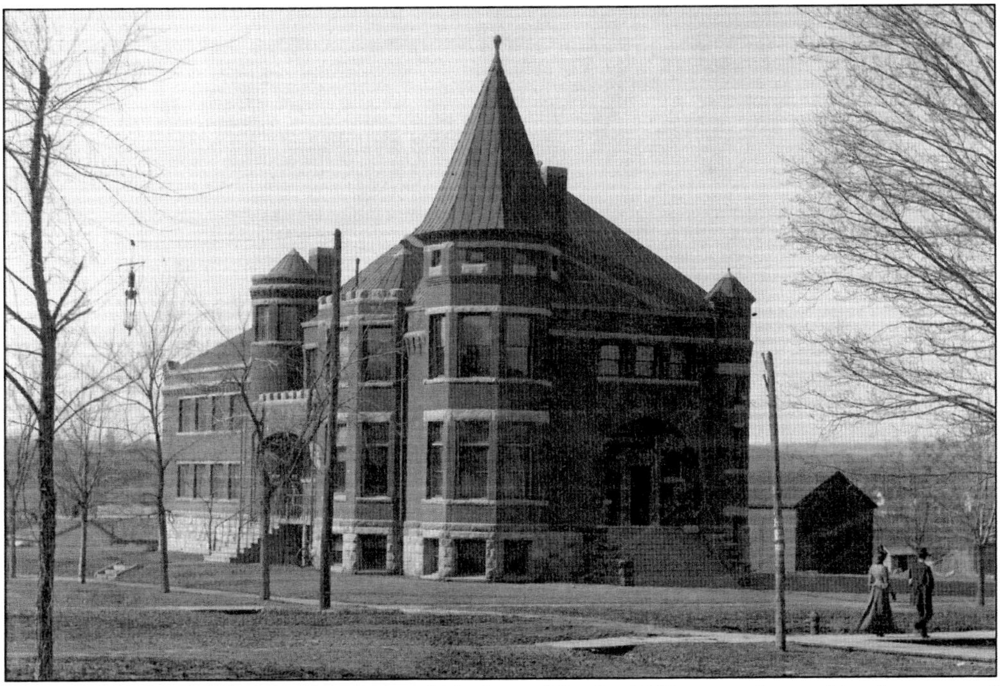

While the old jail sufficed as long as could be hoped for, by 1890 it was deemed inadequate and a new jail and sheriff's residence were designed by Conover and Porter of Madison. While not only looking the part with its battlements and fortress-like appearance, the building was also deemed one of the best designed in the state for its purpose. The building was razed in the 1960s, when the new jail in the courthouse annex was completed.

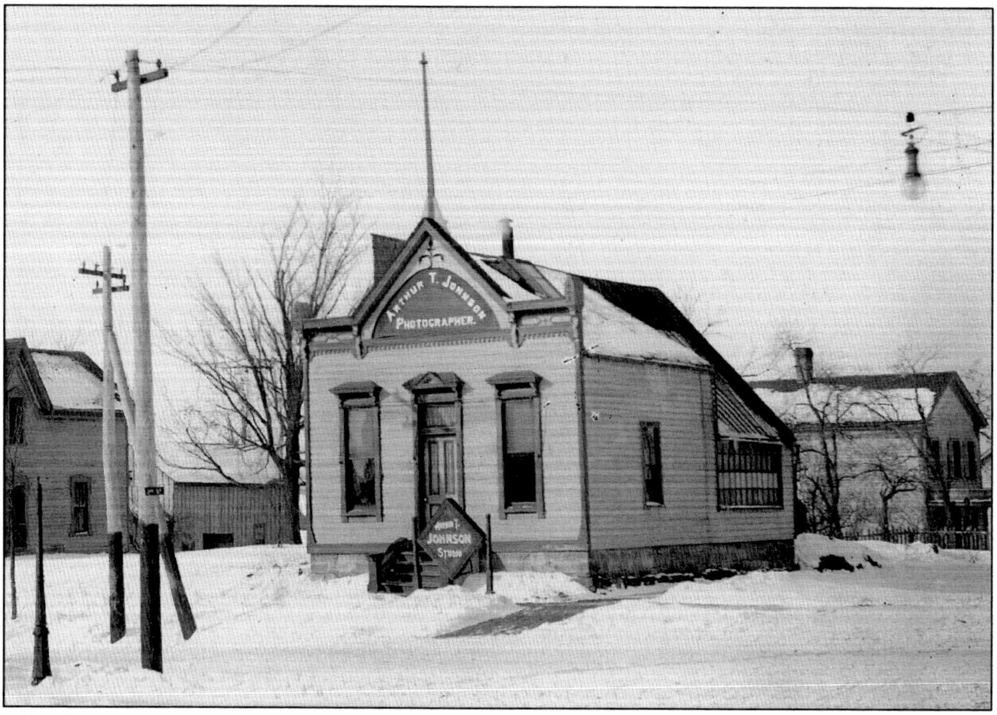

The photography studio of Arthur T. Johnson stood for many years on the southwest corner of Oak and Second. Owned earlier by Adolph Baer, it was bought out by Johnson in 1892. The neat little building contained a studio with north-facing skylights to take advantage of natural lighting.

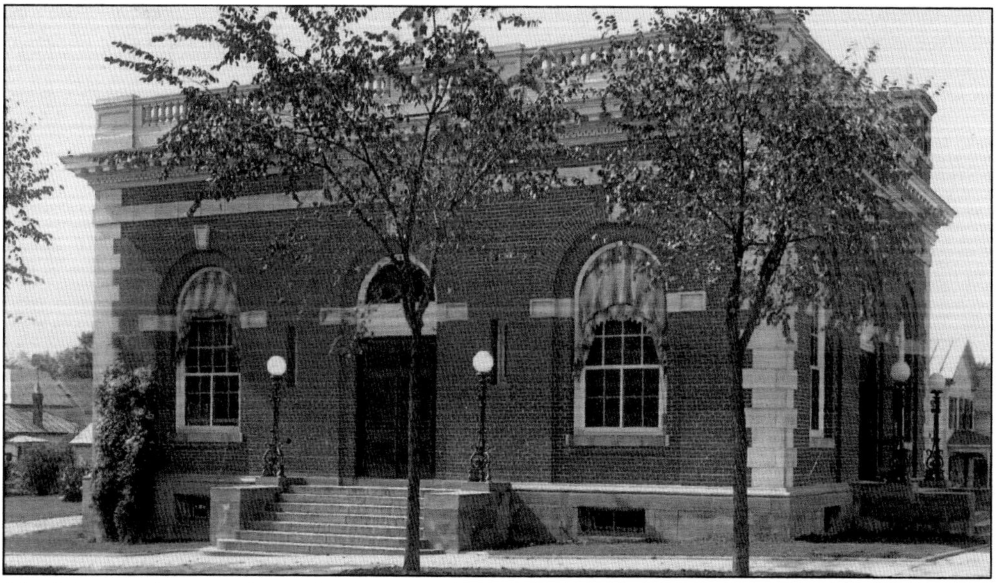

The Johnson photography studio lot was sold and the building moved in 1904 to make way for a new post office. A year and a half later, a new building with all the modern conveniences stood on the corner. It was not to everybody's liking however, as many thought the exterior looked cheap and could not understand where $45,000 had been spent. The building was soon improved with the addition of a decorative balustrade at the roof line.

Four

South Side

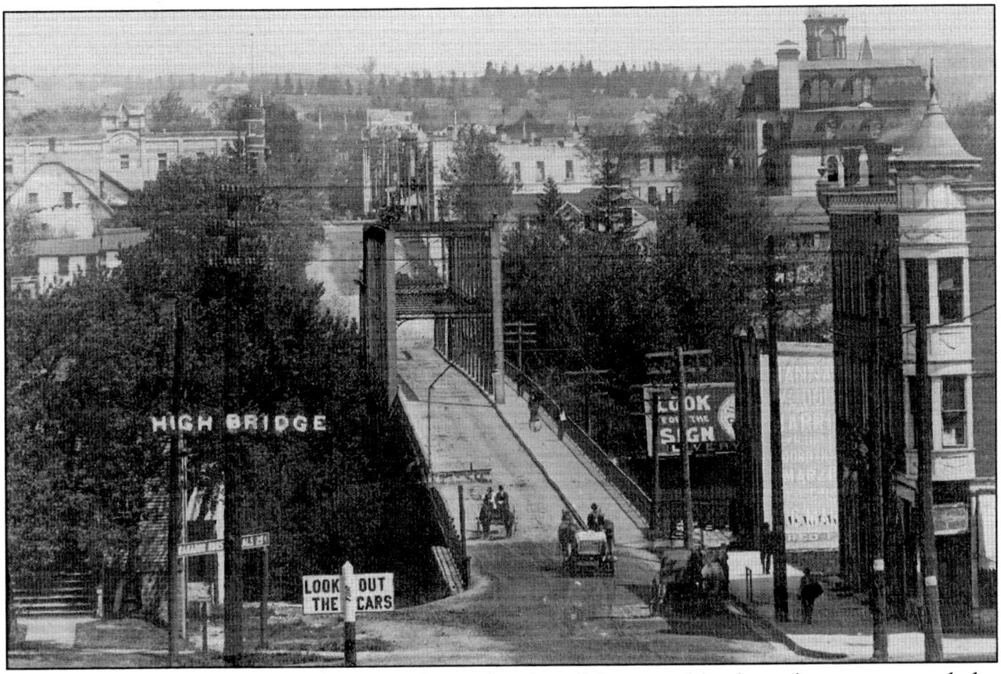

While the south side of Baraboo may have developed less quickly than the area around the square originally known as Adams, it can nonetheless claim the title as the original Baraboo. It was on this land in 1846 that George Brown platted the village he named "Baraboo." This included land north of the river on Water Street, which was called "under the hill" due to its geography. Later in 1849, the county board ordered that the two plats of Adams and Baraboo be named Brooklyn. The name Baraboo seems to have been preferred by the residents however, as in 1852 the post office officially became known as Baraboo. While the square and surroundings may have contained the buildings of city and county government, fine hotels, and prominent shops, it was the south side that was the soul of Baraboo. It was there that some of the prominent mills, factories, and breweries were located along with the bridges that spanned the river. The railroad arrived there in 1871 and employed hundreds of railroad men. The south side was also home to the Ringling Brothers headquarters and had its own commercial sections primarily at both ends of the Ash Street bridge. These grew substantially after the arrival of the railroad.

The south side is shown at its most spectacular at about 1900, above, when the High Bridge spanned the river at Oak Street and provided access to the depot at the same level as the square. The three-story Effinger Hotel sat prominently at the south end of the bridge, while the view to the north shows the 1869 high school with cupola on the right. (Baraboo National Bank Collection.)

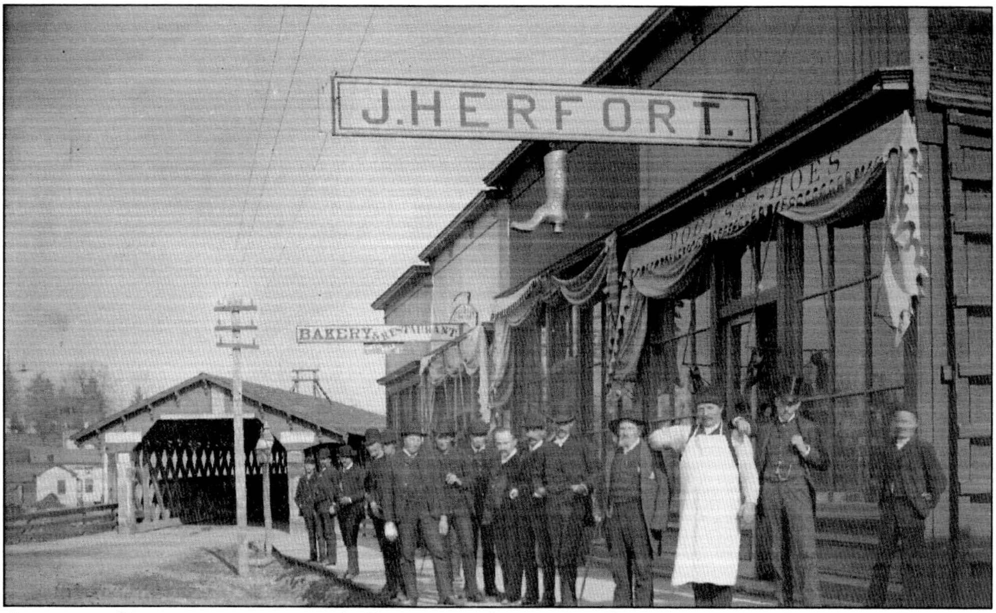

A group of business owners and clients posed outside of a new crop of buildings that were constructed just south of the Ash-Walnut Street bridge after the arrival of the railroad in 1871. The thoroughfare was also improved in 1875 with the construction of a covered bridge, one of at least six built in the county at this time. The bridge contained 83,000 board feet of lumber, 54,000 shingles, and spanned the river at 166 feet with no center support.

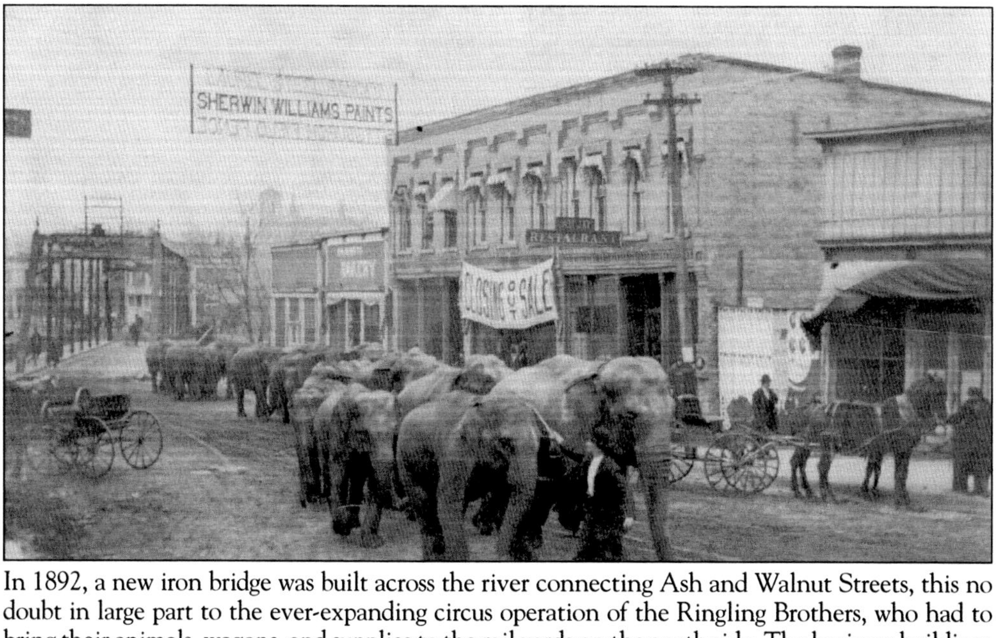

In 1892, a new iron bridge was built across the river connecting Ash and Walnut Streets, this no doubt in large part to the ever-expanding circus operation of the Ringling Brothers, who had to bring their animals, wagons, and supplies to the rail yards on the south side. The business buildings in this area were slowly improved to brick structures, often after a fire destroyed the old ones, as was the case for two of the buildings in the photo at top. (Courtesy of Don Dietsch.)

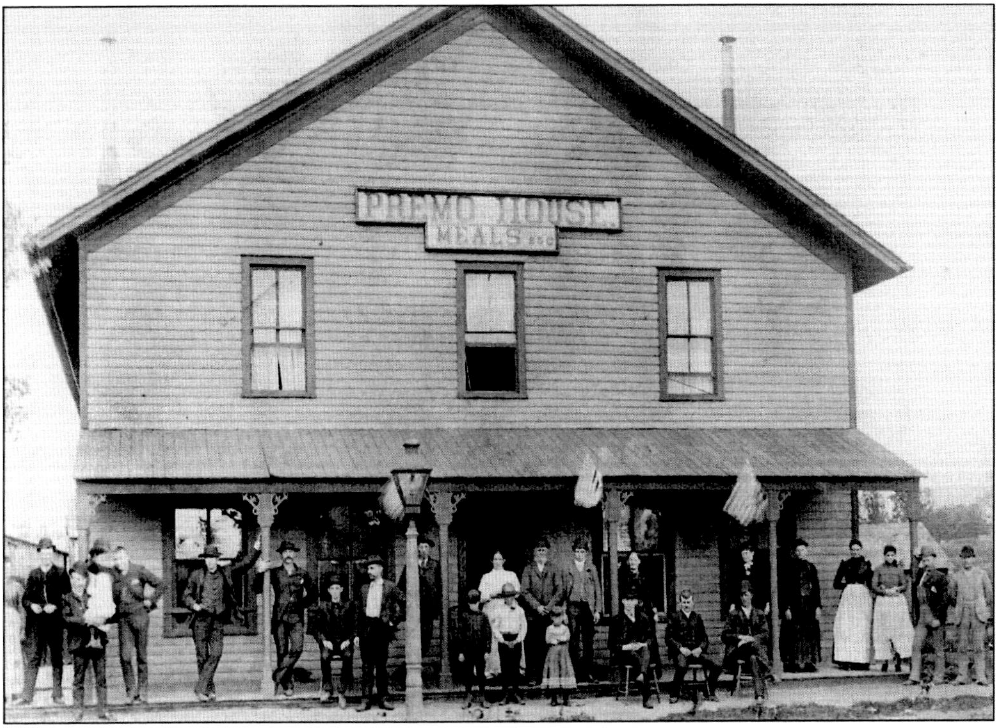

The Premo House, located at 423 East Lynn Street on the south side, was a boarding house for unmarried working men and women. Located near the rail yards, it offered affordable room and board, primarily to railroad employees. At the time of this photo, from around 1880, meals were advertised at 25¢.

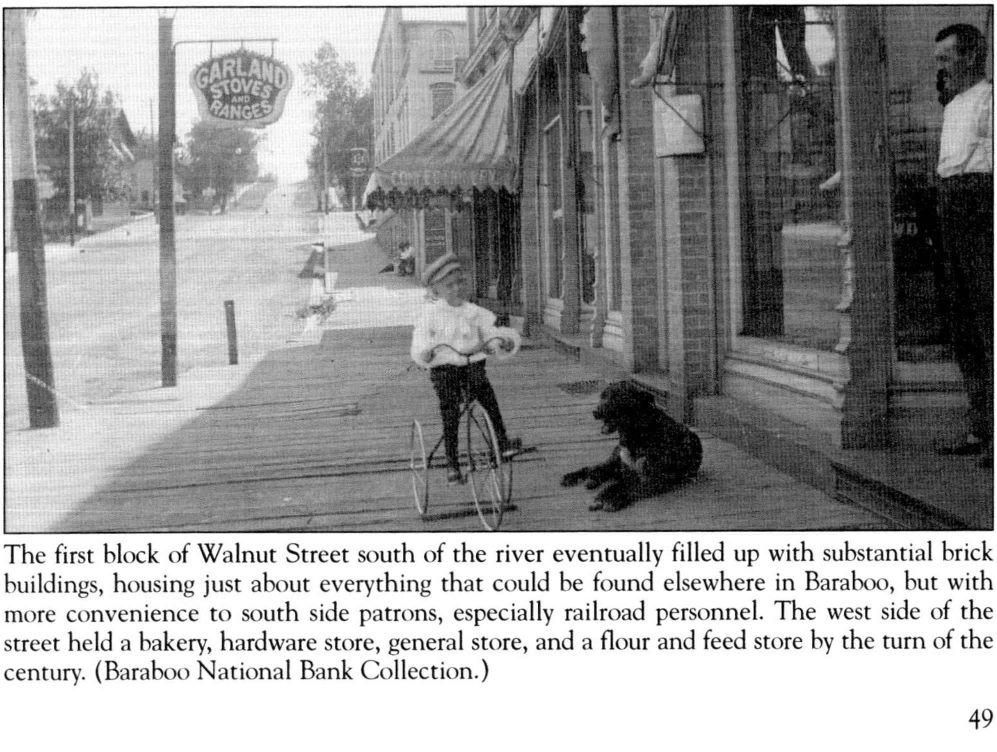

The first block of Walnut Street south of the river eventually filled up with substantial brick buildings, housing just about everything that could be found elsewhere in Baraboo, but with more convenience to south side patrons, especially railroad personnel. The west side of the street held a bakery, hardware store, general store, and a flour and feed store by the turn of the century. (Baraboo National Bank Collection.)

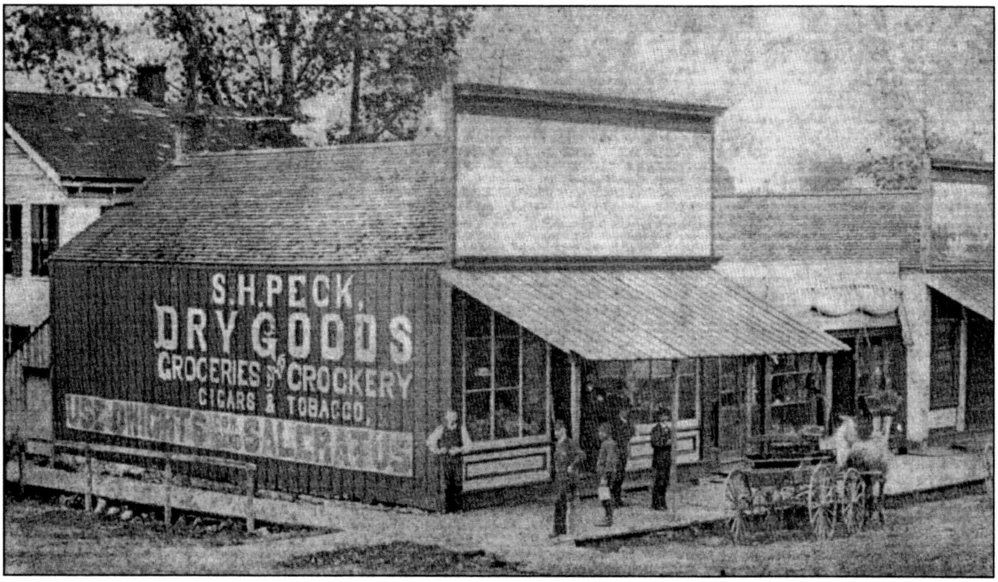

One of the earliest stores in Baraboo was that of Judge Hoxie, erected at the southeast corner of Ash and Water in the early 1850s. At that time, Water Street was busy with the traffic going to and from the enormous Bassett Mill west of the store. For many years, the only bridge was at Ash Street, which made for a good location for business. The building was demolished in 1902, when a substantial brick building was built on this corner.

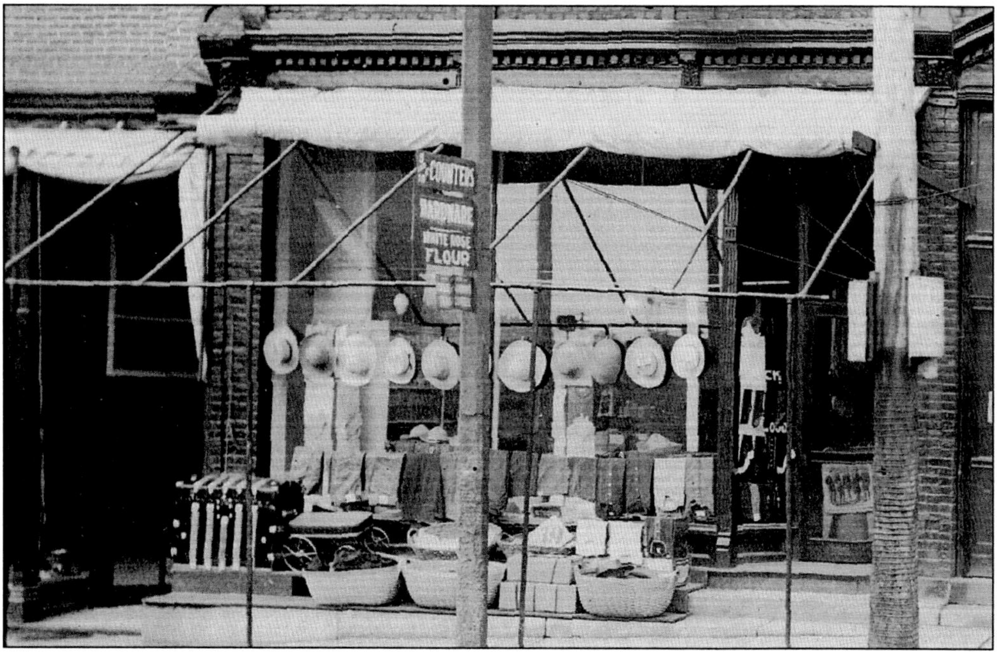

Peck's South Side Department Store was a fixture at 127 Walnut Street for over 50 years, beginning in 1885 when the building was built to house the seven-year-old firm of Peck and Herfort. Frank Herfort was only 18 when he went into business with 22-year-old Fremont C. Peck. Though Herfort later sold out and eventually opened a canning factory, Peck remained at the location, eventually selling the business to a nephew.

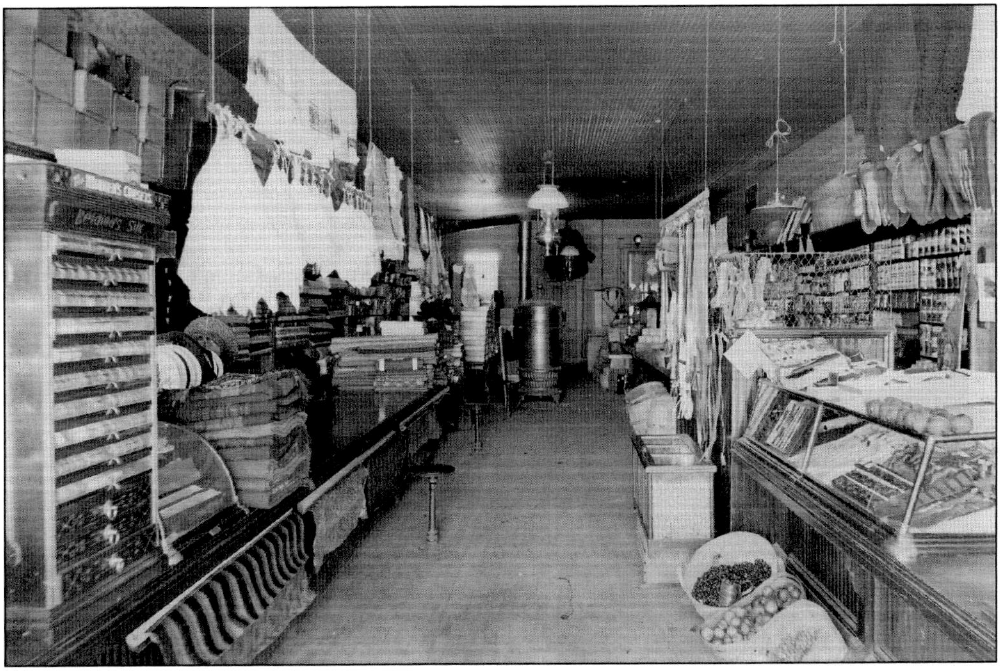

The interior of Peck's South Side Department Store featured everything a homemaker could want. On the left side, a large array of fabrics and sewing notions could be had, with the convenience of a stool for waiting while your selection was cut. The right side of the store contained gloves and belts, wallets and purses, and some seasonal food items, such as those in the baskets on the floor.

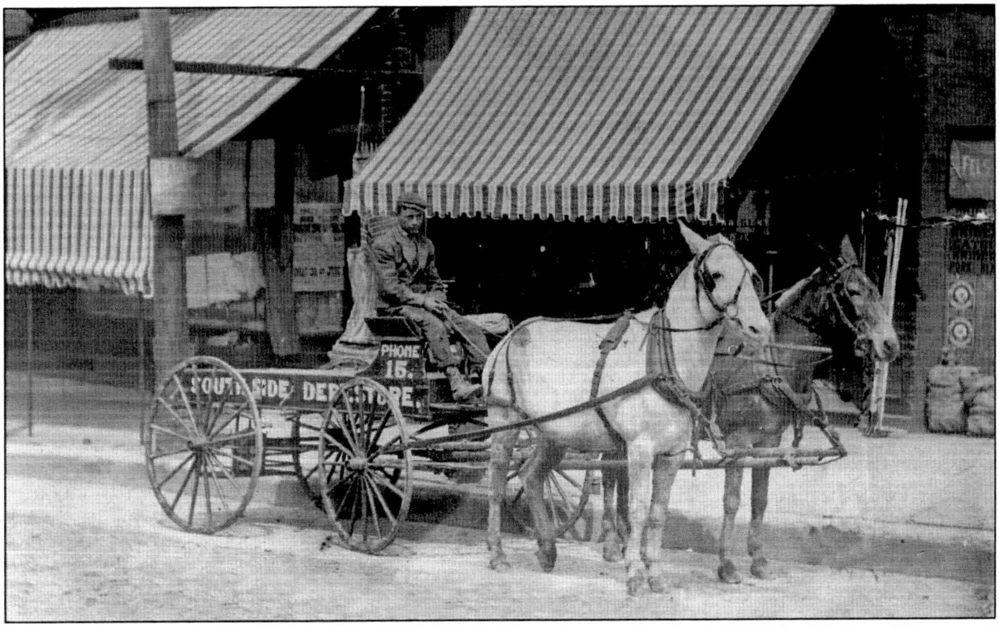

The delivery wagon of Peck's South Side Department Store was operated by Nelson "Brownie" Bartley in 1907 and offered something in the way of convenience for patrons who couldn't make it in to the store. A quick phone call to No. 15 meant that your goods were on their way.

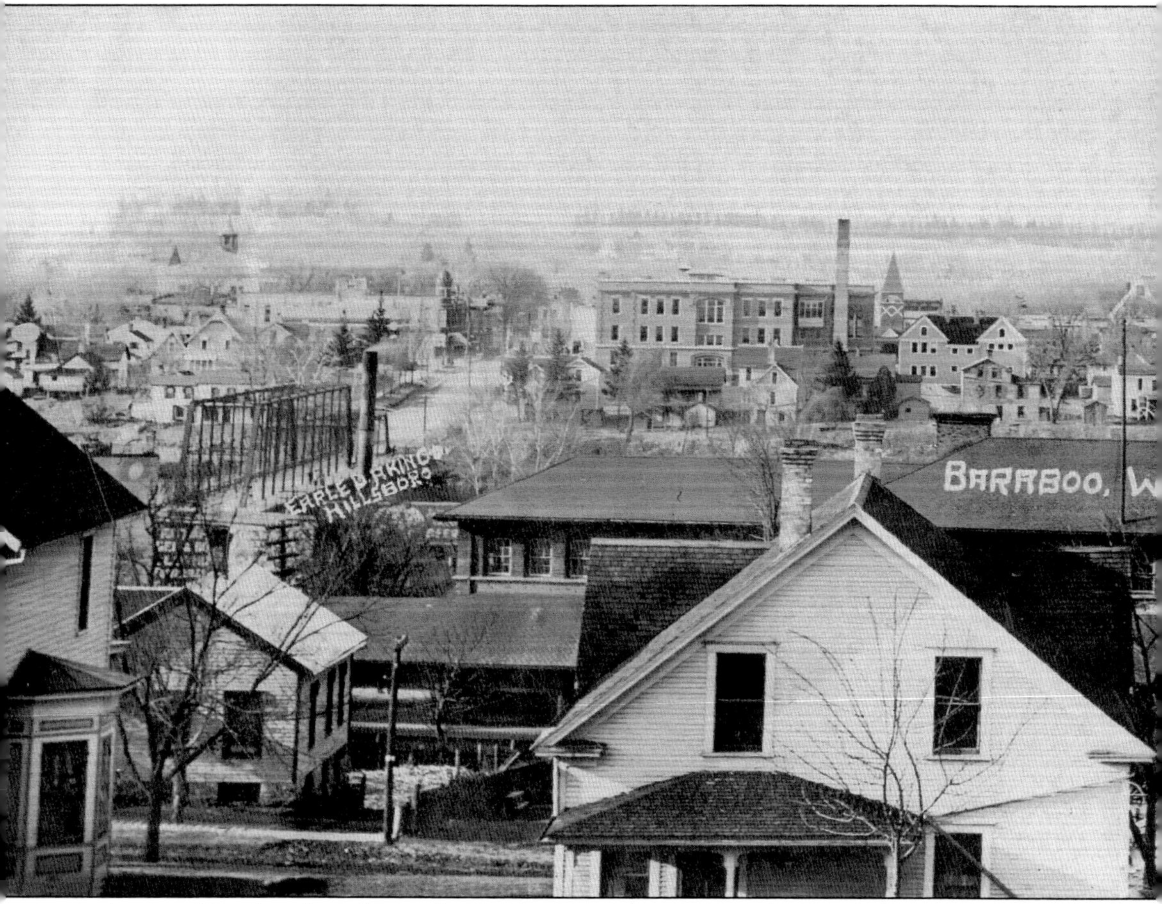

A view of Baraboo from the south side about 1910 (compare with page 2) shows a city that had quadrupled its population since the arrival of the railroad 40 years earlier. The crowning jewel of the railroad era was the depot, completed in 1902, in the center of the picture. At left, the high bridge connects the south side with Oak Street on the north side. The thoroughfare runs

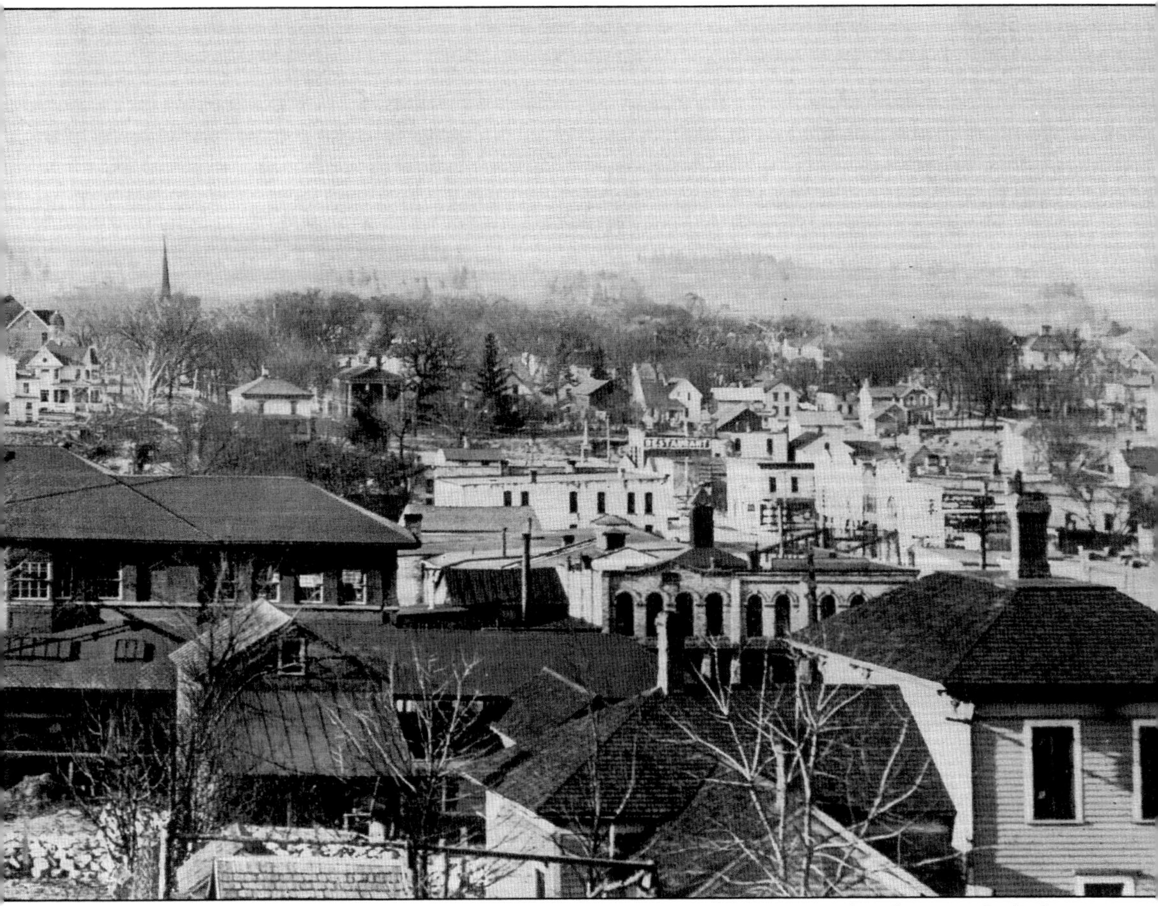

past the new red brick high school, completed in 1907. To the extreme right, the new Catholic church stands with its two steeples bathed in sunlight. The houses in the foreground on Maple Street are simple, but functional, homes for Baraboo's working class.

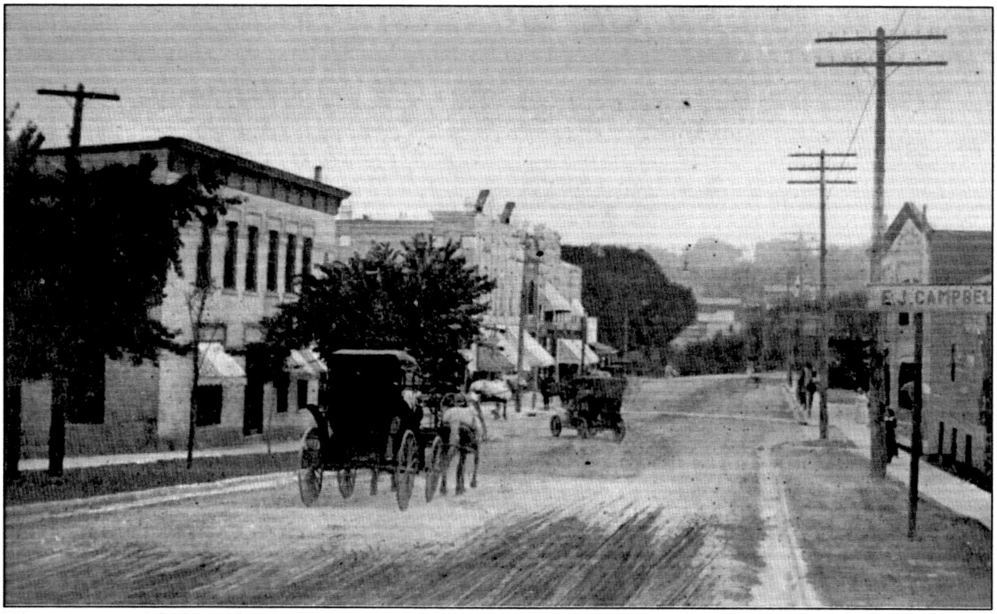

The corner of Ash and Water Streets has always been a bustling place. The corner was one of the first to be developed in early Baraboo and by 1902 it had two hotels: the Thompson House (at left), completed in 1899, offered 23 rooms, and the Urban House (diagonally opposite) offered about the same. The southeast corner contained the new Effinger Block, housing a saloon and bottling works.

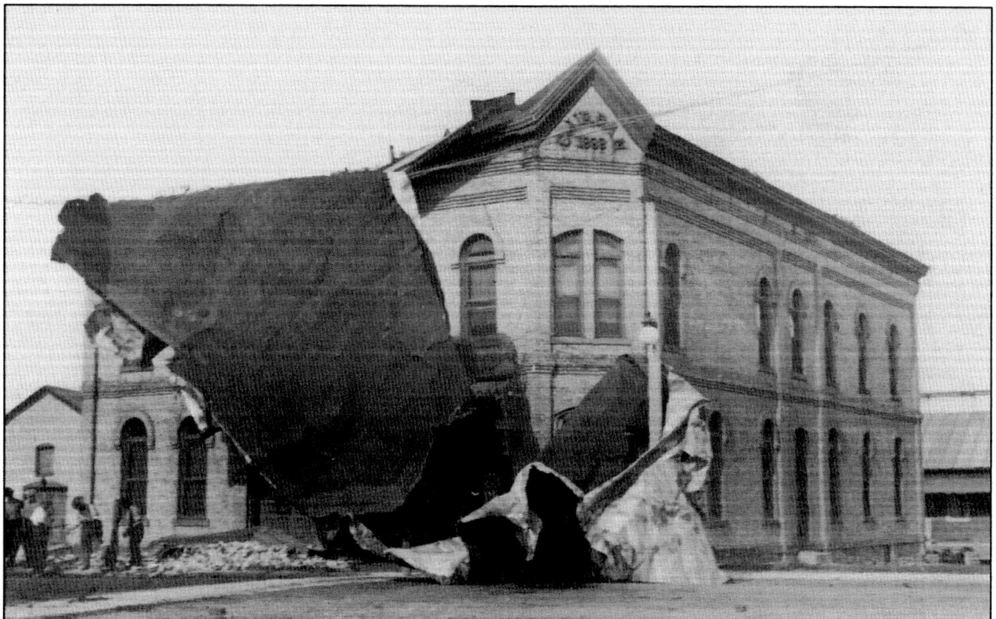

The Urban House at the southwest corner of Ash and Water was built in 1888. It was dramatically damaged on the night of June 25, 1914, when a terrific wind storm hit Baraboo, causing much damage. The wind peeled up the metal roof, weighing over a ton, and laid it over the front of the building, on top of the power lines and around a light pole. (Courtesy of Joe Ward.)

Five

Circus Days

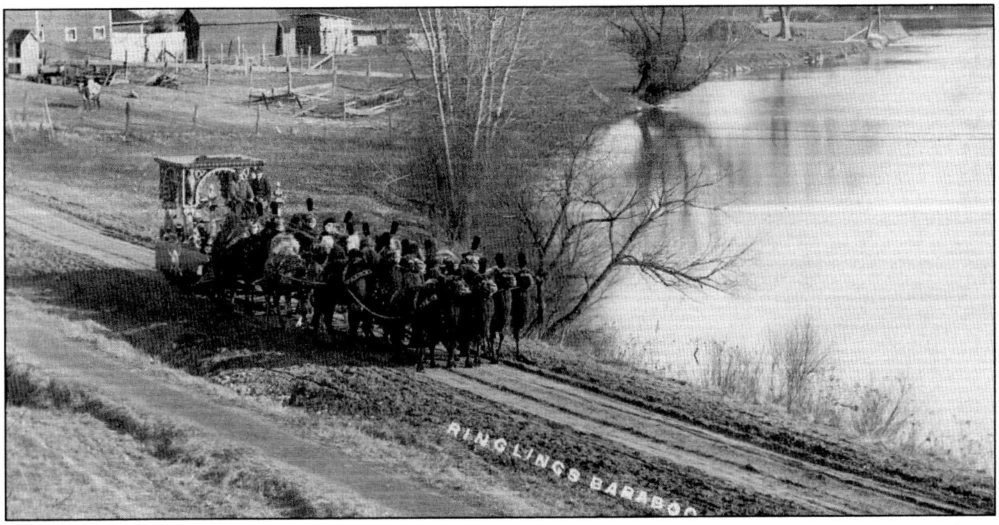

It was somewhat by chance that Baraboo became the birthplace of the Ringling Brothers Circus. The nomadic patriarch, August Rüngeling, later Ringling, moved his family in and out of Baraboo three different times starting in the 1850s. The family happened to be there in 1882 when Al., the eldest son, organized the Ringling Brothers' Classic and Comic Concert Company, the forerunner to the circus. Their tented circus opened in Baraboo on May 19, 1884, with the help of veteran circus man "Yankee Robinson," who prophetically announced before each show that, "the Ringling Brothers are the future showman of America." Despite the fact that Robinson died during the first season, the show grew quickly and soon the brothers were acquiring old industrial land next to the river for their winter quarters. In 1890, the circus switched to a railroad operation and grew exponentially. By 1900, the Ringling Brothers were acquiring other circuses and were well on their way to becoming the largest circus in the United States. Their cousins, the Gollmar Brothers, also started a circus in Baraboo in 1891. Another set of cousins, the Moeller brothers, made circus wagons for both operations. The effect on Baraboo's economy was enormous. Off-season operations included everything from a large wardrobe department to caring for the hundreds of exotic and domestic animals used in the shows. This was good news for area farmers and businessmen. In 1918, the Ringling Brothers moved their winter quarters to Bridgeport, Connecticut, former headquarters for Barnum & Bailey, which Ringlings purchased in 1907, thus ending a 34-year legacy in Baraboo. The Gollmar Brothers sold their outfit in 1916. Today, the circus heritage is carried on at Circus World Museum, located at the historic Ringling winter quarters.

A hitch of 16 camels, above, pulls the Egypt float along the Baraboo River at the Ringling's winter quarters, getting ready for the next season. The Egypt float was built in Baraboo by the Moeller brothers in 1903.

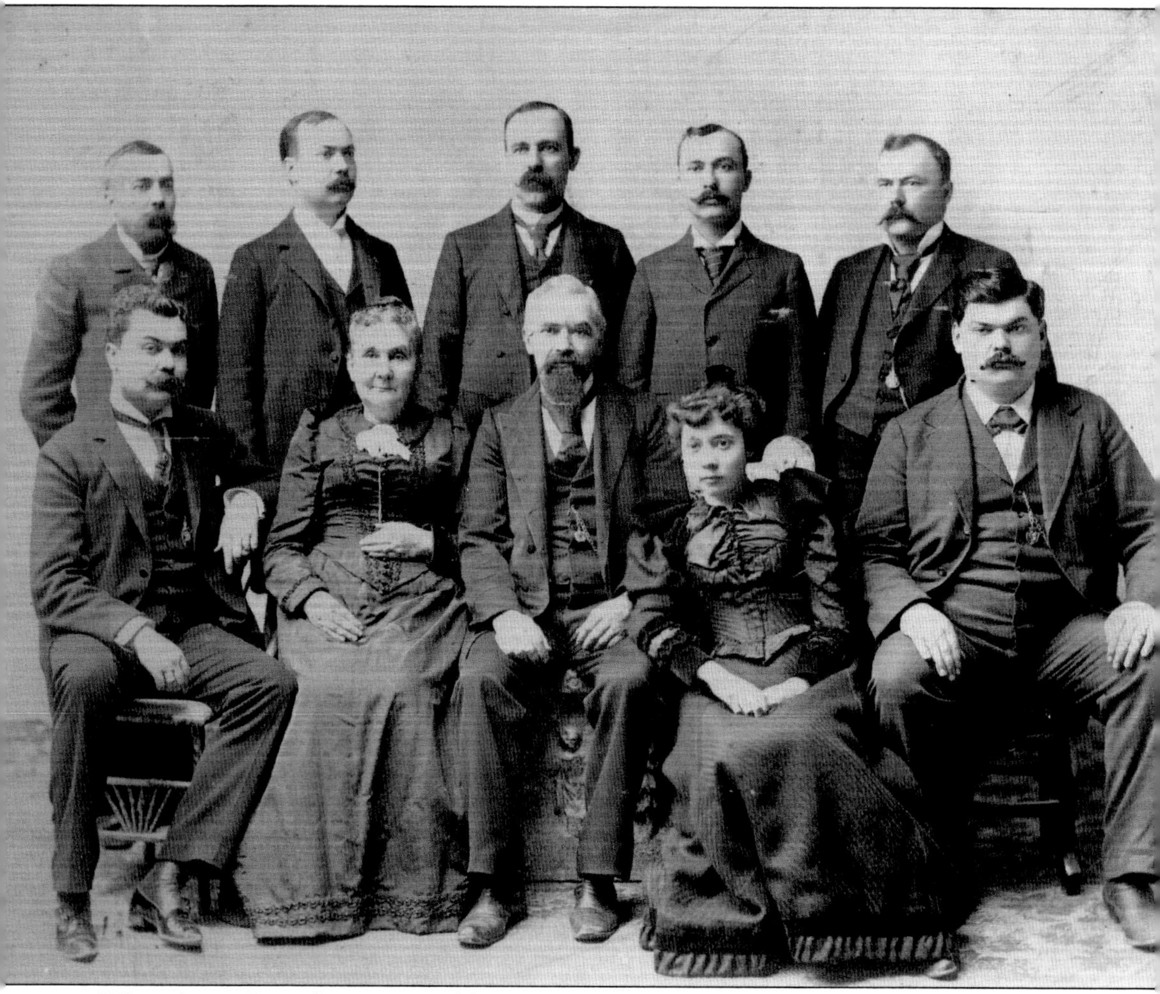

When August Rüngeling emigrated from Hannover to Canada, and later to the United States in the late 1840s, he probably could not have dreamed of the success his sons would achieve. Blessed with seven sons and one daughter, who lived to adulthood, he moved his family many times, always looking for a better market for his harness shop. This portrait, taken a few years before August Ringling Sr.'s death in 1898, shows the prosperity the family had achieved. Pictured, from left to right, are: (sitting) John, Marie, August Sr., Ida, and Henry; (standing) Al., Charles, Gus, Alf. T., and Otto. (Courtesy of Circus World Museum, Baraboo, Wisconsin.)

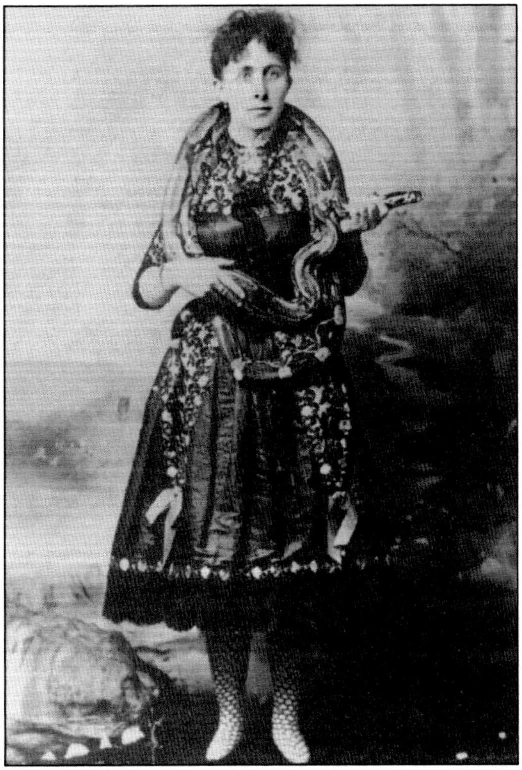 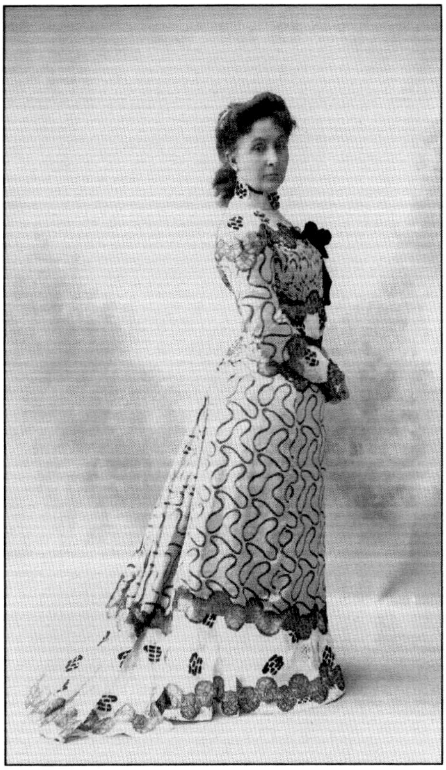

Lou Ringling was undoubtedly the most efficacious of all the Ringling wives. To be fair, she was the only Ringling wife when the circus started, but was probably as instrumental to its success as any of her many brothers-in-law. She performed a multitude of tasks, from performing in the side show as a snake charmer to supervising the wardrobe department, which grew to 20 girls under her care. Her life and marriage to Al. remain something of a mystery, as they were allegedly married in December 1883, but later were secretly married in Hoboken, New Jersey in 1890. No matter the case, by the turn of the century Lou was not reticent to enjoy some of the family's hard-earned wealth. After Al.'s death in 1916, she devoted her life to various real estate projects, but lost nearly everything during the Depression. (Dresser Collection.)

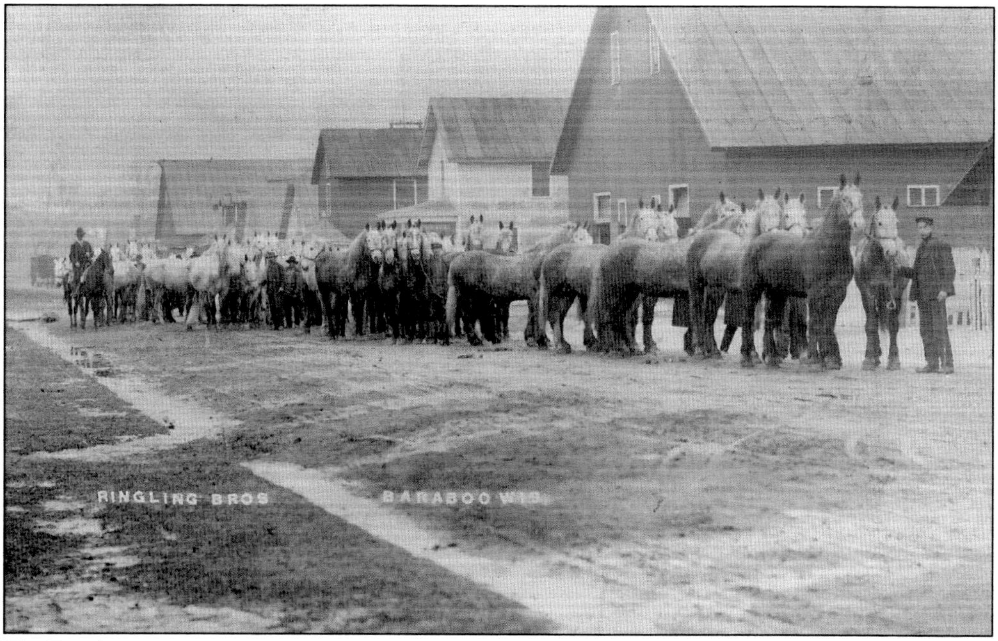

The Ringling winter quarters on Water Street grew to include over a dozen buildings, many of which were used to house the hundreds of animals, from the exotic to the mundane. As many as 400 dappled Percheron draft horses were kept to perform the task of pulling the scores of wagons.

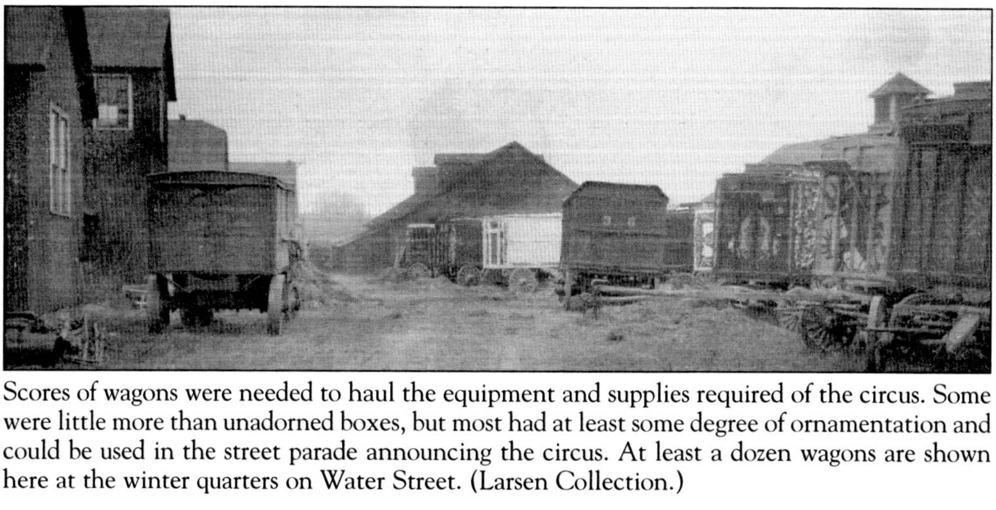

Scores of wagons were needed to haul the equipment and supplies required of the circus. Some were little more than unadorned boxes, but most had at least some degree of ornamentation and could be used in the street parade announcing the circus. At least a dozen wagons are shown here at the winter quarters on Water Street. (Larsen Collection.)

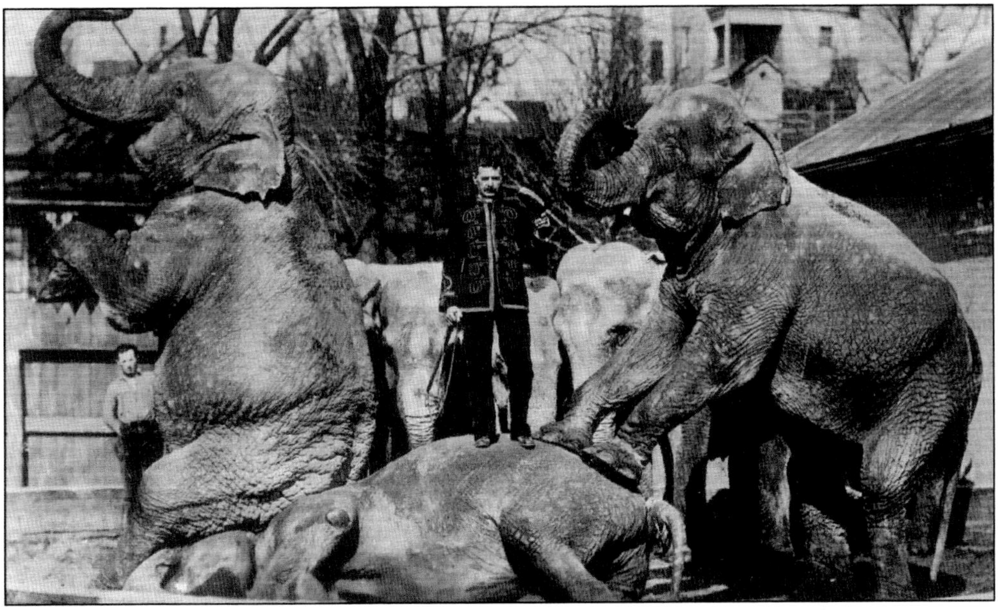

Elephant trainer Pearl Souders posed with about seven of the Ringling Brothers elephants in the practice ring on Water Street for this photo, taken about 1908. The Ringlings bought their first elephant in 1888 and soon added more. The herd grew to about two dozen by the turn of the 20th century.

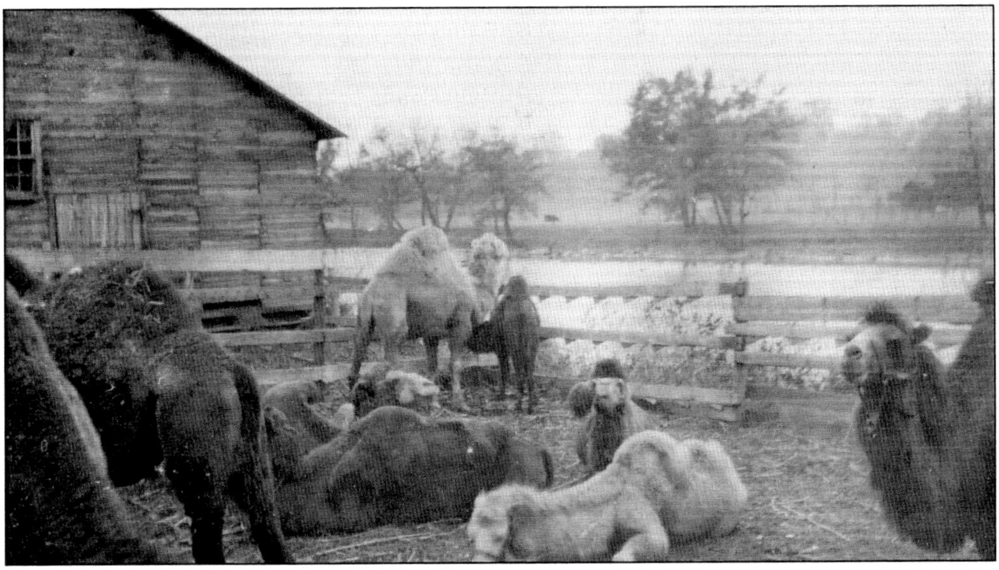

Ringling Brothers' animal holdings became extensive and buildings were constructed at the winter quarters to house a variety of animals, including Bactrian camels and dromedaries, which had their own building and pen along the Baraboo River. (Larsen Collection.)

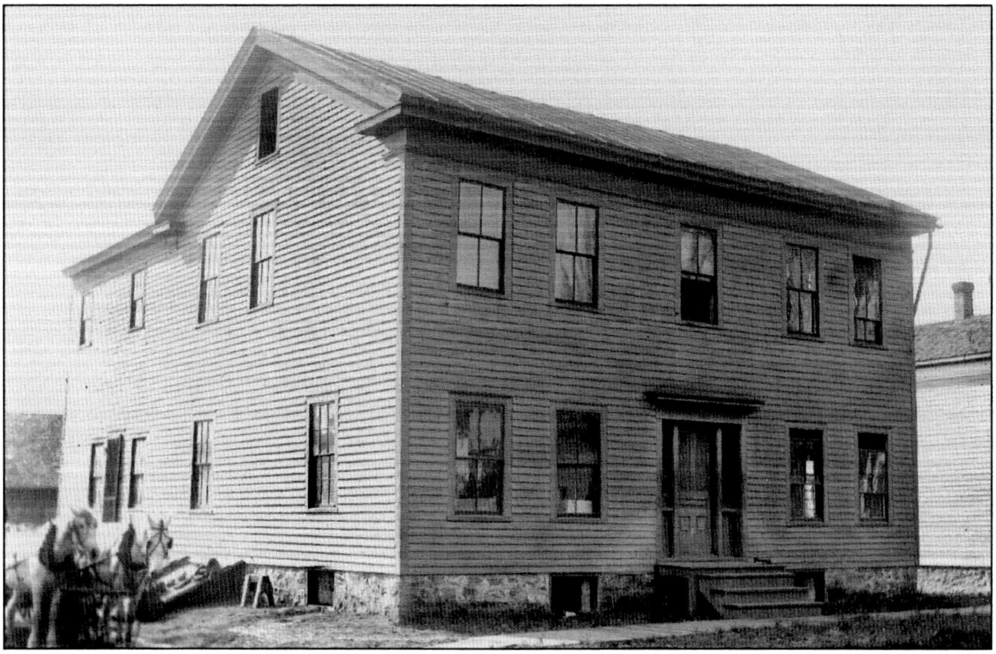

In late 1890, the Ringling Brothers started leasing the Union Hotel, above, at the southwest corner of East and Water Streets to house their growing crew of off-season workers. This convenient spot was nearly adjacent to their winter quarters. Eight years later, the building was purchased, but it was not until 1916 that a new and modern hotel was built. The new three-story brick building, below, included lounge areas, dining rooms, sleeping rooms, and dormitory-style accommodations on the third floor for the spring influx of workers. The new accommodations would not be enjoyed for long however, as the Ringling Brothers moved their winter quarters to Bridgeport, Connecticut, in 1918. The building still stands and is used today as apartments and office space.

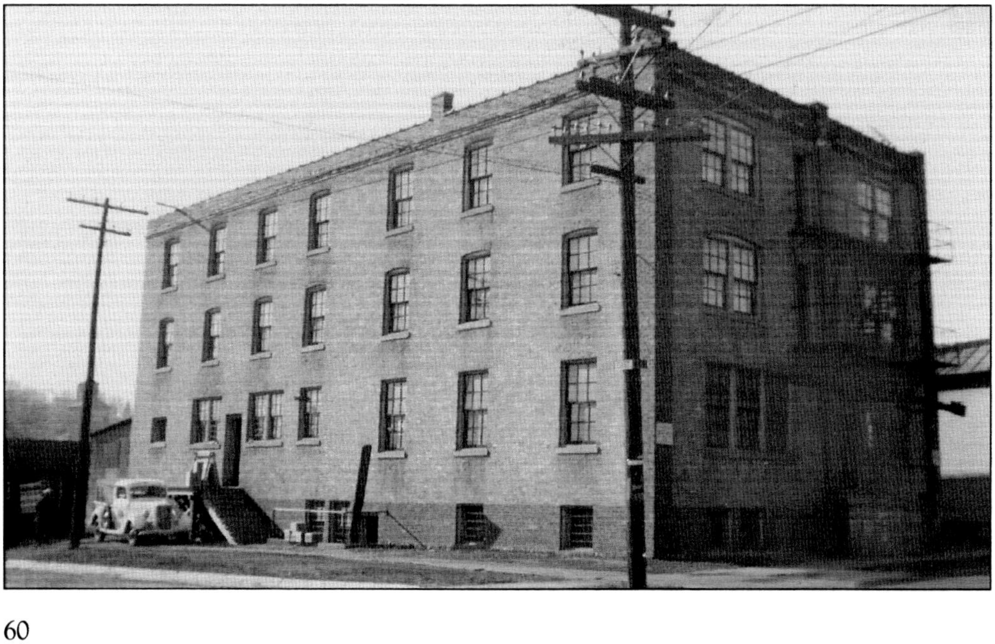

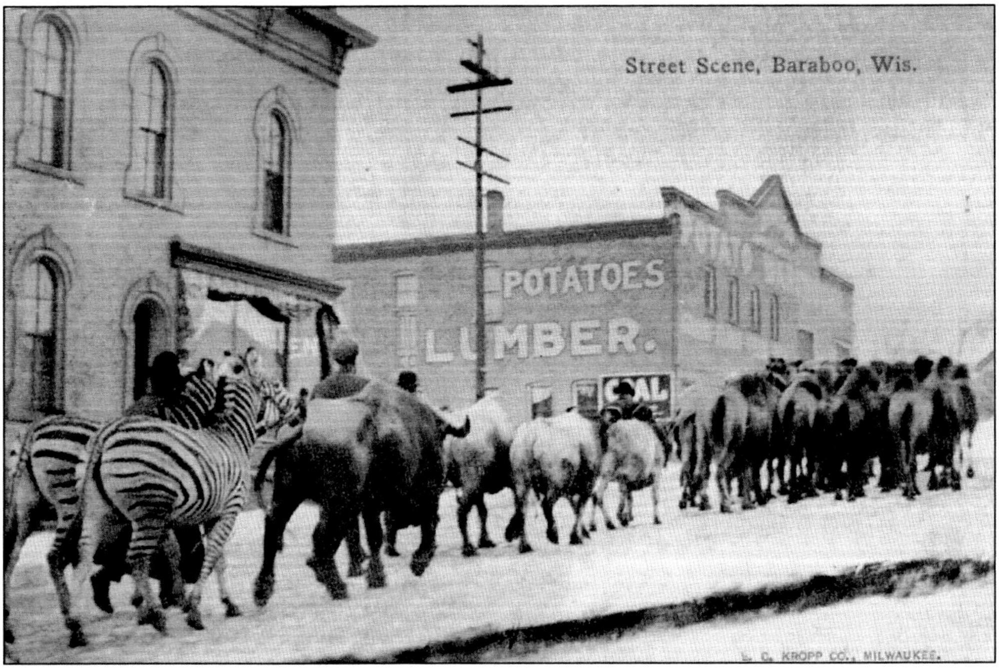

Street scenes like these made great postcards for the citizens of Baraboo, even though they were something of the norm when the circus departed or returned to town. A herd of camels leads the way up Walnut Street at the intersection with Lynn, providing a show for those at the Bender Saloon. Below, a somewhat doctored photo shows the elephant parade going up Ash Street at First with St. Joseph's Catholic Church in the background.

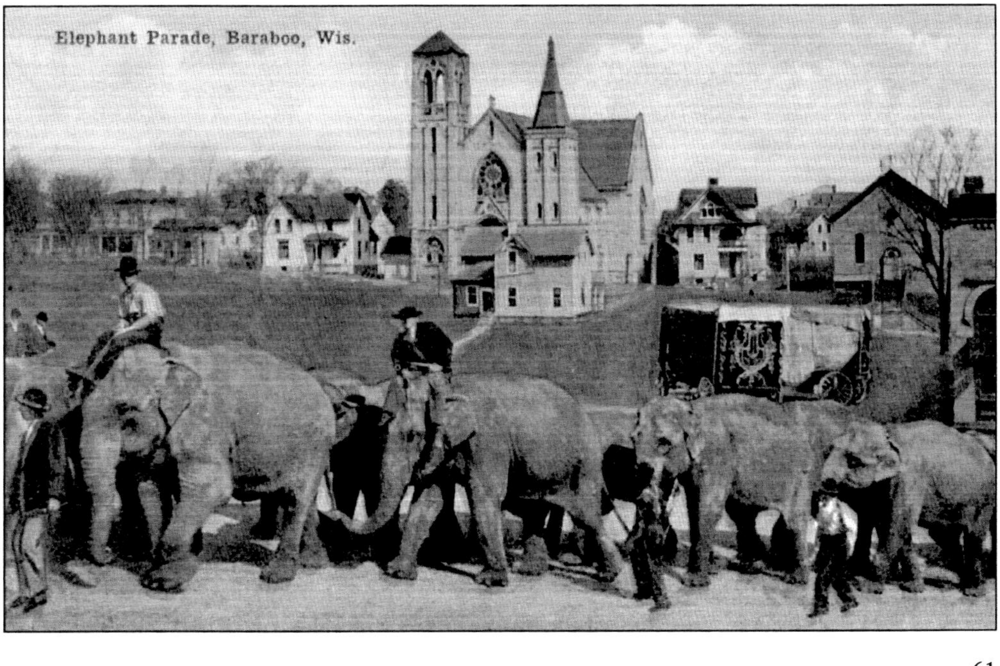

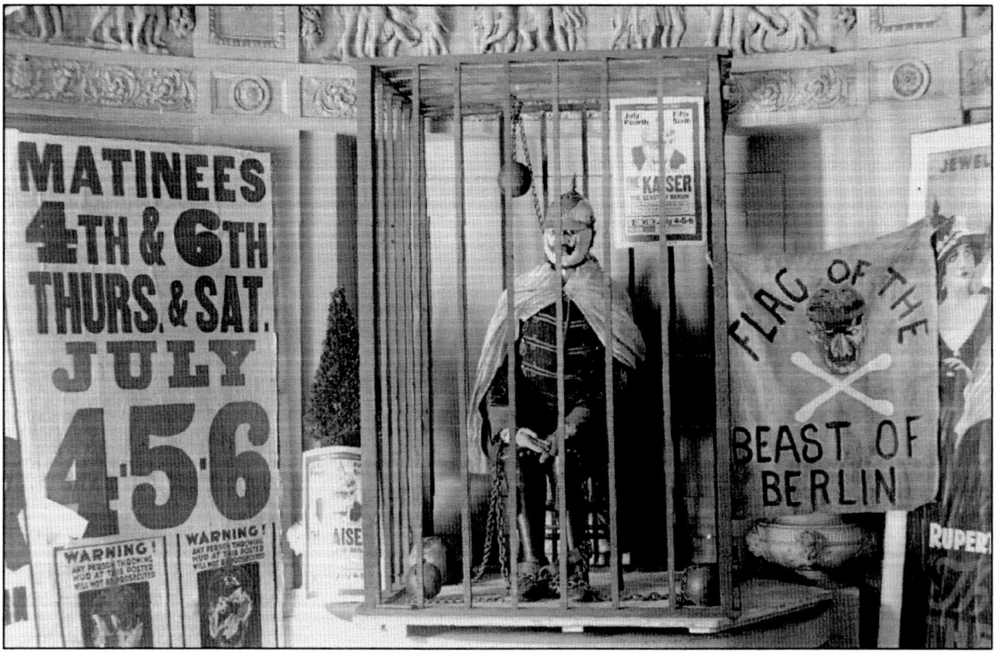

Some items from the winter quarters were no doubt used to help advertise a new movie at the Al. Ringling Theatre in 1918. A leftover cage and an old band coat were used to create this tableau of the evil German Kaiser. The poster at the left reads, "Warning! Any person throwing mud at this poster will not be prosecuted." (Siekert Collection.)

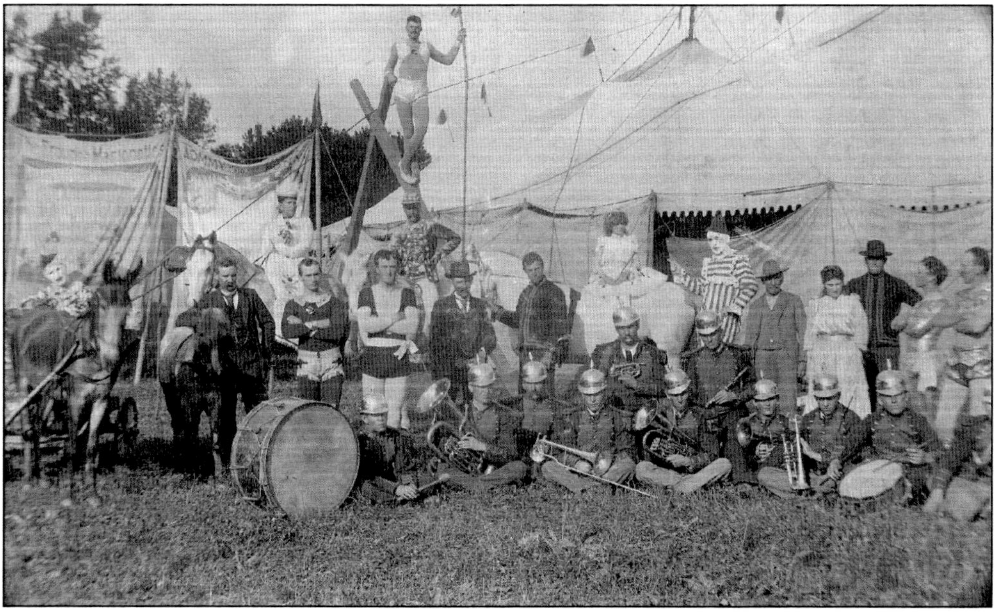

In 1891, four of the Gollmar brothers, the Ringlings' cousins, started their own circus in Baraboo. After its inaugural year, the show opened every season in Baraboo, making it even more of a home-town favorite. It was eventually a rail show, using about 30 railroad cars when it was sold in 1916. (Courtesy of Circus World Museum, Baraboo, Wisconsin.)

Six

INDUSTRY AND ENTERPRISE

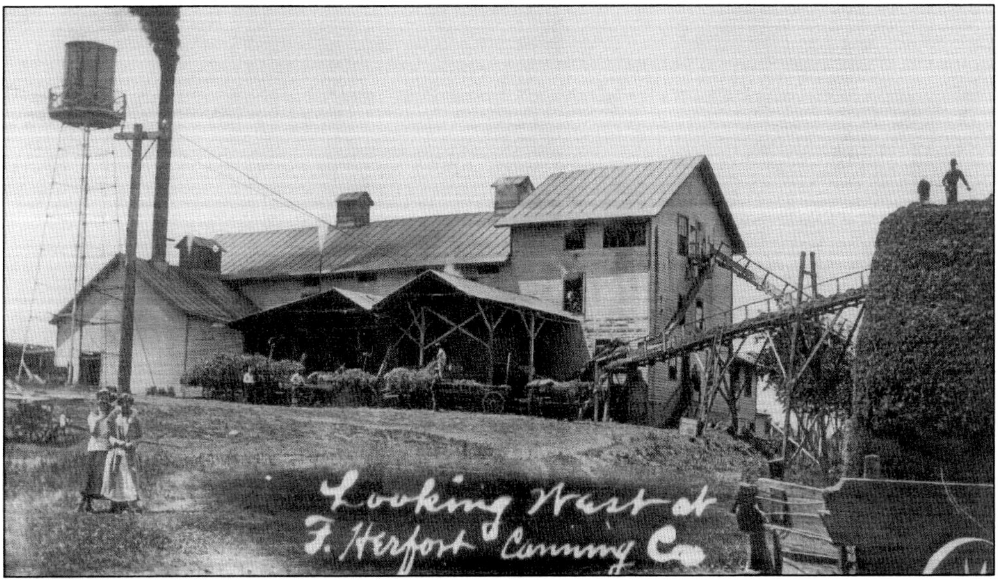

Baraboo's origins are founded in its industrial possibilities. The very first Euro-American settlers who crossed the bluffs found this spot attractive because of the rapids on the river, which meant a drop in elevation that could be harnessed with dams. The first water power was used to power saw and grist mills, but by 1860 textile and furniture mills were built as well. As Baraboo grew, the rising population resulted in the natural development of shops and small businesses. Everything from machine shops to meat markets could be found in the commercial districts. It was a place where local farmers could bring their goods to market and after 1871, with the arrival of the railroad, ship their crops across the country. The railroad initiated a dramatic change for Baraboo, more so than other communities, because it was located halfway between Chicago and Minneapolis and became a division headquarters. Extensive repair shops and offices were built and the railroad soon employed as many workers as the mills. The arrival of the railroad opened many doors for the young city. It enabled the Ringling Brothers, and later Gollmar Brothers, Circus to keep their headquarters here. Other companies took root in Baraboo as well. Two breweries thrived, as did factories like the Hertfort Canning Company, above. By the turn of the 20th century, iron had been discovered in the Baraboo range and just south of town a large mine was in full operation. Throughout the early 20th century, Baraboo continued to grown and develop. By the end of the First World War, the city was home to several major industries.

The canning factory Frank Herfort bought in 1906, above, stayed in the family for over 50 years and provided steady employment for some and seasonal employment for many more. The factory was located at 101 South Boulevard.

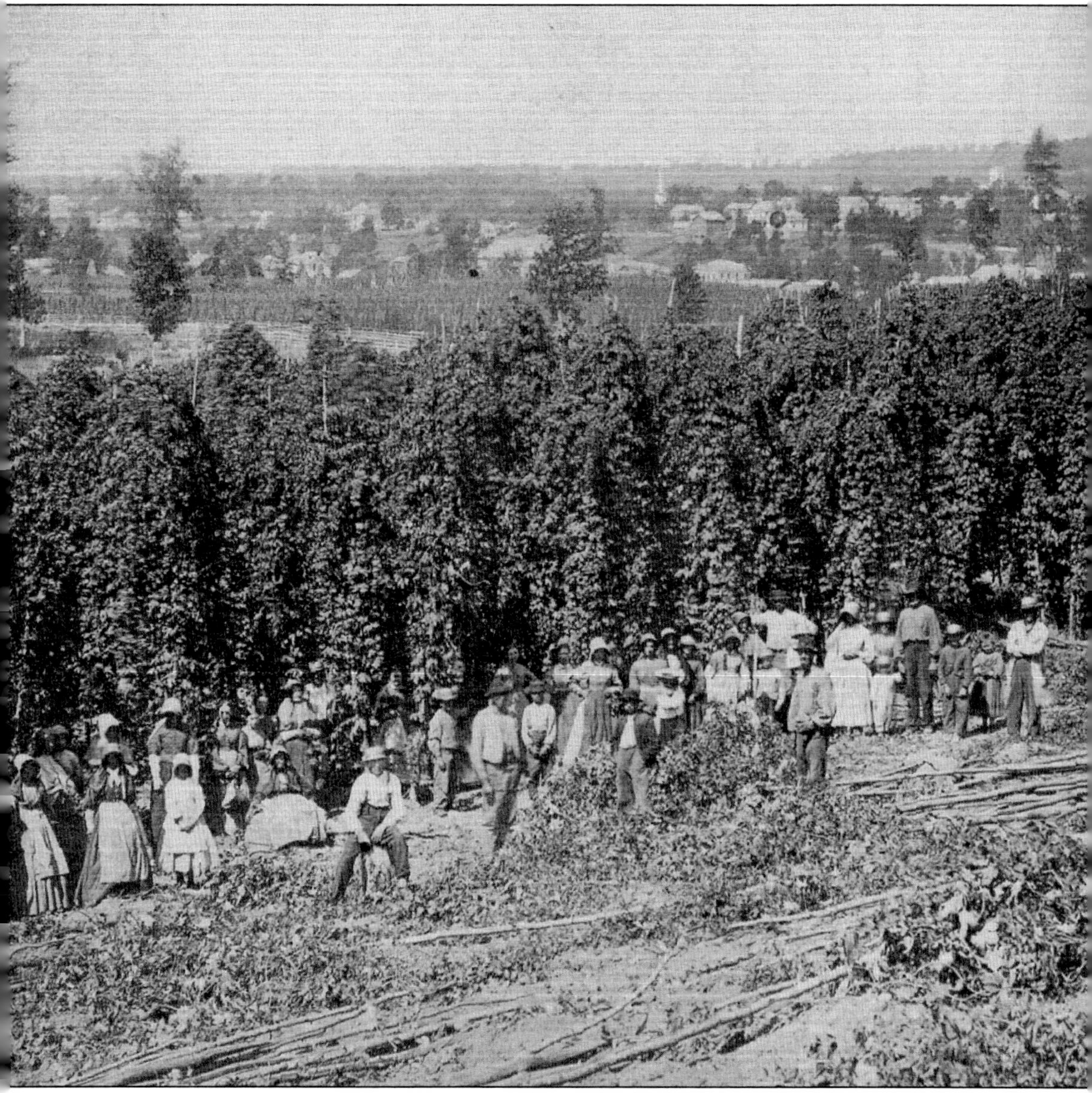

In the mid-1860s, Baraboo and Sauk County were in the midst of a hops boom, when the price for the essential crop in beer making hit an all time high due to the devastation of the crop in the eastern United States. H.H. Potter, who owned this field southeast of Baraboo, was not only a grower but also a dealer in hops plants and in the harvested hops florets. When harvest time came, hundreds of workers were needed to harvest the crop. In 1867 alone, the crop in Sauk County accounted for one-fifth of the nation's production, bringing an income of two million dollars into the county. The boom ended as quickly as it started however, when the eastern crop rebounded and the national markets were glutted with too much crop.

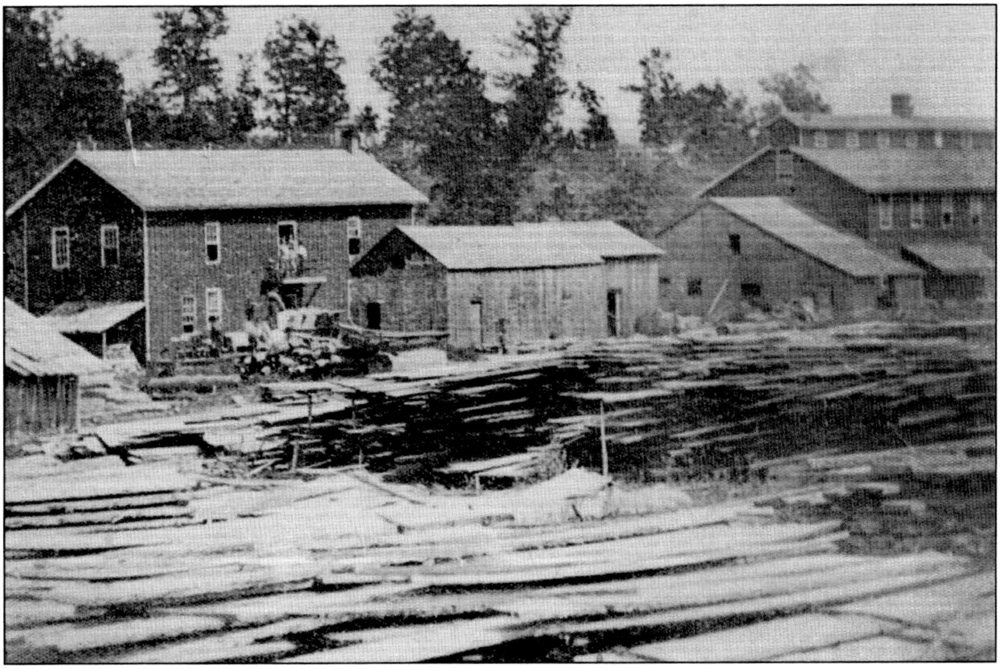

The Baraboo Manufacturing Company was started in 1867 and was located next to the Island Woolen Mill on the west end of Baraboo. The complex was extensive and included a blacksmith shop, warehouse, paint shop, dry house, and steam rooms. The company produced chairs, rocking chairs, and bedsteads. Its furniture was sold all over the upper mid-west and as far away as Texas. The company did not survive a fire in 1885.

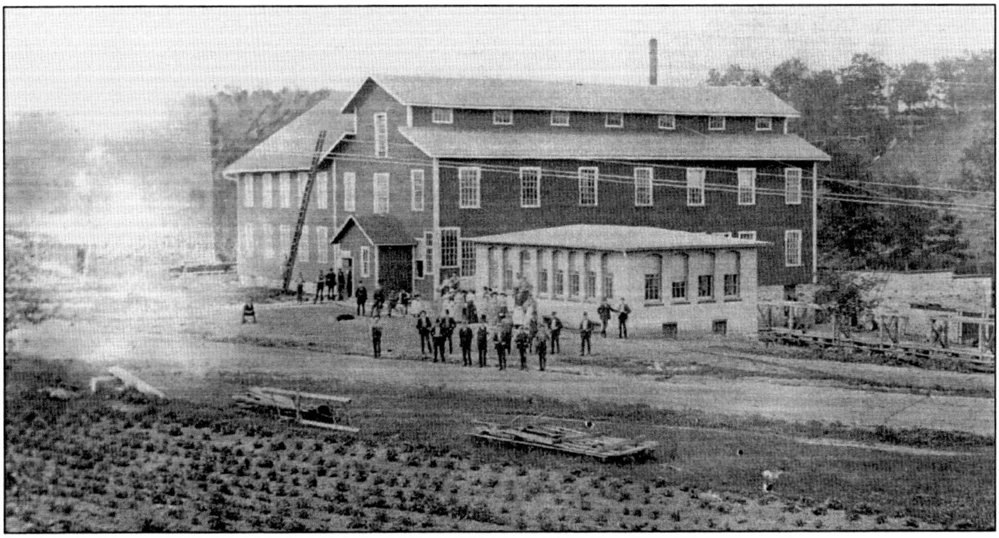

An early historian declared the Island Woolen Mill "one of the heaviest manufacturing houses in the state." The original wool mill was built in 1859, near the "island" created by the water raceway cut across the upper oxbow peninsula. For most of its existence it was owned by the McFetridge family, who nurtured the business until it grew to be one of the largest textile mills west of Philadelphia. By World War I, the mill was at its peak and had grown from the simple structure pictured here to a vast complex of buildings.

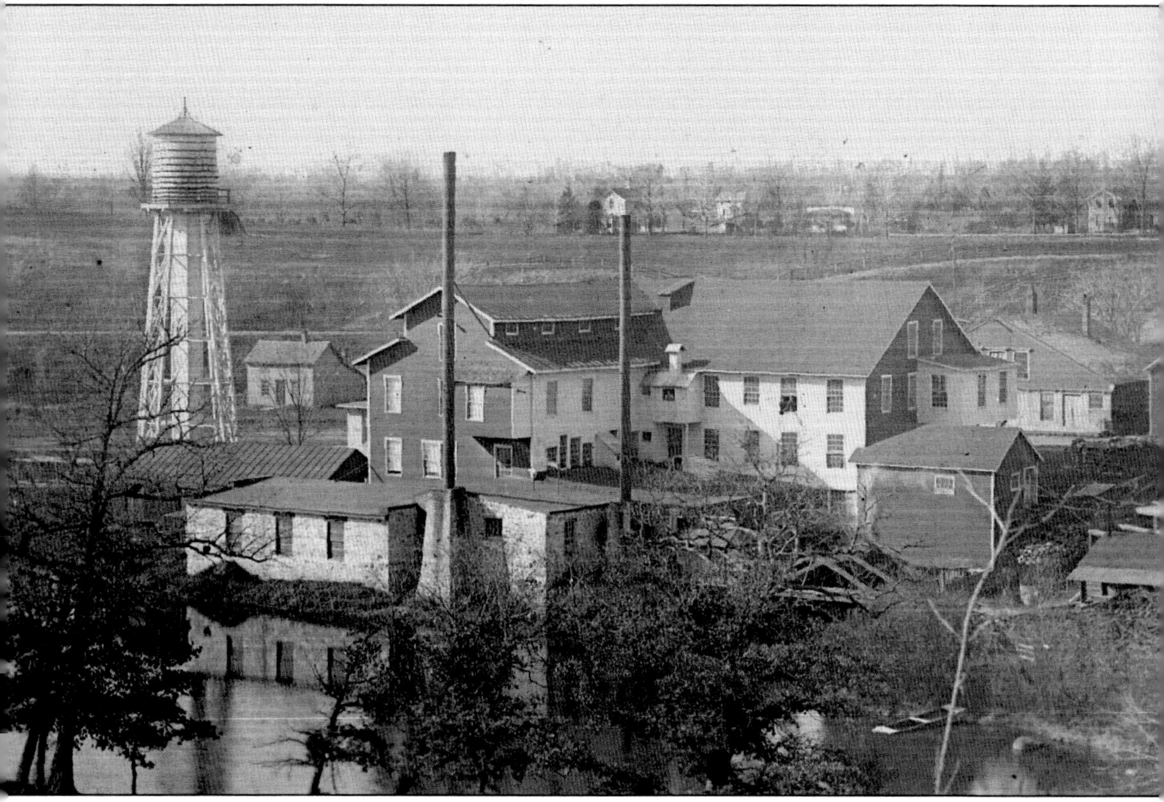

Operational for more than 80 years (1863–1949), the Island Woolen Mill was, at one time, the largest employer in the Baraboo area. It eventually occupied the county's largest building in the 1920s. A producer of diverse goods, the mill carded, spun, and loomed material for clothing, automobile upholstery, and, during World War II, overcoat material for the army. This picture, looking southwest about 1900, shows the mill before a massive building campaign in the 1920s greatly enlarged the operation. After 1949, the mill stood vacant and eventually burned in 1963. (Siekert Collection.)

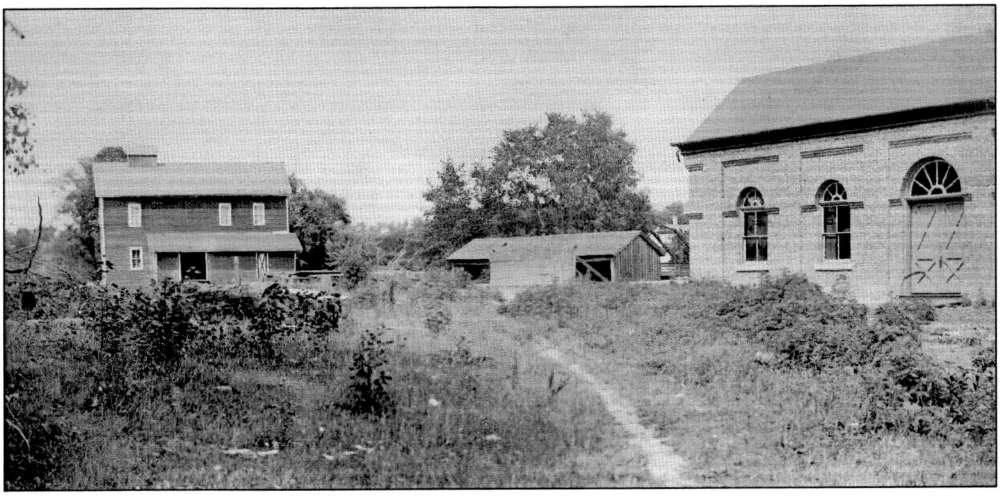

Located at the "lower water power" at the lower oxbow, the Manchester Mill was located on land originally belonging to Eben and Rosaline Peck, early settlers in Madison and later Baraboo. In 1840, claim jumpers attempted to build a dam here, but were forced to stop when papers were served. A subsequent flood and the limited resources of the Pecks kept a working dam from being built here for several years. By 1848, however, James Maxwell of Dane County bought the site, moved his family to the area, rebuilt the dam, and erected a saw mill. Later, a grist mill was added to the site, which was subsequently converted into a woolen mill. In May 1850, the area was platted as the town of Manchester, which never grew to any size beyond the mills and a few houses. In the late 1860s, the woolen mill was known for producing beautiful afghan blankets. The photo above shows one of the mills, probably in the early 1880s. The brick building at right is the original pumping station for the Baraboo City Water Works. Another view of the Manchester mill below was taken around 1890.

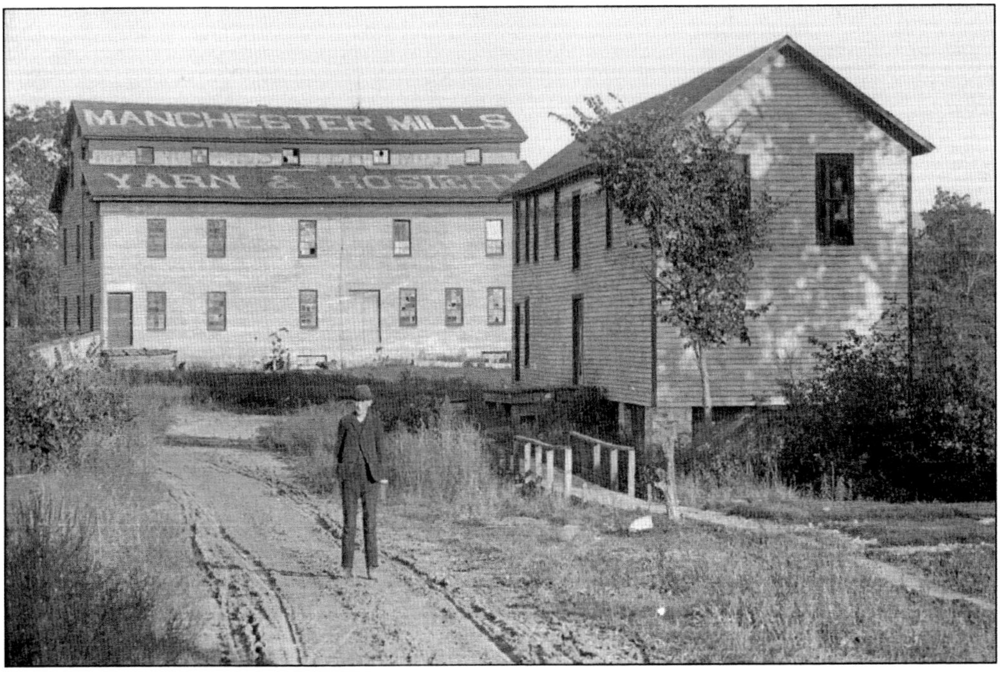

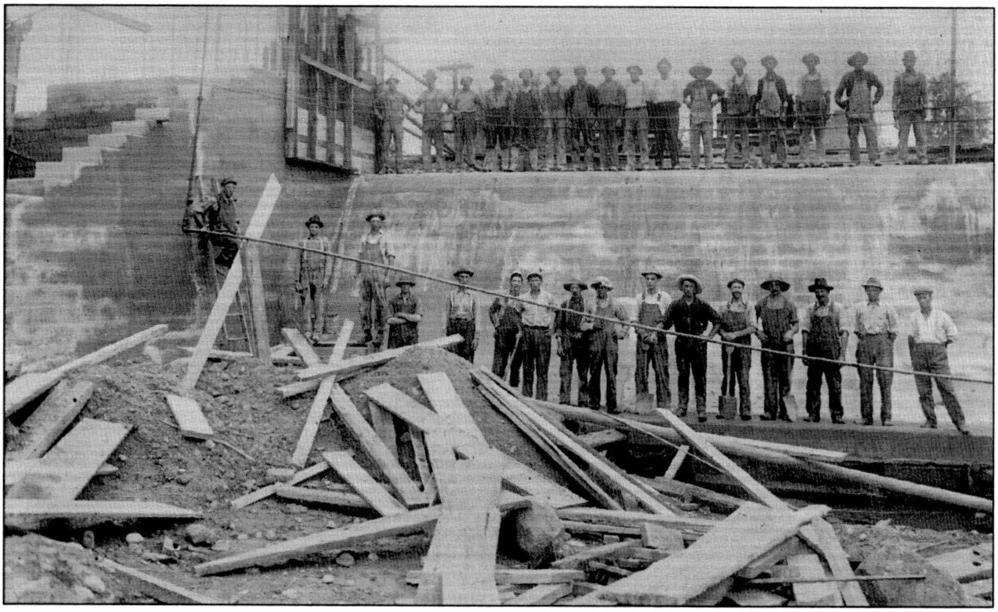

In the summer of 1913, construction was under way for a new dam at the Island Woolen Mill, since the old dam was seriously damaged by high water that spring. The stepped retaining wall to the left would be topped with a decorative viewing area inset with mussel shells taken from the river bed. The dam required 1,500 yards of concrete and was 157 feet in length.

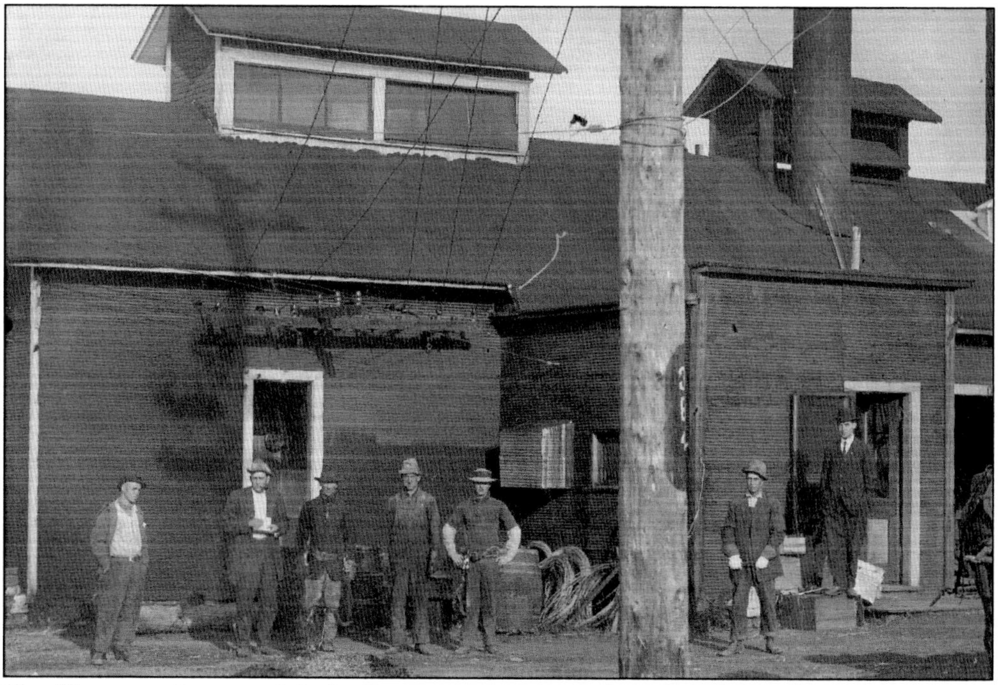

The Wisconsin Power and Light Company was captured in this photo, also taken in 1913. Located on the south side of the Oak Street Dam, where Alliant Energy is now located, WP&L maintained a gas works, among other things. Coal was transformed into gas and then piped to businesses and homes all over town for lighting.

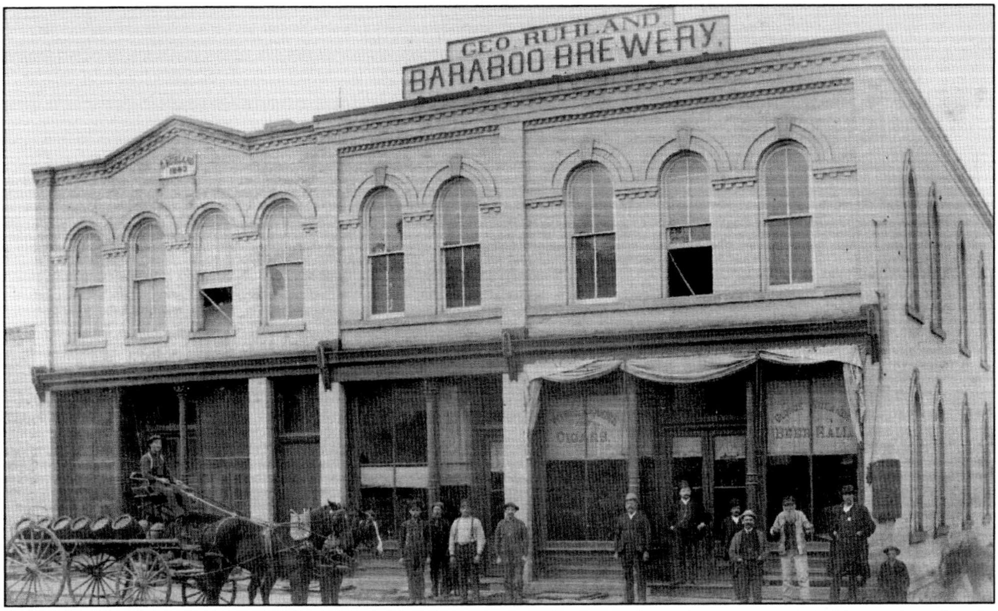

The Baraboo Brewery was built in 1883 by George Ruhland and contained 207,000 bricks. It stood at the northwest corner of Walnut and Lynn Streets on Baraboo's south side. Besides housing the brewery, the building also contained a saloon. The building was mostly demolished in the late 1960s, with only the first story wall of the Walnut street facade visible today.

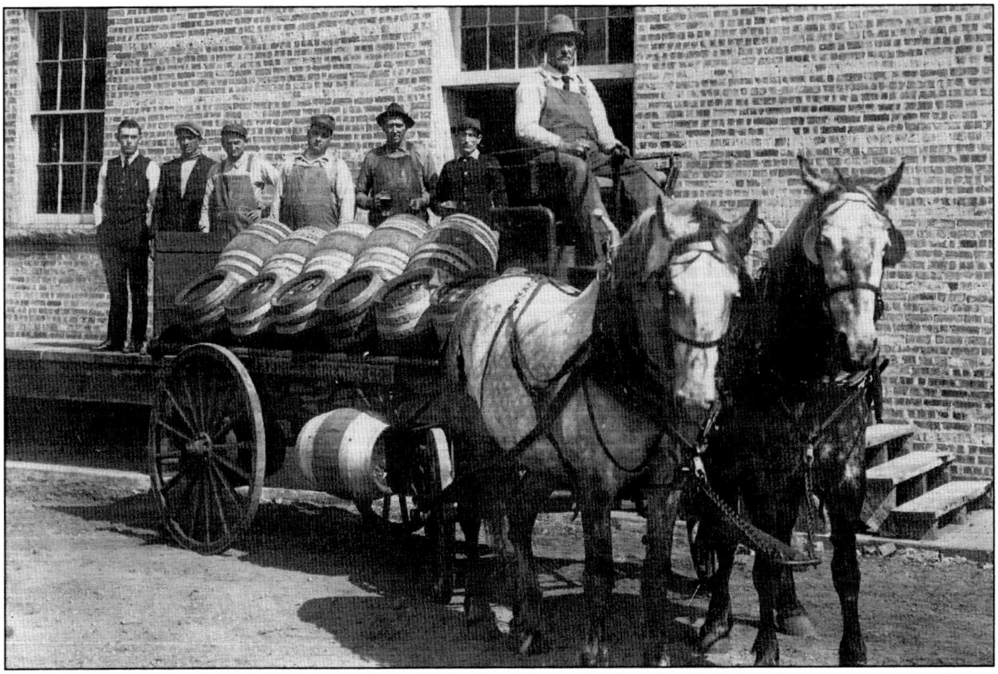

The Effinger Brewery, which was also located on the south side on Lynn Street, was Baraboo's longest running brewery. In the late 19th century and early 20th century, it was not uncommon to see a beer wagon, like this one from the Effinger Brewery, delivering fresh lager to the many taverns throughout town.

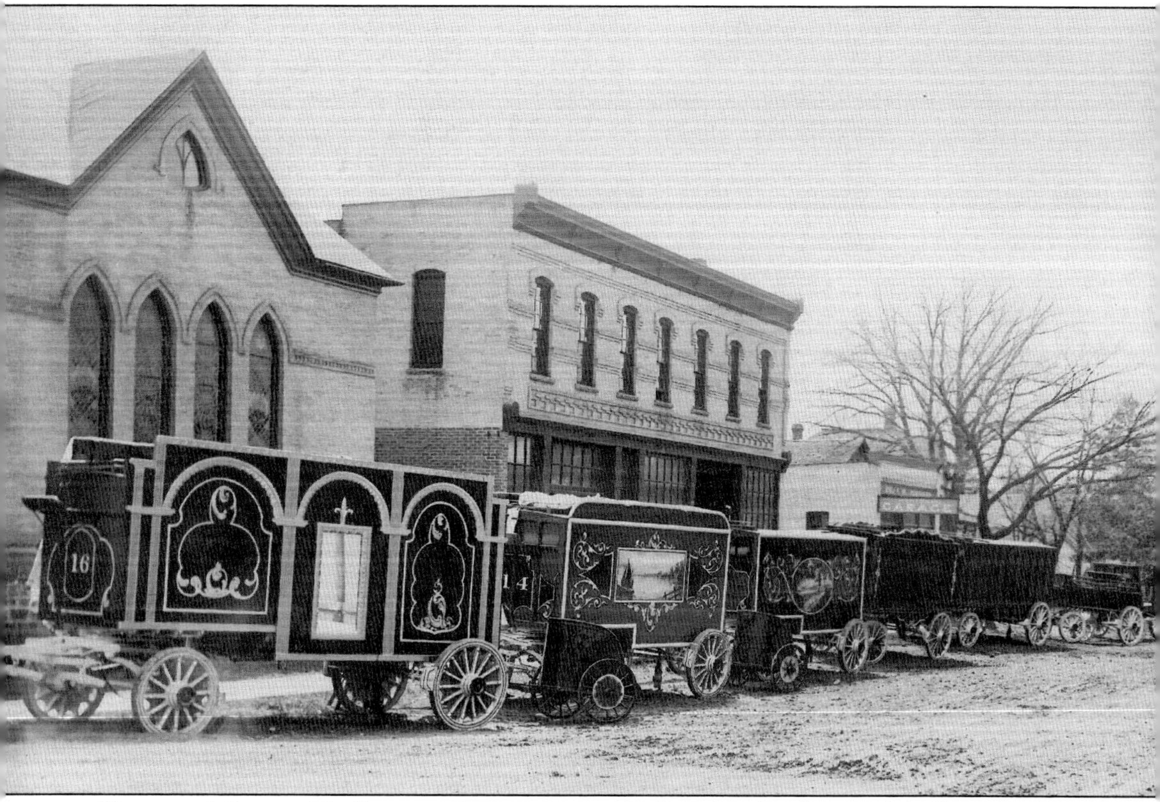

Henry and Corwin Moeller were first cousins to the Ringling brothers and Gollmar brothers, and thus related to both circuses that started in Baraboo. The Moeller brothers contributed their part to Baraboo's circus heritage by making circus wagons for a number of traveling shows, including the Dode Fisk Show of Wonewoc, for whom these wagons were made and displayed on Third Avenue in 1909. (Courtesy of Circus World Museum, Baraboo, Wisconsin.)

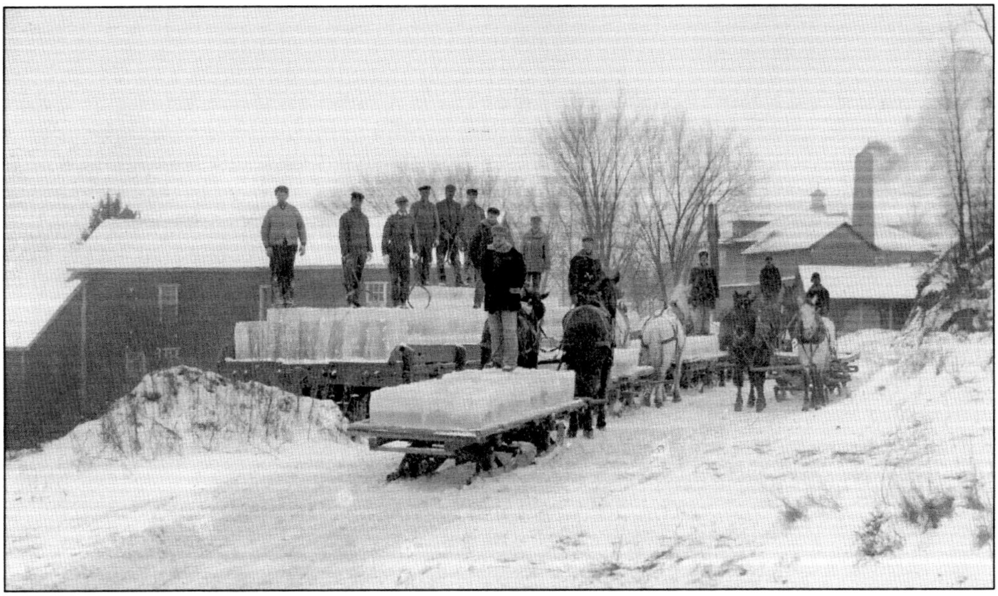

The sight of large wagons full of ice was regularly seen along the Baraboo River during the winter season. These men might be workers of the August Platt Ice Company moving ice to storage. Massive quantities of ice were needed in the days before refrigeration for private homes and businesses.

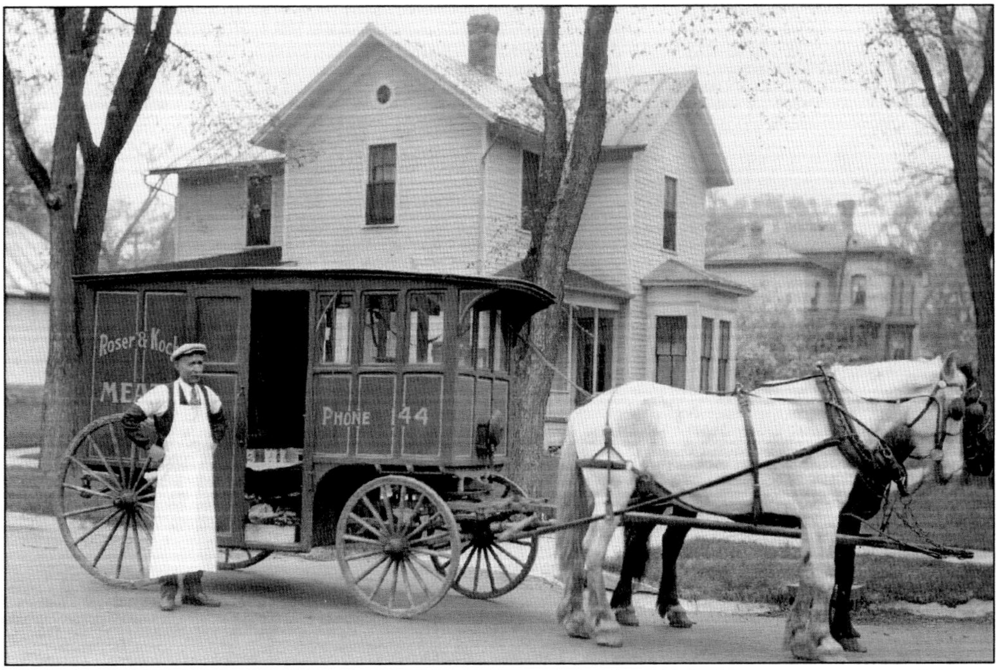

Enterprising businessman, Edwin Roser, ran a meat market and delivery service on Martin Street in 1899. By 1905, he had moved to the west end of town near Ochsner Park, where he set up a grocery business with Walter Koch. His meat delivery wagon held meat in an ice-cooled compartment in the rear and had a large scale in the front. His proud rig was photographed at the northwest corner of West and Third.

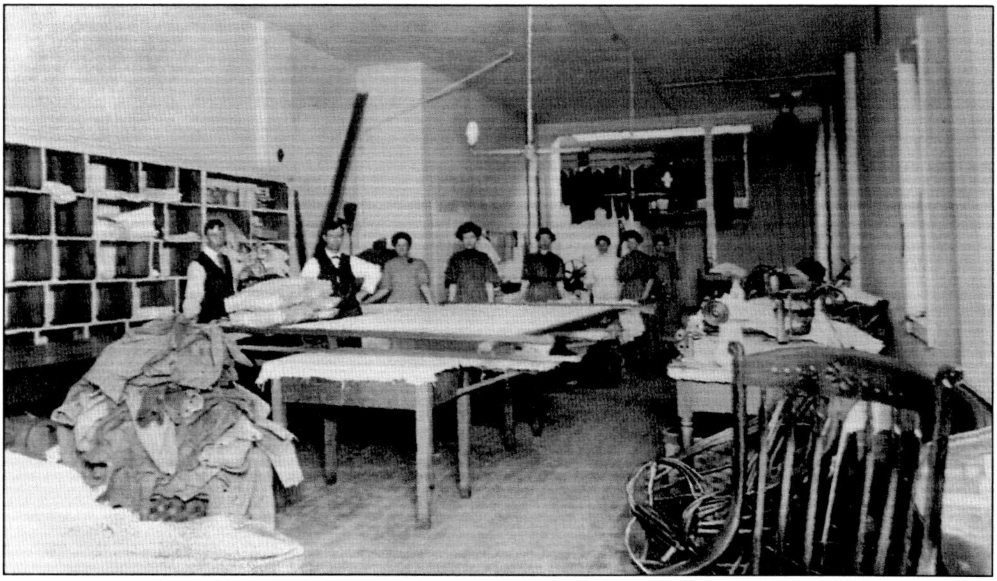

In 1886, the Gem Steam Laundry opened at 120 Fourth Avenue in a new building built by Sheriff Jedediah Ashley. The new laundry business served a growing need in Baraboo and the building was destined to remain a laundry shop for generations. In 1918, the Gem Steam Laundry was replaced by Pierce's Laundry, which in turn became the Baraboo Laundry and Cleaners in 1946.

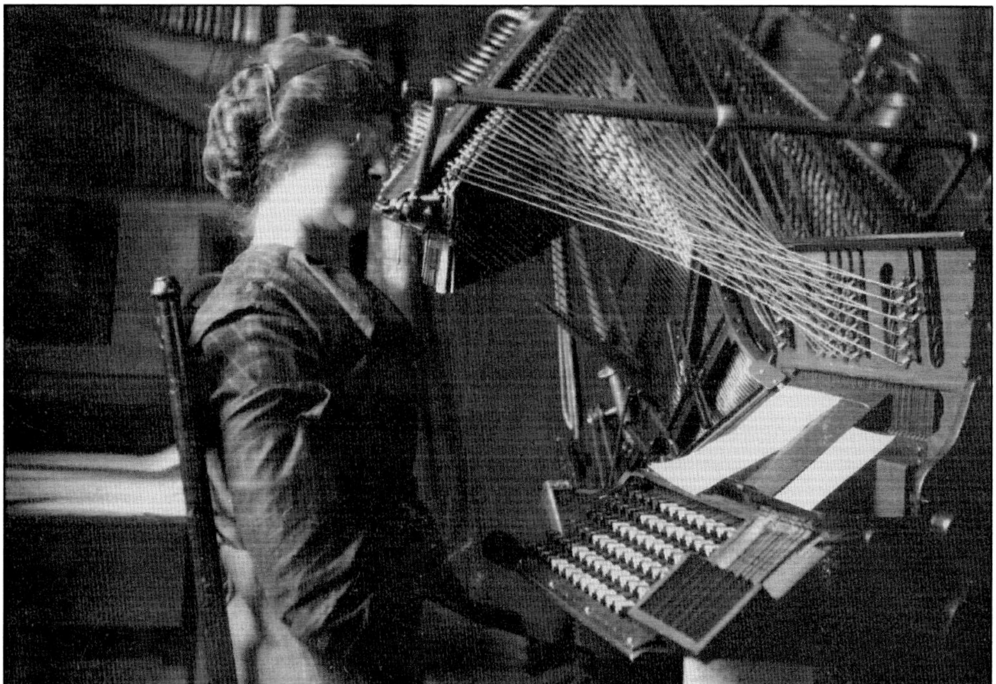

Eleven different newspaper publications had come and gone in Baraboo by 1911. This unknown typesetter poses with her machine at the Baraboo News, which started in 1884. The laborious job of manual typesetting was made easier with the invention of typesetting machines.

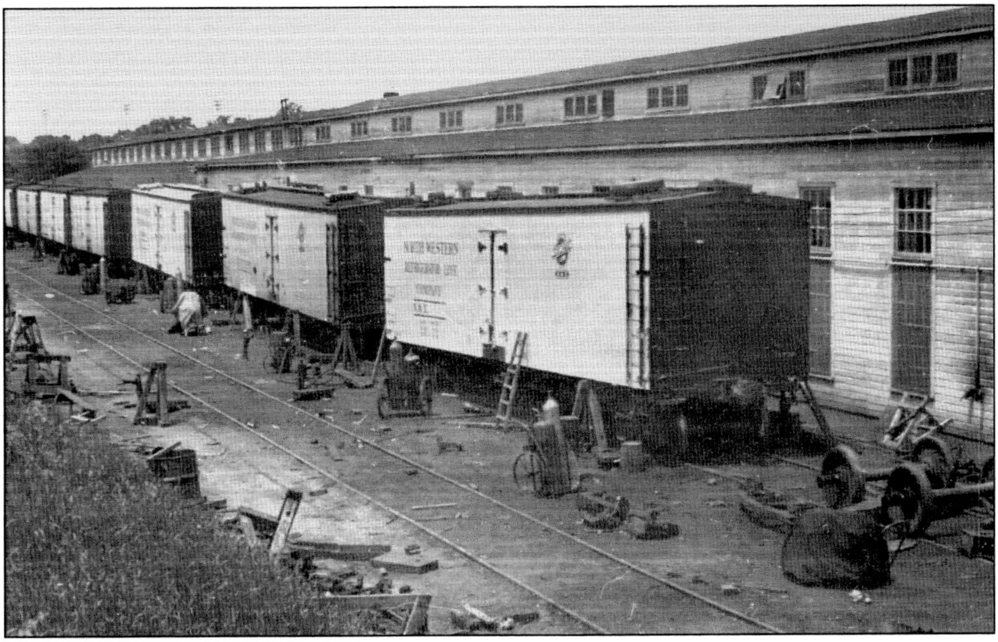

The old Ringling car shops, located on the south side of the river east of Broadway, were purchased by the North Western Refrigeration Line Company after 1918. The shops specially modified existing boxcars, making them rolling iceboxes. The walls of the rail cars were built with 12 elements, including wood, cork, and felt. The operation employed 100 men and produced an average of three refrigerator cars per day.

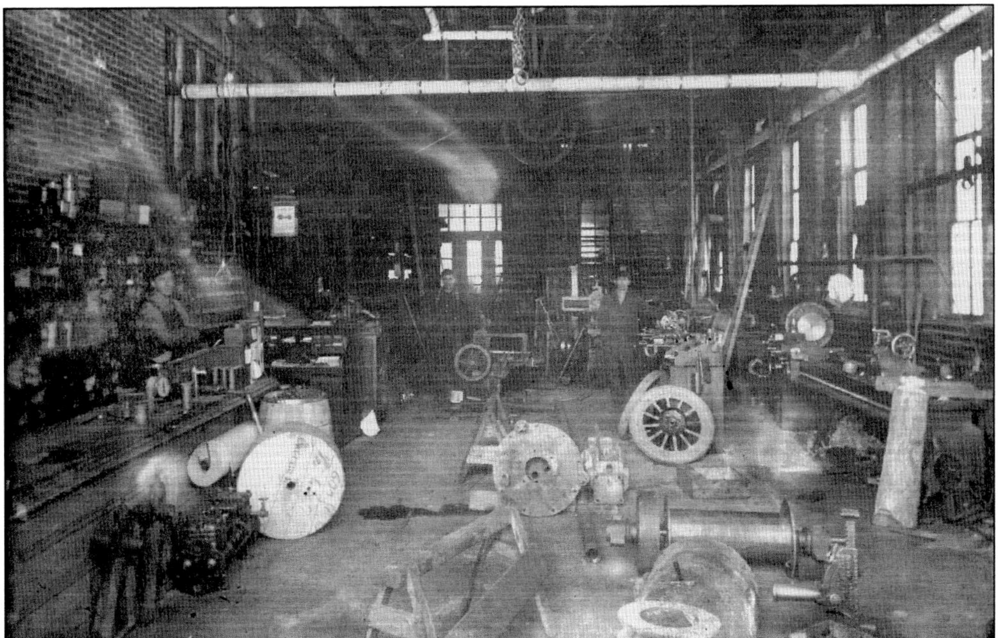

William Platt bought the Gollmar machine shop and garage in 1913 and ran the business out of this shop at 218 Third Avenue until 1920. The Platt's then moved on to 108 Fifth Street and kept Baraboo cars on the road until the 1950s.

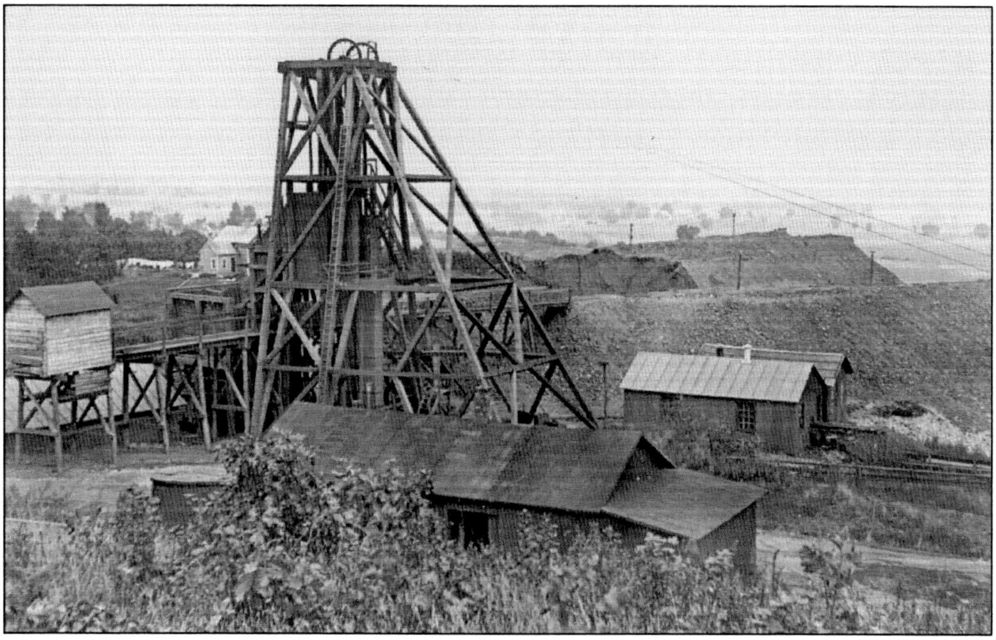

Sauk County was once the site of many iron mine operations, from Ironton in the western end of the county through LaRue and North Freedom and into Baraboo. The Cahoon Mine was located about halfway between Baraboo and Devil's Lake. The mine was first dug in 1911 and ran until 1925. The ore was considered very high grade, but mining in the Baraboo area was very difficult, primarily due to constant flooding in the mine shafts. Work inside the mine was cramped, dirty, and not for the faint of heart. Note the boots to keep feet dry inside the damp tunnels.

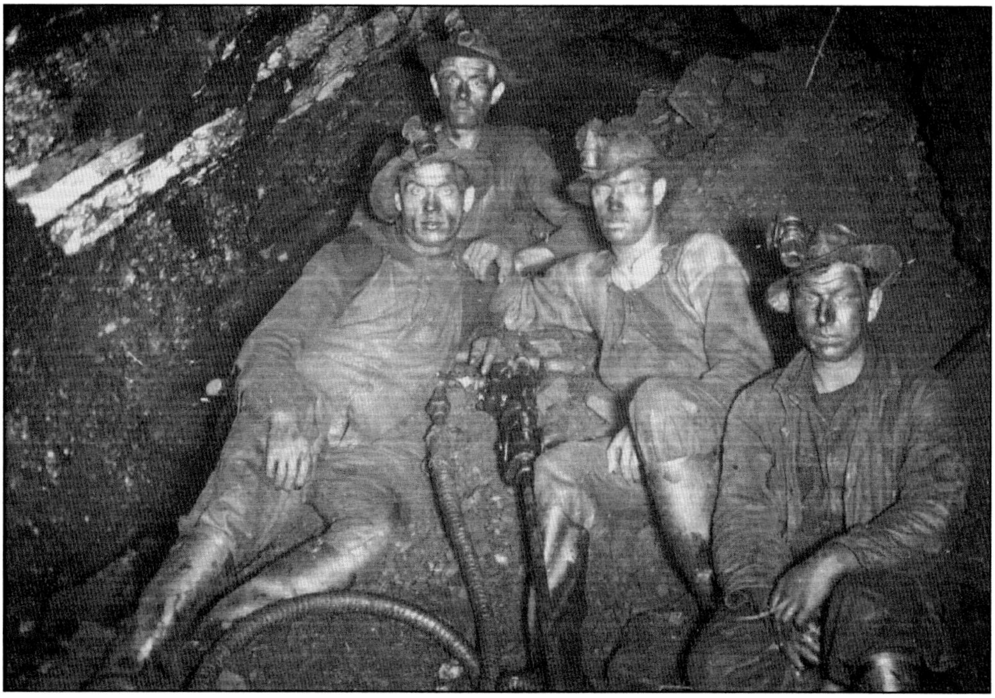

Seven
PEOPLE AND PERSONALITIES

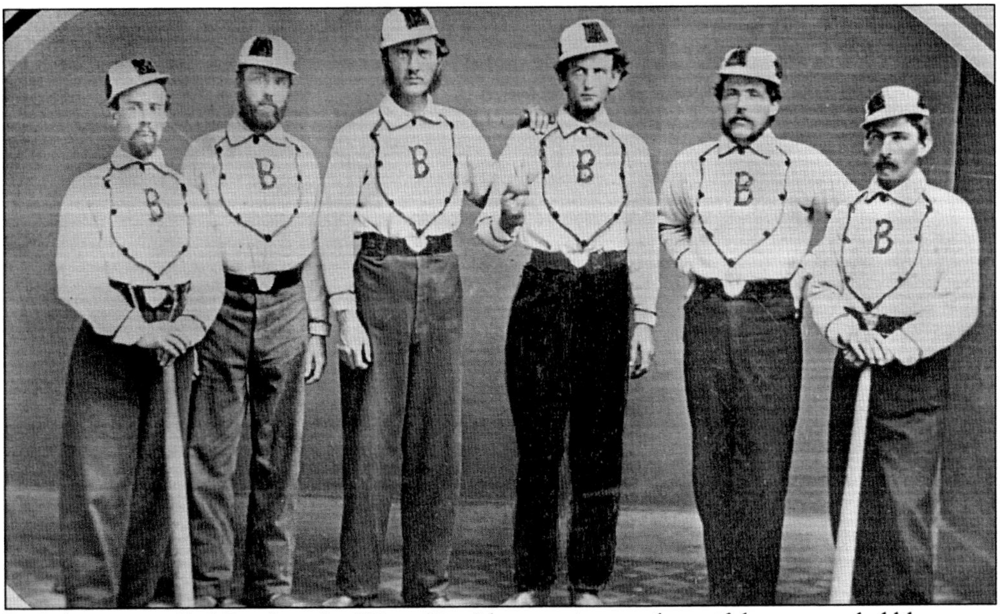

Early boosters called Baraboo the "Gem City," because it was a beautiful town nestled like a gem amidst the surrounding bluffs. This sobriquet belied a pride that many residents could relate to. Baraboo evolved out of the wilderness, taking its name from the river that flows through it. Early on, the community was made up of unique personalities like Abe Wood, a rough and tumble character, and Rosaline Peck, a survivor if there ever was one. And right from the start people relied on the help of those nearby to erect shelter, take care of claim jumpers, and provide the friendship needed to survive. By the late 1870s, Baraboo had become a thriving community. Its people worked at various mills, in the railroad yards, or in the countless shops surrounding the courthouse square. Churches of many denominations had been established, as had numerous fraternal organizations. Baraboo was also the county seat and more than a few were involved in the government. The community was also well educated. In the 1860s, the village could boast a number of small schools and the Baraboo Female Seminary. The city was one of culture-supporting literary societies and a series of opera houses, culminating in the construction of the lavish Al. Ringling Theatre in 1915. People gathered for all types of reasons: leisure, enlightenment, entertainment, and education.

Purportedly the first baseball team in Sauk County, this team, above, formed in Baraboo in 1869. Baseball became a popular sport in Baraboo in the latter half of the 19th century and local teams sprang up around the county. Between 1869 and 1918, Baraboo supported at least four different teams. The teams were often associated with companies, such as the Island Woolen Mill or the C&NW Railroad.

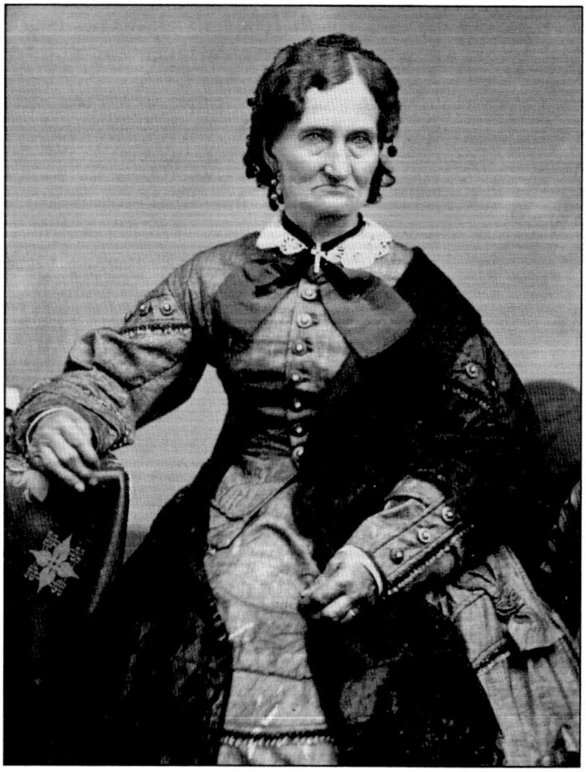

Rosaline Peck is remembered as the first white woman in Madison and Baraboo. She suffered tremendous hardship and misfortune throughout her life, yet is remembered by those who knew her as gracious, generous, and a "benefactress and true friend." She raised a son and daughter single handedly when her husband left her to seek his fortune further west. She fell prey to land grabbers and nearly lost her home. Despite this, she hosted numerous public events in her home, cared for the sick, welcomed and helped establish new settlers, lent money and time to individuals and fledgling organizations, and was a good cook and an "excellent fiddle player."

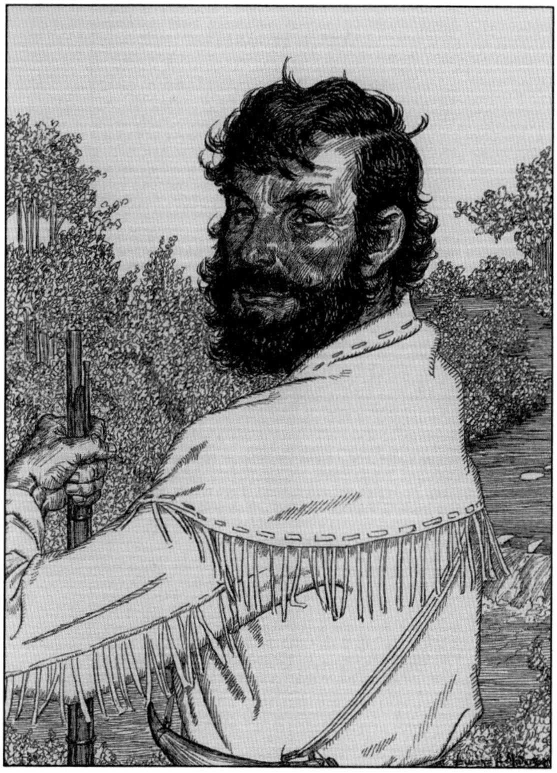

Abe Wood is known as the first permanent settler in Baraboo. Abe was a trapper and trader who moved through the Madison area during the time that area was being developed as the State Capitol. He moved to the Baraboo area in 1839, and with his partner Wallace Rowan built the first dam on the Baraboo River at the upper oxbow. Abe was a huge man both physically and in personality. His flaring temper and great strength led him to frequent trouble with authorities.

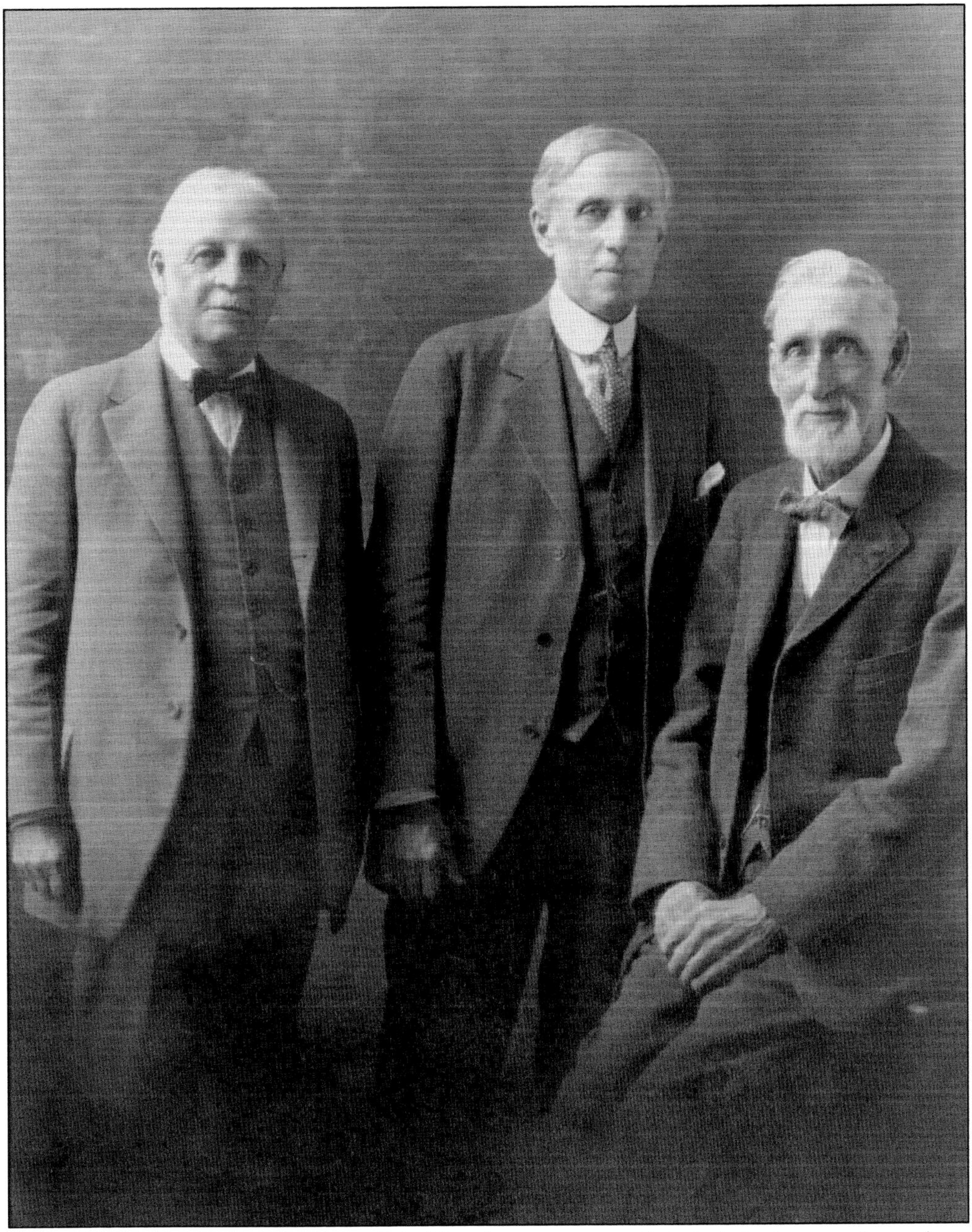

Baraboo incorporated as a city in 1882. The first city council included nine members, three from each ward. Thirty-eight years later, the three survivors from that first council gathered to take a photo in Trimpey's studio. On the left is Henry P. Barlow, who represented the Third Ward, in the middle is Jacob Van Orden from the First, and on the right is James S. Worthman from the Second. Worthman went on to become City Clerk for 32 consecutive years and Van Orden became mayor in 1887.

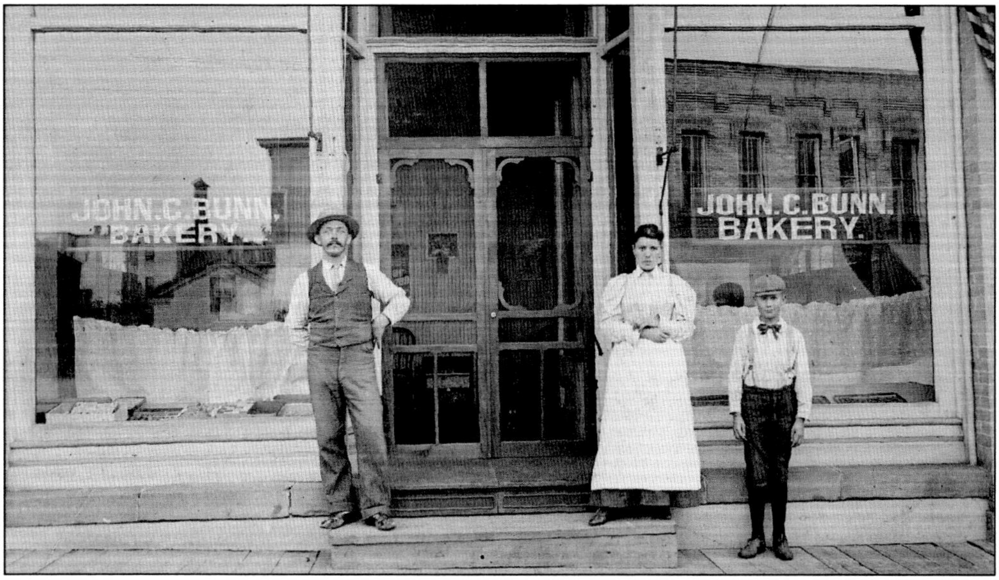

John C. Bunn was born in Germany and apprenticed as a baker. After immigrating to the United States, he eventually set up a bakery in Baraboo in 1896. He probably would have lived out the rest of his days in quiet anonymity, except for his last name which was immortalized when it was discovered by a reporter from the Chicago Tribune. Forever after he became "Bunn the Baker of Baraboo," and was featured in short poems in the Chicago paper. Later in life, Bunn used his fame to promote Baraboo and became an alderman and also a county commissioner.

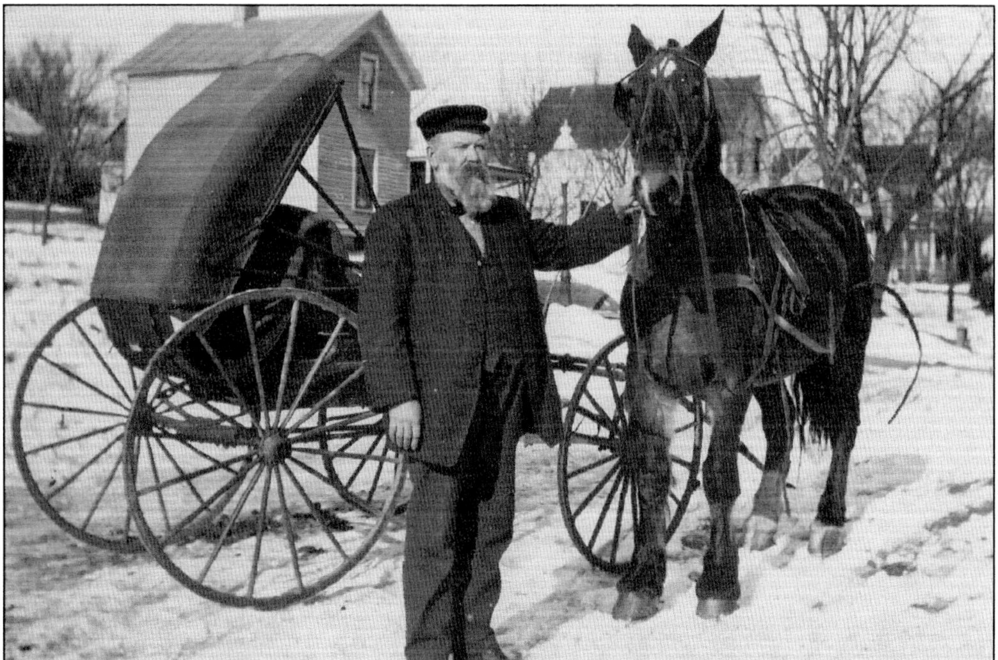

In the old days, doctors did indeed make house calls, especially animal doctors. Veterinarian W.H. Thompson was one of Baraboo's animal doctors, who poses here with his buggy and horse around 1909. (Krueger Collection.)

Baraboo photographer, Arthur T. Johnson, joined the volunteer fire department in January 1890 and served the city with the organization for the next 47 years and 7 months. He witnessed many of the great fires in Baraboo's history, from the burning of the old courthouse in 40-degrees-below-zero weather to the destruction of the old high school. He posed at the end of his career with his original uniform from Phoenix Hose Company No. 1.

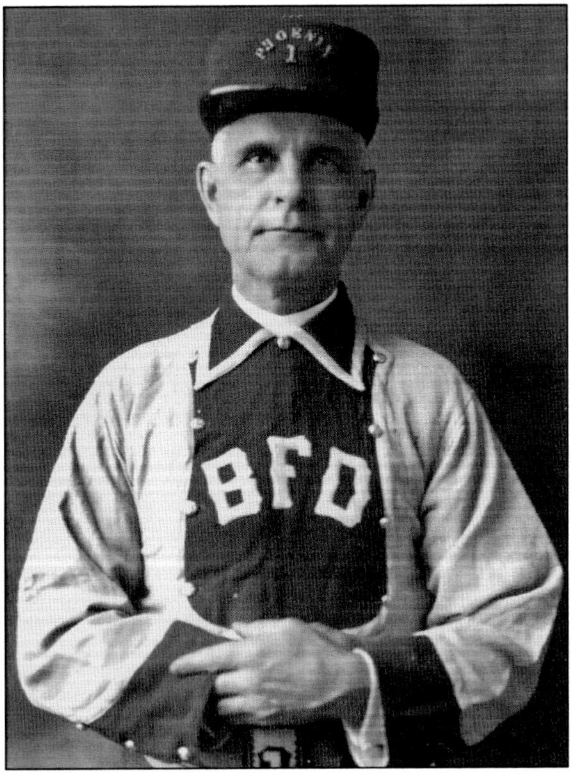

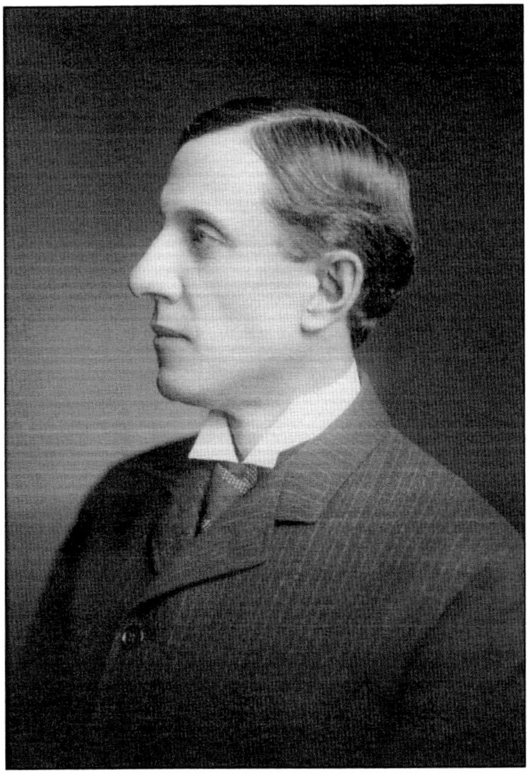

Jacob Van Orden's life and career exemplified the American dream of working hard and climbing the corporate ladder. He moved to Baraboo in 1874 with his widowed mother and started with the Bank of Baraboo as a bookkeeper. He eventually climbed the ranks to become president of the bank. During his career, he was instrumental in helping the fledgling Ringling Brothers Circus succeed with judicious lines of credit.

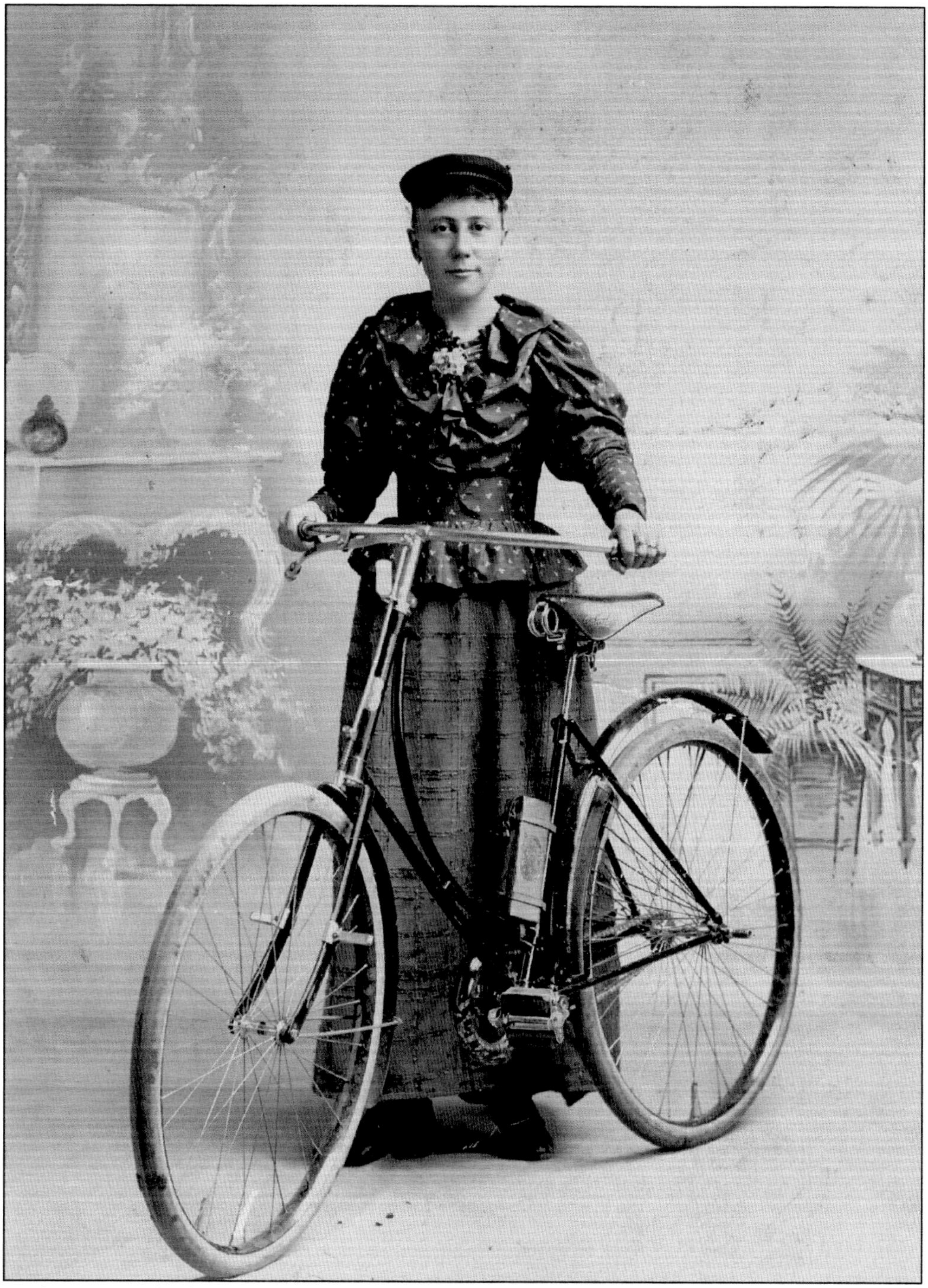

In the 1890s, the bicycle craze hit Baraboo's men and women. The advent of better street conditions and the arrival of mass produced bicycles meant that just about anyone that wanted to could enjoy the freedom of self propulsion. This unknown Baraboo woman posed with her two-wheeler at Arthur Johnson's photography shop. (Siekert Collection.)

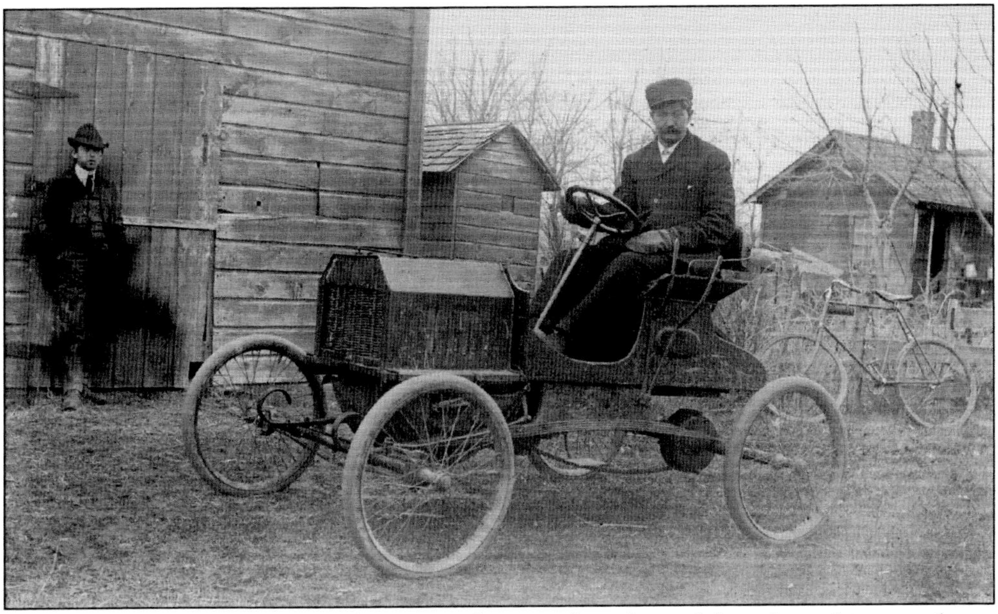

Automobiles soon eclipsed bicycles in popularity with early models such as this one, above, borrowing heavily from the bicycle industry. Ward Shepard is shown about 1905 sitting in his early automobile.

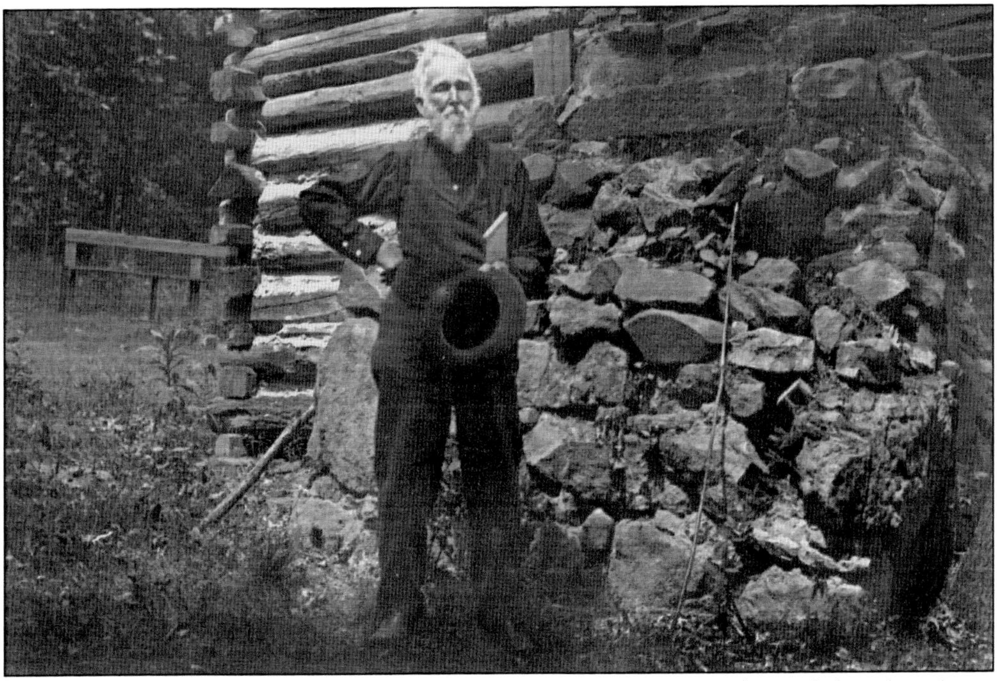

William H. Canfield was one of the Baraboo valley's early pioneers and most beloved residents. He settled on Skillet Creek in 1842 with his pregnant wife and lived under their dry goods boxes until he could erect a cabin. He wrote several volumes of Sauk County history and started the Old Settlers' Association in 1872, which eventually had grounds and some buildings at Devil's Lake, above. Canfield died at the age of 94 in 1913.

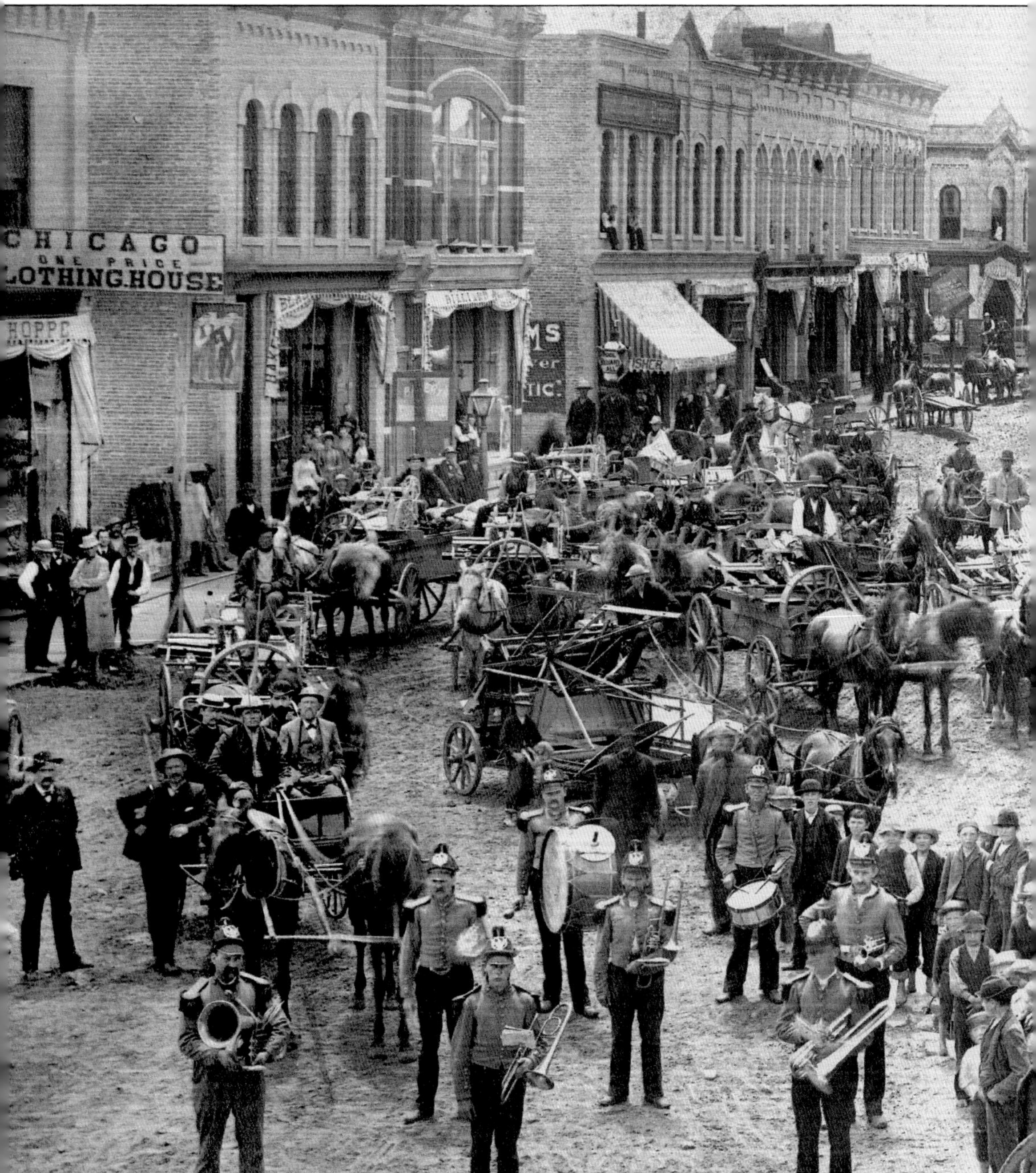

On Saturday June 20, 1885, the principle streets of Baraboo were lined with crowds of spectators who came out to witness the delivery of the new Excelsior Twine Binders and Mowers. The whole event was orchestrated by Peter Wilkinson, an agent for an Ohio firm selling the machines. Wilkinson had spent considerable time in the preceding months delivering sales pitches and his sales tour culminated with the dramatic delivery of the machines. A grand parade was planned, beginning with the unloading of the new machinery at the railroad depot, followed by a procession through town. The parade was led by Wilkinson and other dignitaries

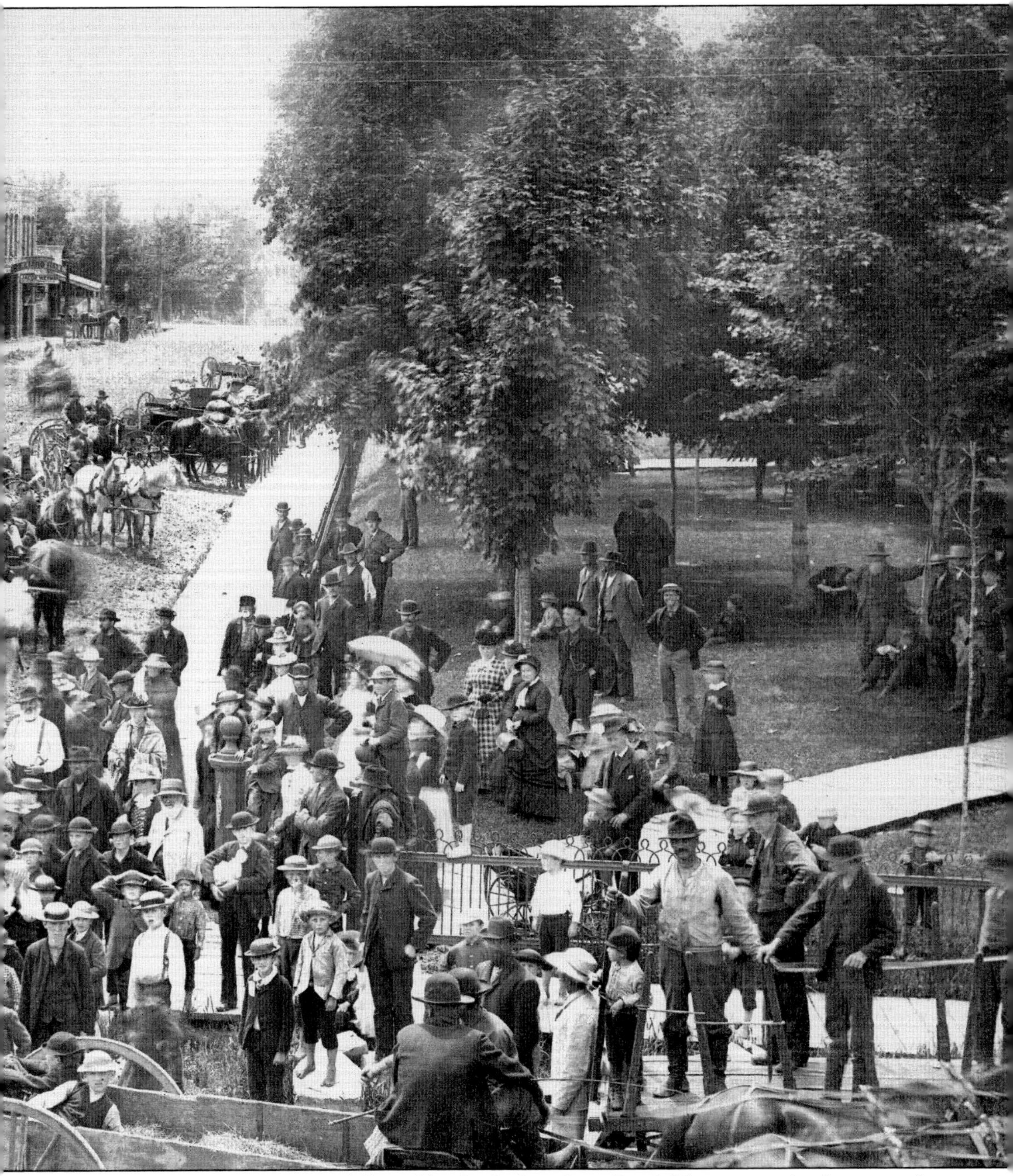

who rode in a double carriage followed by the Badger State Band. Then came the farmers with their new machinery loaded upon their wagons. The highlight of the parade was a brand new Excelsior specially mounted on trucks "which showed the machine to perfection." The event culminated with this photo taken on Oak Street in front of the Warren Hotel. For Peter Wilkinson, the affair was bittersweet. His sales drive was so successful that he had more orders than he could possibly deliver. When realizing the situation, the salesman reportedly "went out and wept bitterly." (Baraboo National Bank Collection.)

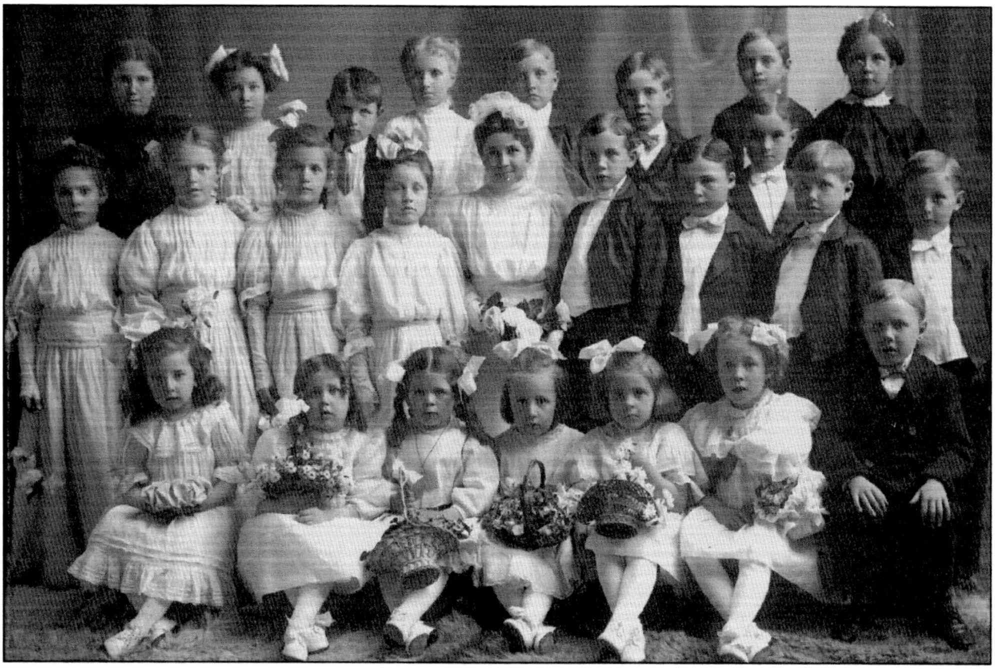

Baraboo's children were not always to be "seen and not heard." In 1890, some of them were seen and heard in a performance of *Tom Thumb's Wedding*.

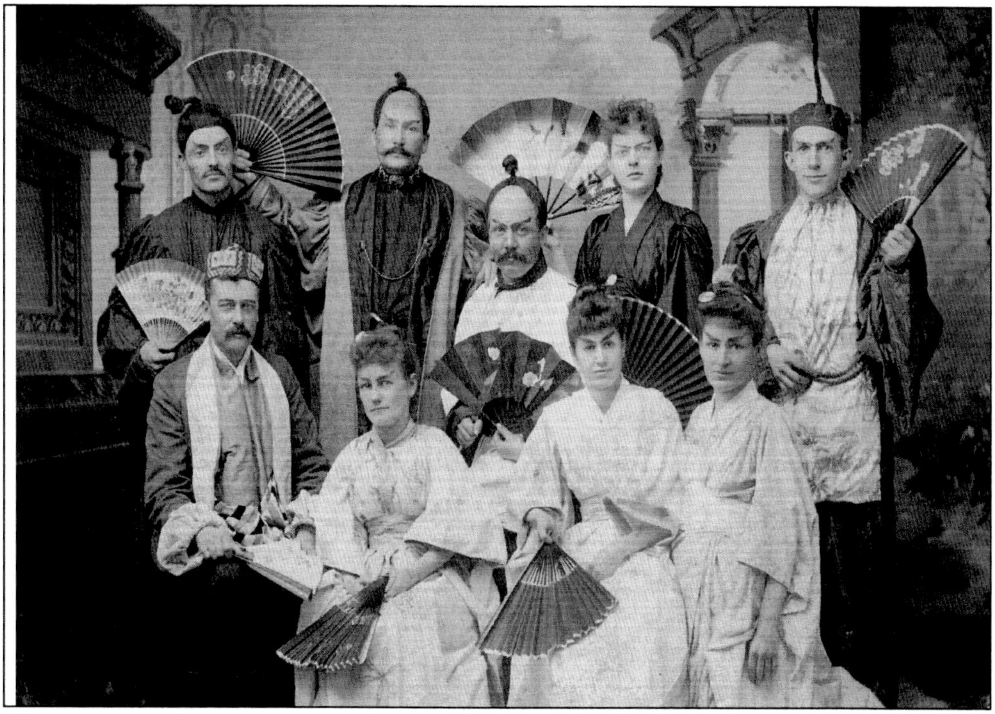

While traveling shows often came to Baraboo's early opera houses, local talent was also featured periodically. During the Christmas season in 1890, this collection of actors performed for a Baraboo audience, perhaps doing their rendition of the *Mikado*.

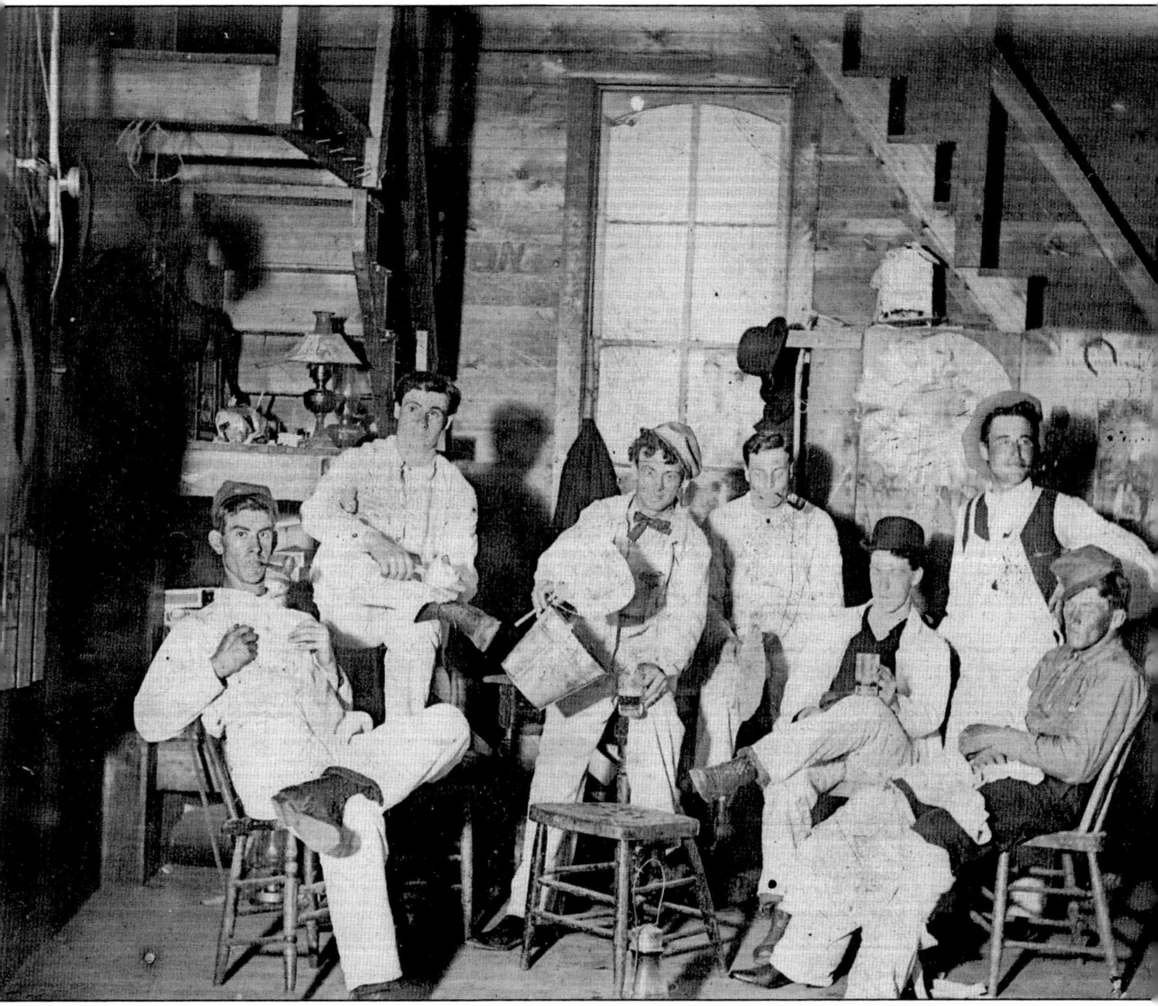

Every stage performance needed actors, but also needed a crew to handle things backstage. This group of seven young men helped out at one of Baraboo's opera houses, probably Capener's at the northwest corner of Oak and Fifth. Originally built as a roller skating rink in the early 1880s it became an opera house in 1887. William Jennings Bryant and Robert LaFollette spoke on its stage. The Opera House burned on February 22, 1905.

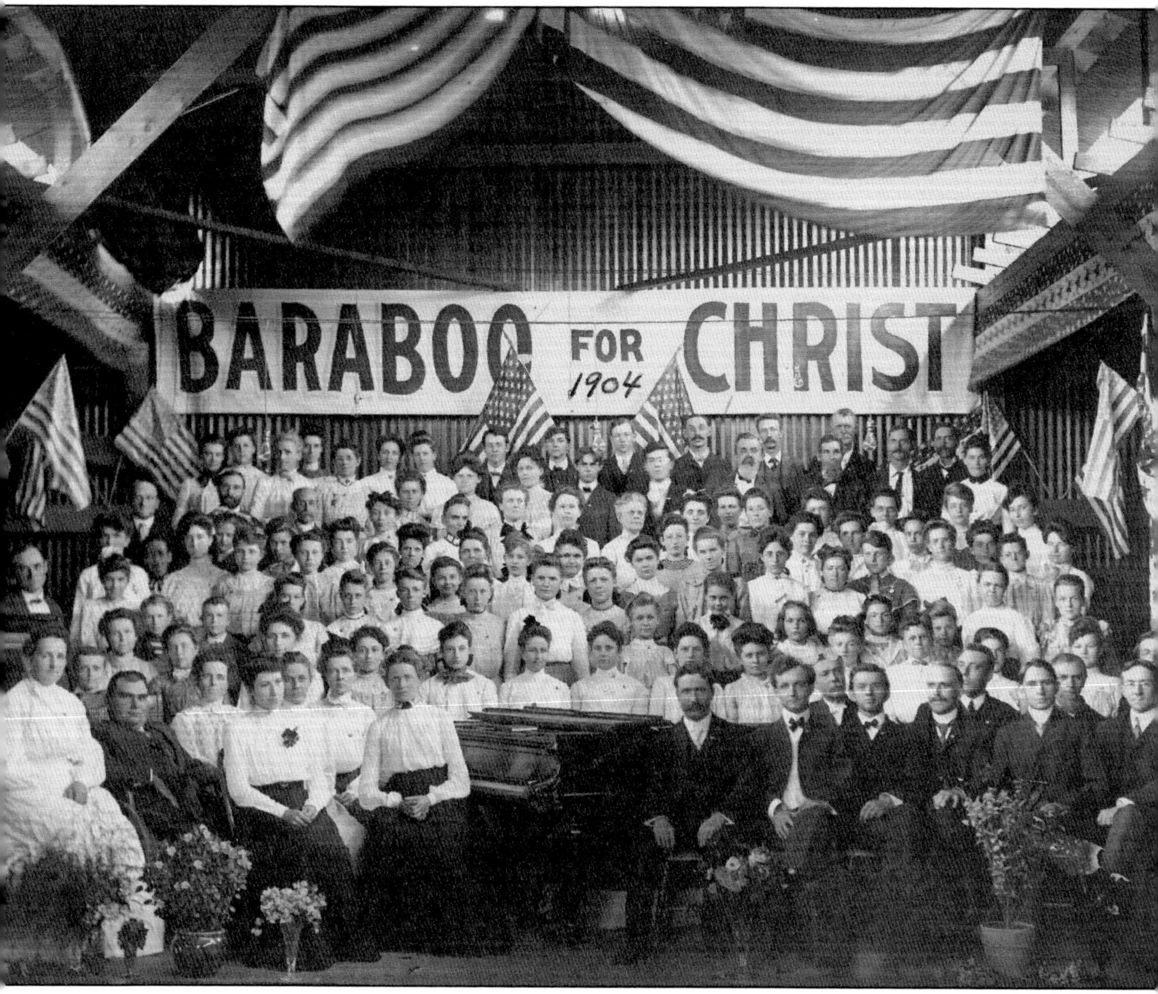

In June 1904, Baraboo was host to a series of lectures given by Reverend M.H. Lyon, an evangelist who traveled the country spreading the gospel. Arthur Judevine was contracted to erect a 64 x 125 ft. temporary building, capable of seating 2,000, at the southeast corner of Broadway and Fifth. A choir of "over 100 of the best voices of the city" was formed and rehearsed several times before and during the lecture series. Businesses closed early and Fred Morley's First Marine Band rearranged their concert schedule so the citizens of Baraboo could attend Rev. Lyon's sermons. Even rains could not dampen the enthusiasm. Most accounts reported that over 1,300 people attended each of the meetings.

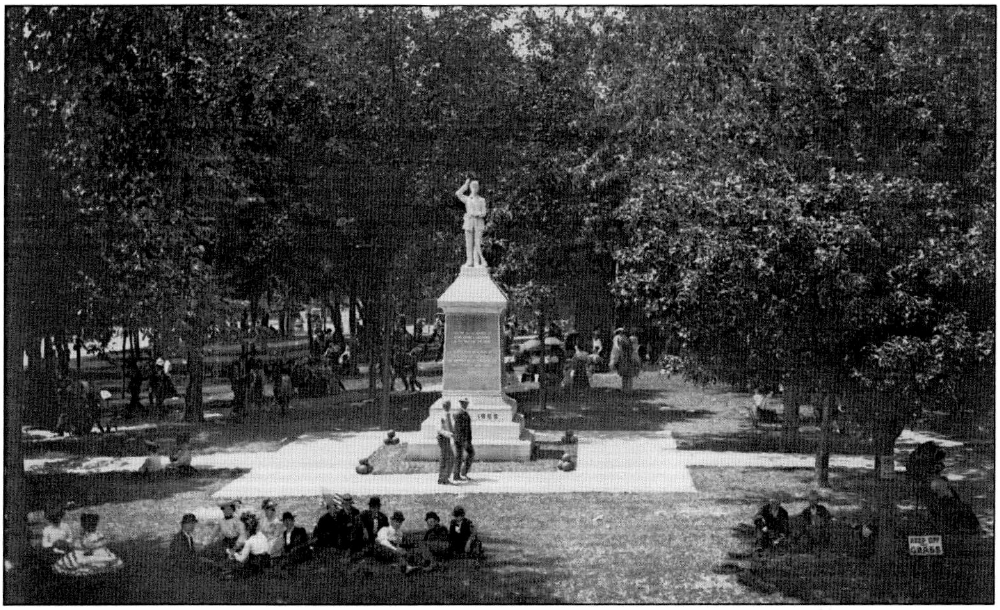

Baraboo's beautiful courthouse lawn has always been a favorite gathering place. Since 1896, major events and intimate gatherings have taken place under the watchful eye of the Civil War soldier depicted in the monument placed there by the Joe Hooker Post of the Grand Army of the Republic (GAR) and its auxiliaries. The small sign to the right reads "Keep off the grass."

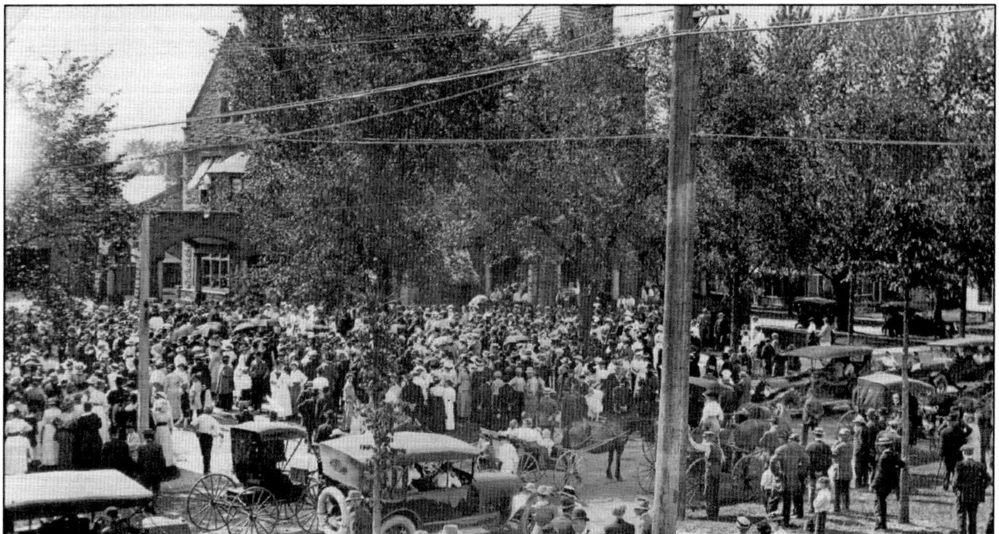

On June 24, 1915, a rally was held in front of Al. Ringling's home on Broadway to thank him for the theatre he was constructing on the square. The rally was held before the theatre was even finished, due to the questionable health of the elder circus showman. City school superintendent, A.L. Kingsford, in his address remarked, "It is eminently fitting and proper that he who with his brothers has given more pleasure to more people than anyone else since the beginning of time, should leave to his own townspeople as a lasting memorial, not a hospital, nor a library or institution of learning, but a palace of pleasure." Al. Ringling died January 1, 1916, just six weeks after the opening of the theatre.

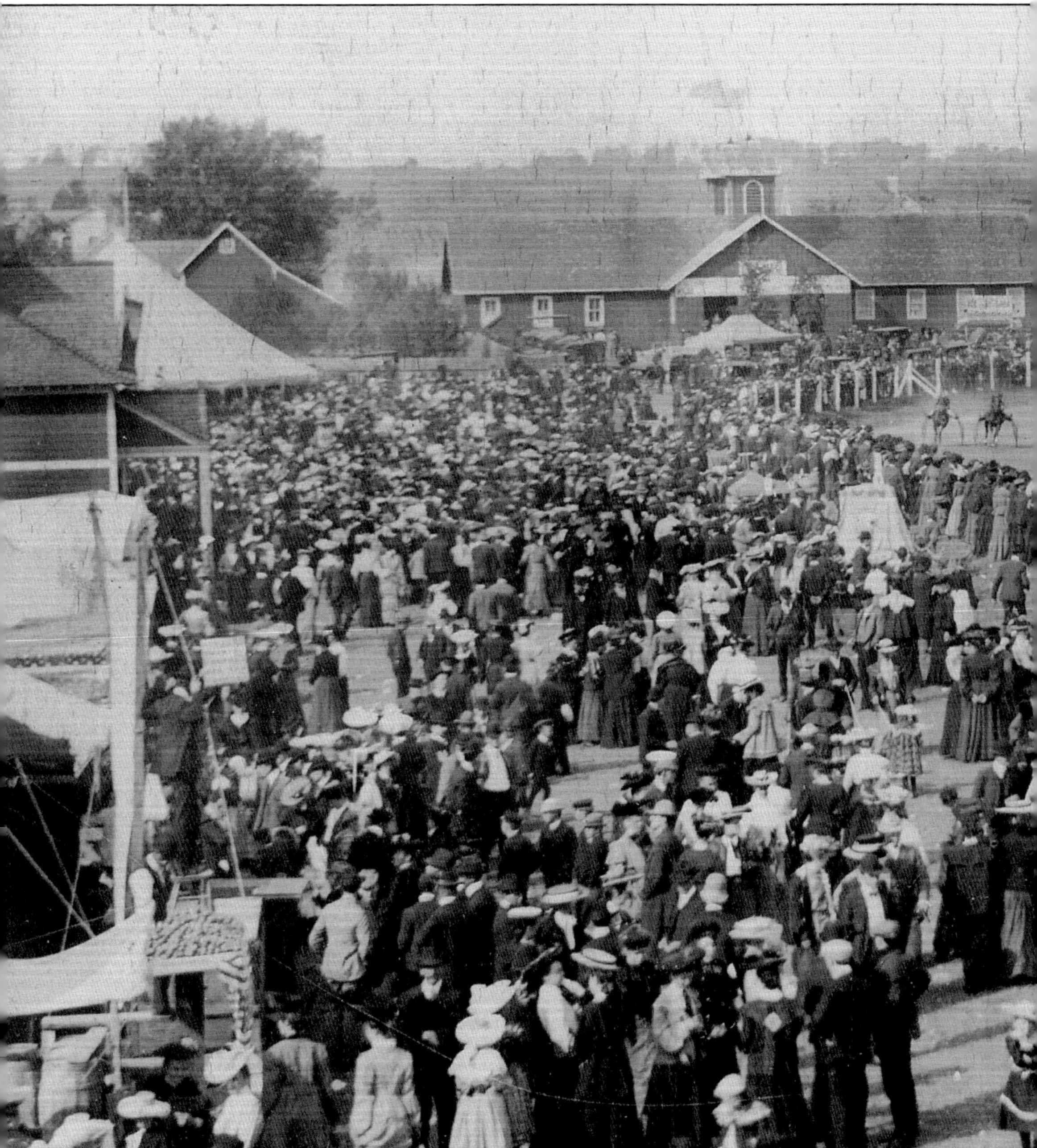

The Sauk County Agricultural Society was formed in 1855 for the "promotion and improvement of the condition of agriculture, horticulture, mechanical, manufacturing and household arts." The first fair was held on the square. In 1870, the society purchased land east of the village for

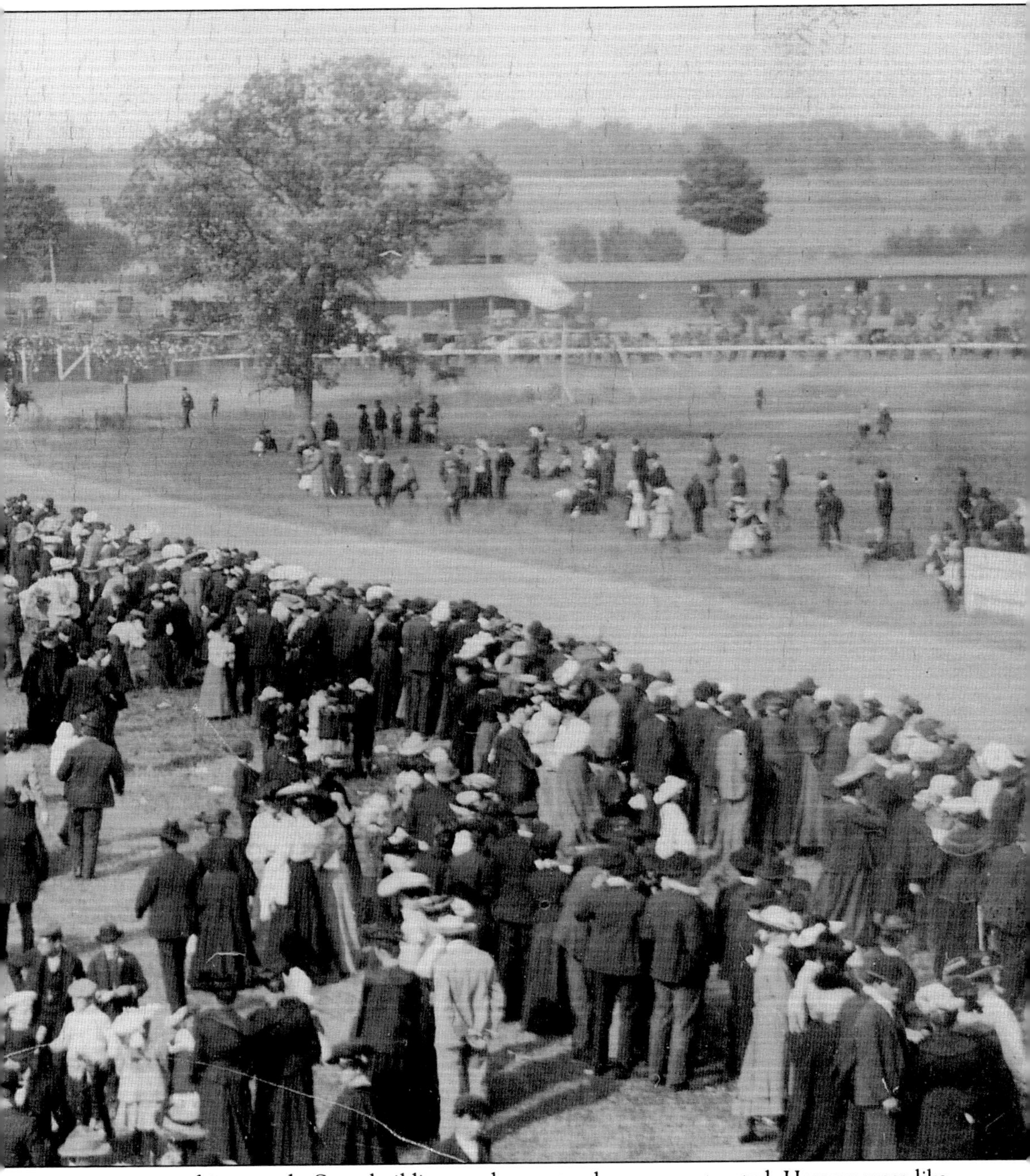

a permanent fair grounds. Soon buildings and a racetrack were constructed. Harness races like the one shown above were a very popular attraction at the fair well into the 1950s. The embankments that formed the corners of the track are still visible on the grounds today.

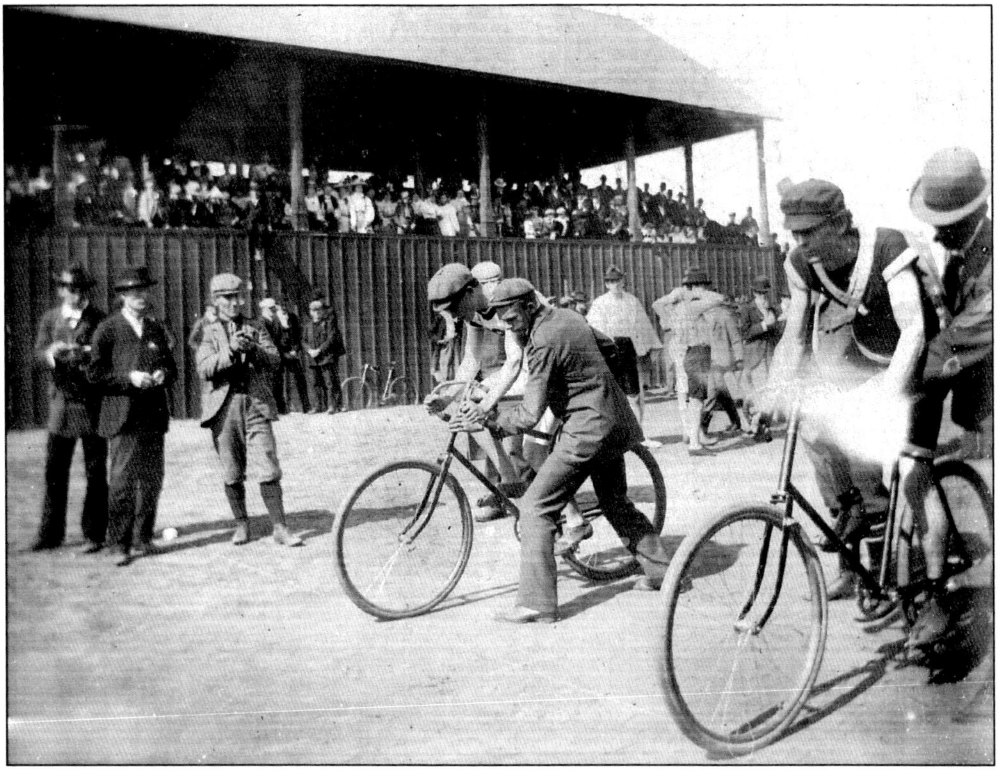

The grandstand at the Sauk County Fairgrounds was always a good place to see something interesting. At the turn of the 20th century, bicycle races filled the stands with enthusiastic spectators.

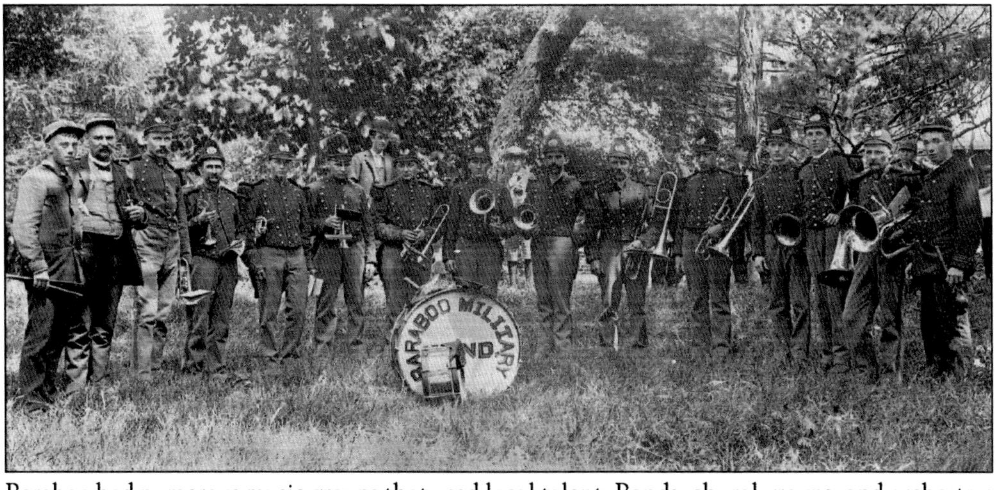

Baraboo had numerous music groups that used local talent. Bands, choral groups, and orchestras were frequently organized and enjoyed a loyal local following. In times of war and conflict, these groups responded with patriotic tunes and military style uniforms. Some of these local bands eventually became attached to the military and performed far from their Baraboo roots.

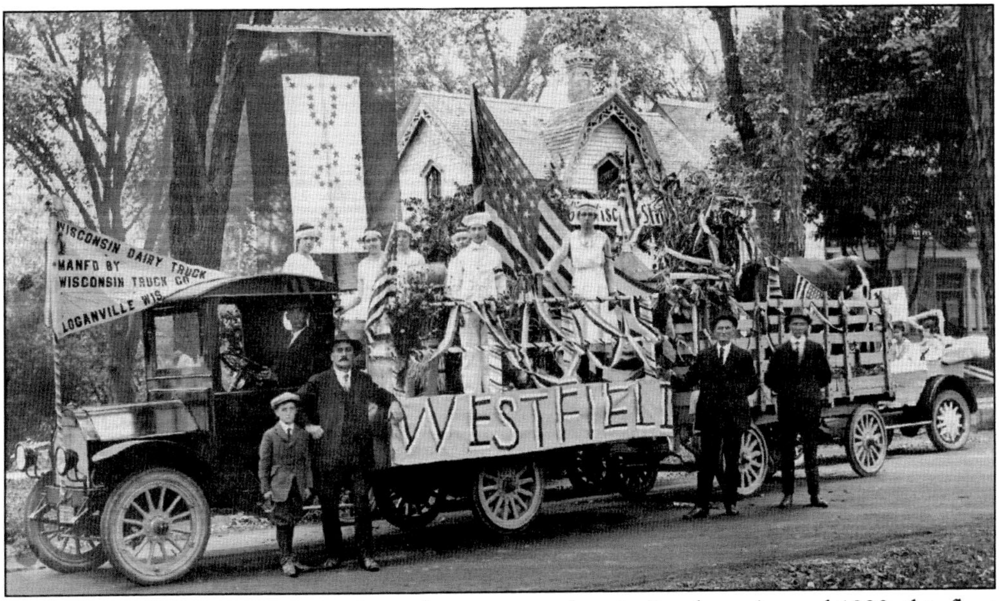

People have always enjoyed parades and no more so than in Baraboo. Around 1920, this float from Westfield Township stopped on Second Avenue for a photo. The truck was built in Loganville by the Wisconsin Truck Company established in 1919. The truck came fitted with an electric starter and a "specially designed dairy body," and the company boasted that it was easy to handle, designed for dairy work, and ran "as smooth and quiet as the finest touring car." Connected is a wagon carrying a real dairy cow.

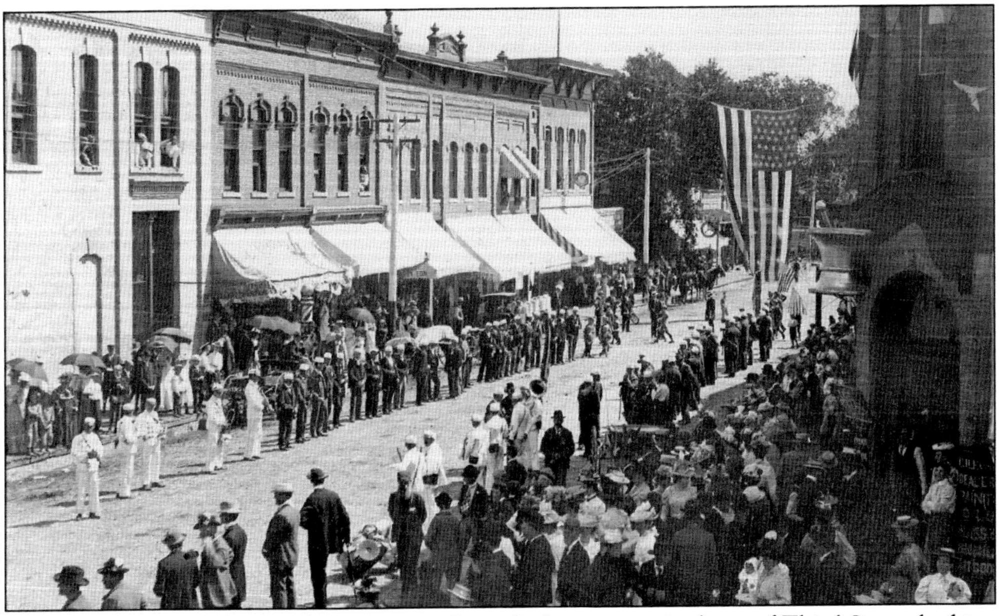

No parade was complete without passing through the square. A photo of Third Street looking east shows a parade about to start in the early 20th century. The men lining up are probably part of one of Baraboo's fraternal or secret societies, such as the Knights Templar, Knights of Columbus, International Order of Odd Fellows, Ancient Order of United Workmen, or the Masons. (Baraboo National Bank Collection.)

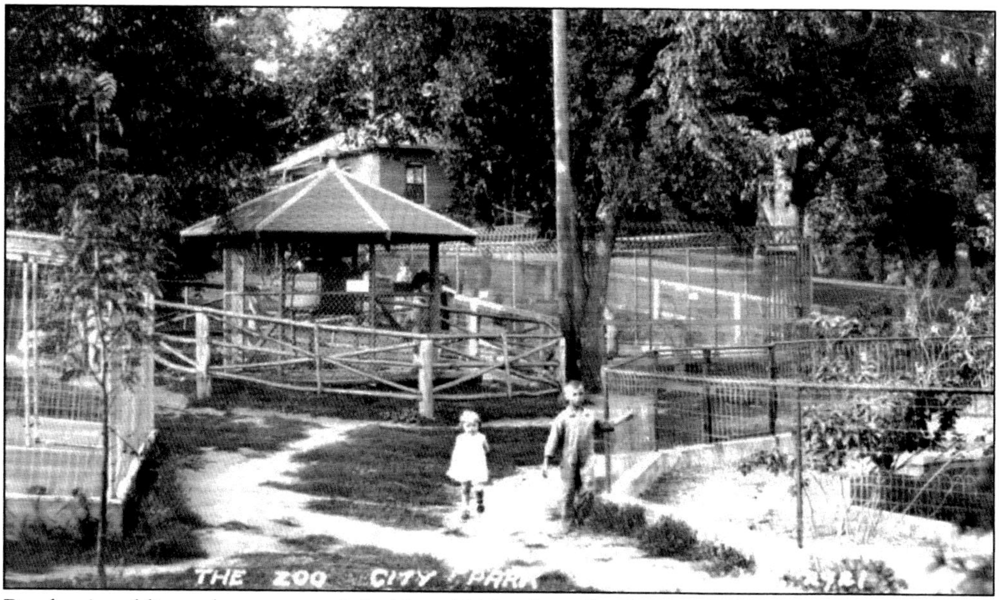

Baraboo's public park system took hold in 1918, when the former Ochsner estate was partially gifted to the city, comprising 12 or so acres on the hill above the upper oxbow in the river. A zoo was soon developed and expanded, perhaps filling a void that was felt when the Ringling Brothers moved their winter quarters out of Baraboo, taking all of their exotic animals with them.

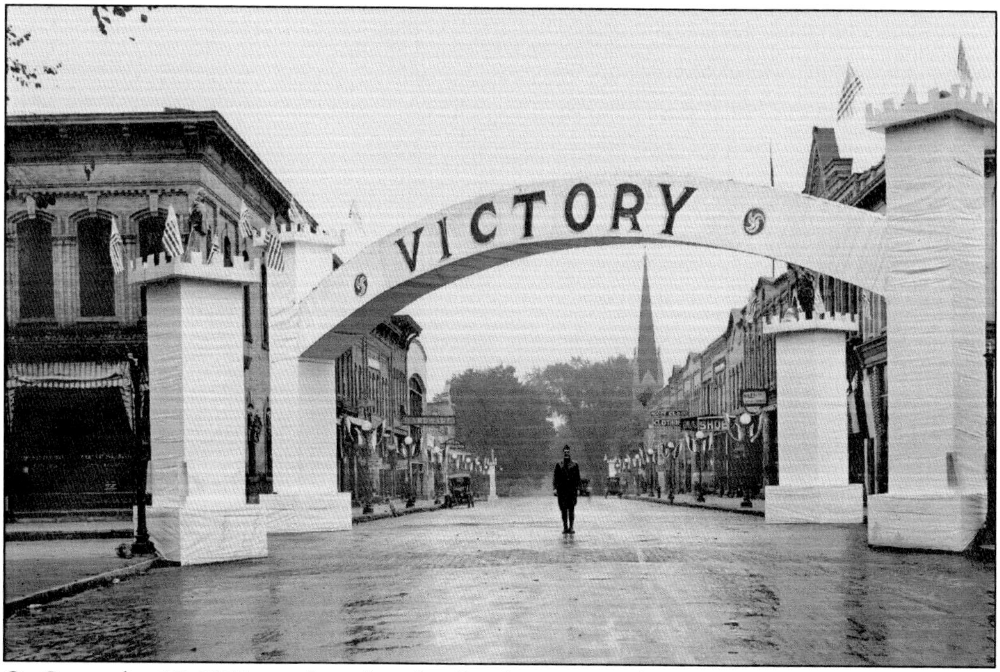

On September 17, 1919, people gathered in Baraboo to attend a Victory Parade, which was held to honor the returning veterans from the Great War. Local papers hailed the event as the "Greatest Day in Sauk County's History." Beneath the white "Victory" arch at the corner of Oak and Third, marched "fine floats and bands." The soldiers proved a most "inspiring sight that will be lasting to all who witnessed it."

Eight

Homes and Havens

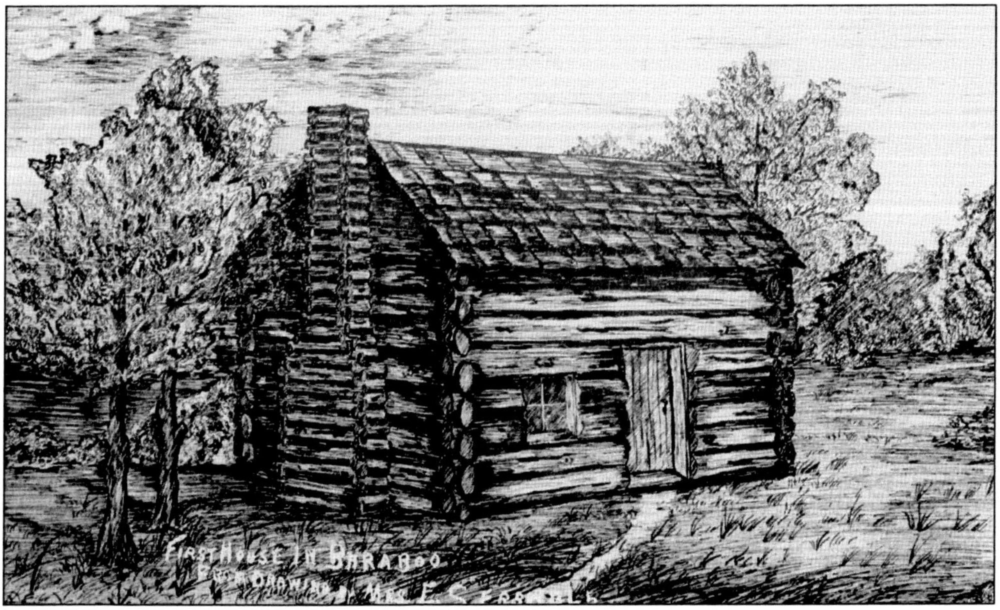

A shelter, whether a crude cabin or stately brick home, has always been a necessity for man, and Baraboo was no exception. Early pioneers built log cabins and lived under even more temporary accommodations while they built them. Such was the case with early Baraboo valley pioneer and historian, William H. Canfield, who slept under his dry goods boxes with his pregnant wife for several weeks while he built their first log cabin. As dams and saw mills were built on the river, the housing stock in Baraboo improved quickly. Even more durable materials like bricks were also available after a few years, either made locally or shipped in. While some fine homes were within the original city limits, larger homes were often built around the outskirts on large plats of land, which eventually became part of the expanding community. As time went on and fortunes developed, homes became more than mere shelters, but an indication of wealth, class, and stylishness. More choices for home construction also became available. Early carpenter designed dwellings gave way to architect designed mansions. Architects from Madison, Milwaukee, and Minneapolis have left their mark on Baraboo.

The first occupied pioneer dwelling to be built in Baraboo is reported to have been a log cabin built by Abe Wood in 1839, above. It was about 16 x 18 ft. in size and had a dirt floor that became so compacted from constant use that the depression was still visible in 1926 when a marker was placed on the site. The marker still exists today at Ochsner Park. Wood was a Kentucky native who came to Baraboo in the fall of 1839 and with his friend, Wallace Rowan, built the first dam on the river at the upper oxbow. He lived in the cabin with his Indian wife, Sarah, who was actually part white, and two daughters.

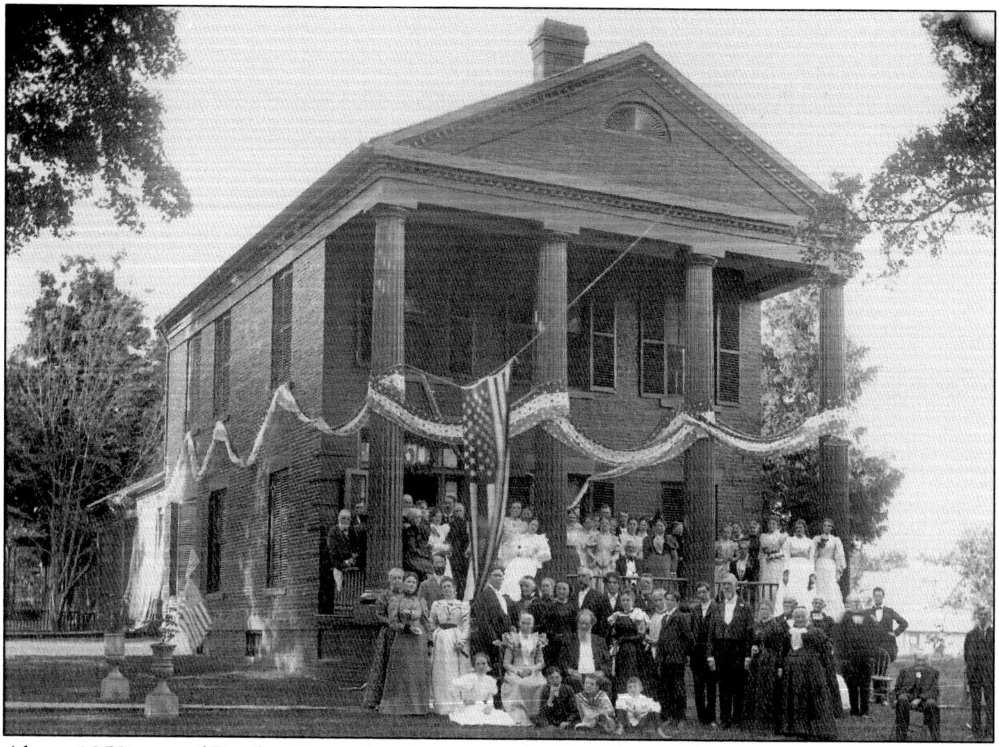

About 1850, one of Baraboo's grandest homes was built at the northeast corner of First and Ash for David K. Noyes and his wife, Lucinda, who were married in 1848. The house was designed by Walter Pashley in the Classical Revival style with four enormous Doric columns. In 1898, Mr. and Mrs. Noyes celebrated their 50th wedding anniversary at the house, above. The house was demolished in 1927 to make a lot for the Peck house, below.

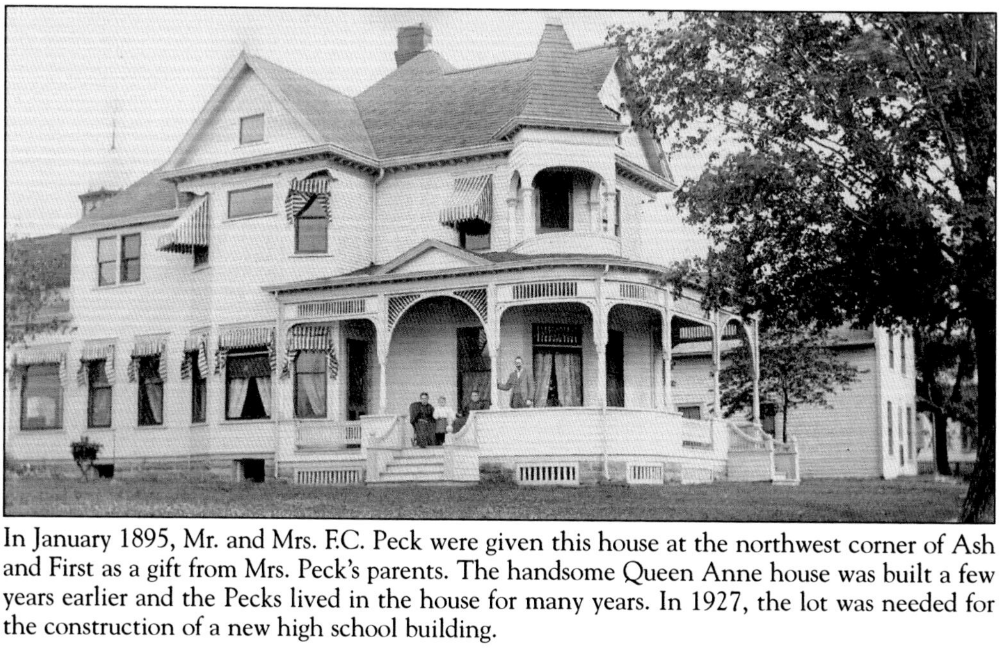

In January 1895, Mr. and Mrs. F.C. Peck were given this house at the northwest corner of Ash and First as a gift from Mrs. Peck's parents. The handsome Queen Anne house was built a few years earlier and the Pecks lived in the house for many years. In 1927, the lot was needed for the construction of a new high school building.

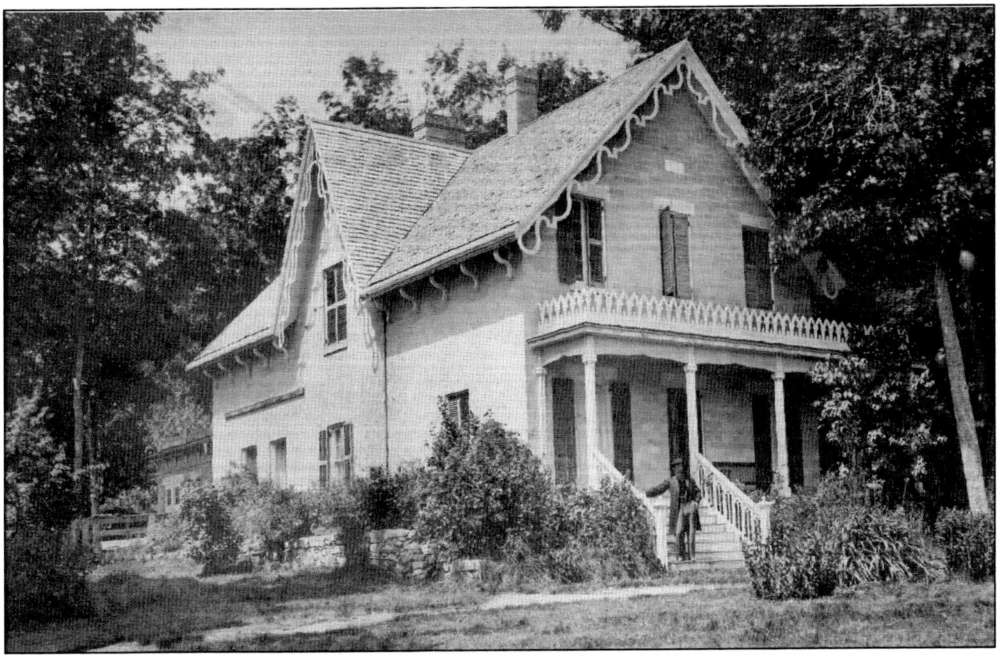

Early pioneer, James Maxwell, constructed a unique house southeast of the village in 1856. The building materials were hauled in from Milwaukee, including lime for making the bricks, which were of unusual size. The house was over 100 feet in length and had a commanding view of the Devil's Lake valley to the south. Gothic ornament on the house was finished in time for the marriage of Maxwell's daughter in the fall of 1856. The home, also seen below, was used during the Civil War to harbor fugitive slaves, one of whom stayed the rest of his life in Baraboo. By 1907, the bricks were starting to crumble and the house was demolished. The once wild surroundings of thick forest had given away to new houses.

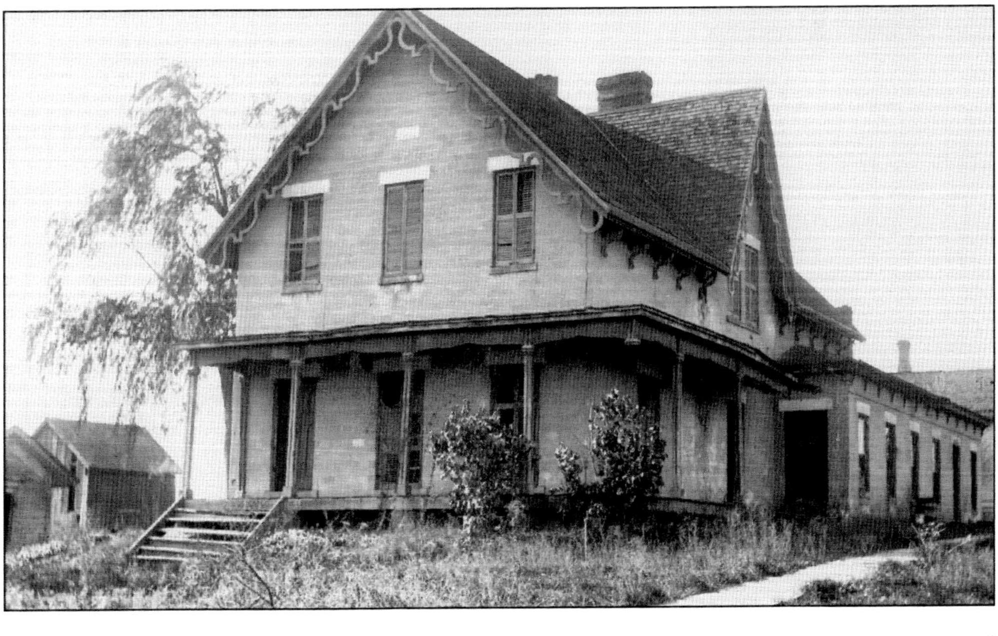

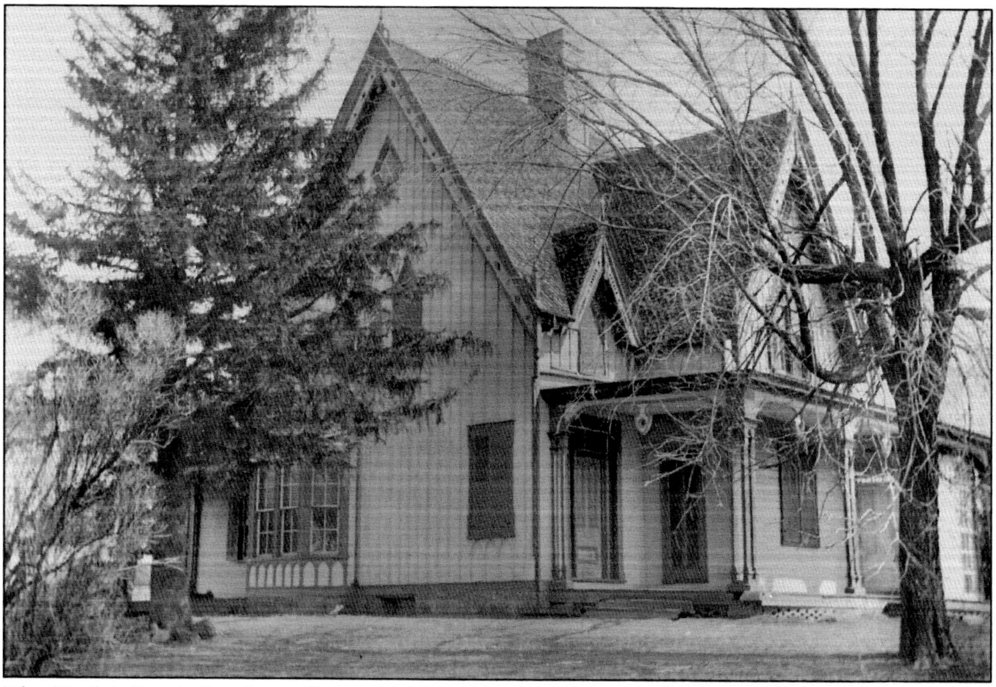

The Gothic Revival style, with its steeply pitched roofs, vertical lines, and pointed arches, was used to good effect on the A.G. Tuttle house, built in 1869 northeast of the village. Tuttle established the Baraboo Valley Nursery Company about 1860 and soon the acreage around the house was filled with fruit bearing trees, especially apples. The house still stands in remarkable condition on Elizabeth Street, which was named for Mrs. Tuttle.

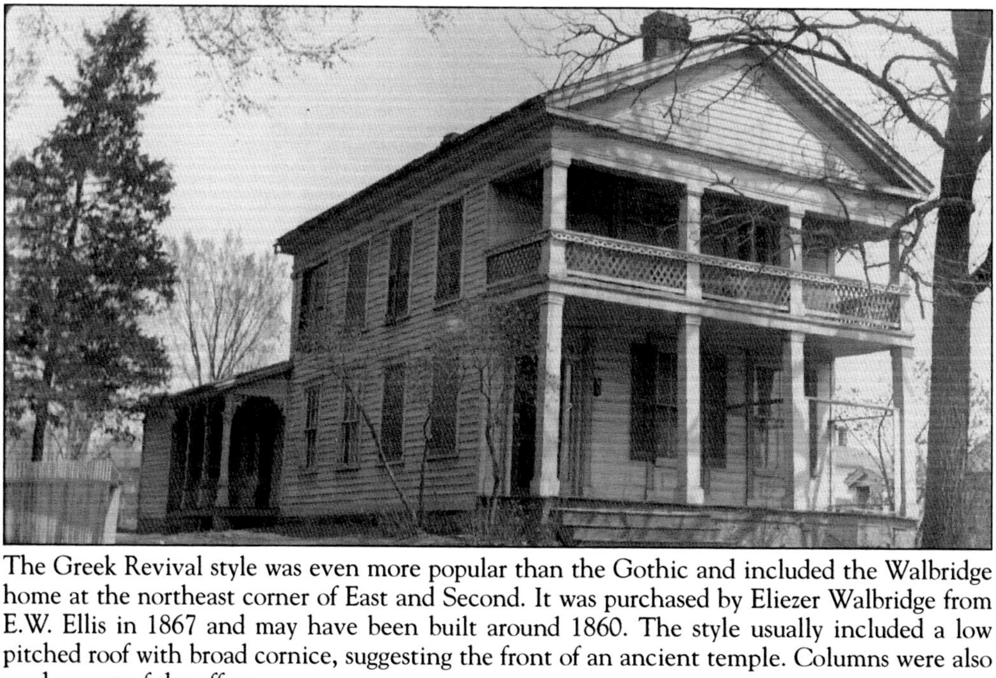

The Greek Revival style was even more popular than the Gothic and included the Walbridge home at the northeast corner of East and Second. It was purchased by Eliezer Walbridge from E.W. Ellis in 1867 and may have been built around 1860. The style usually included a low pitched roof with broad cornice, suggesting the front of an ancient temple. Columns were also used as part of the effect.

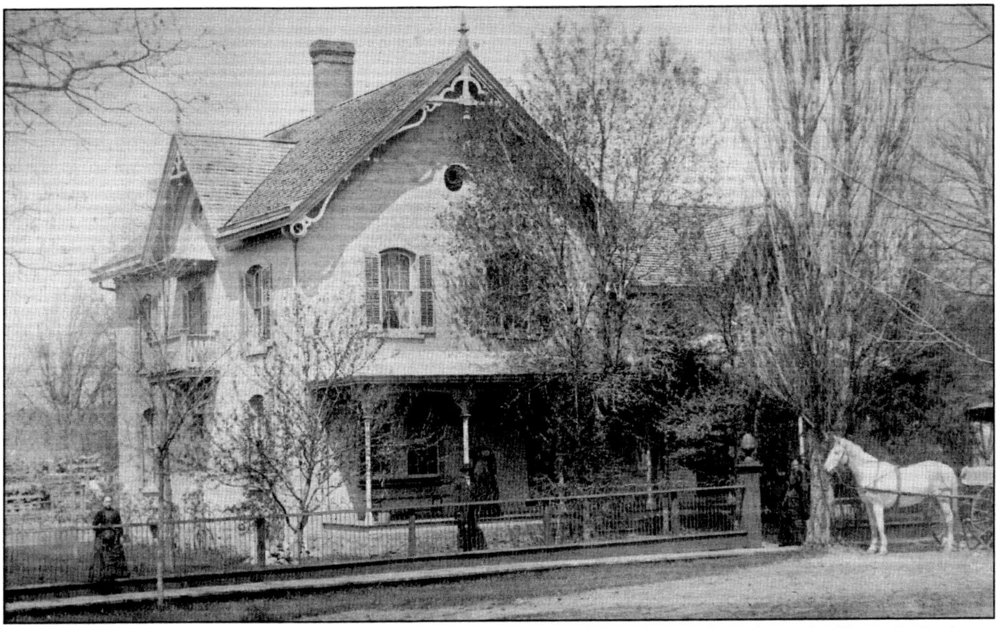

J.J. Gattiker was born in Switzerland in 1826. He was highly educated and taught French, Italian, and mathematics before immigrating to the United States in 1855, settling in rural Sauk County. Just three years later, he became county clerk and later moved to Baraboo. In 1871, he had a handsome Gothic revival style house constructed at the northeast corner of Oak and Seventh. The clock tower was placed on the courthouse in his honor by his daughters in 1915.

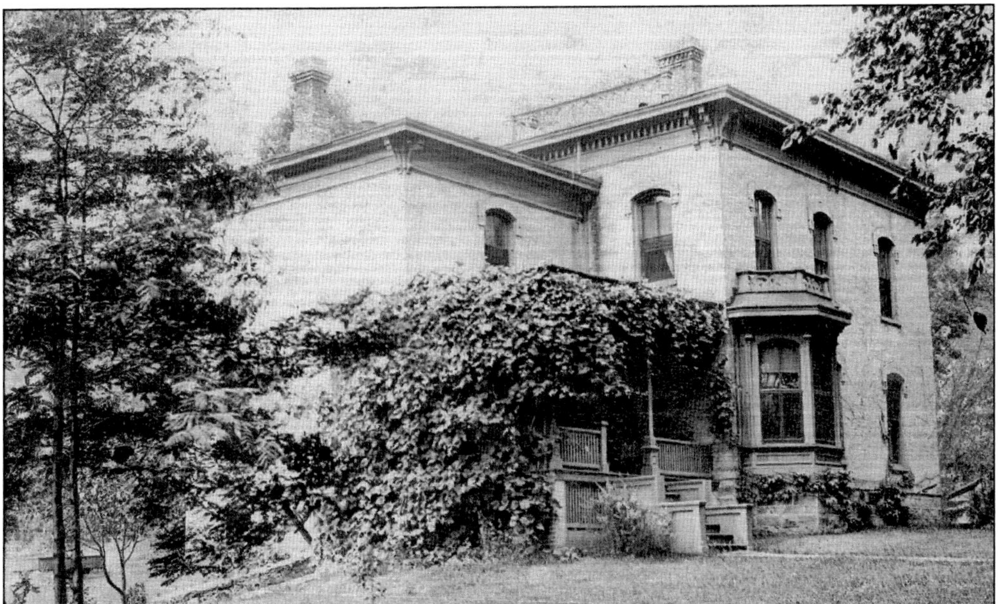

Alfred A. Gattiker was a partner in a hardware business with his brother, J.J. Gattiker, for many years in downtown Baraboo. Alfred had a house built for himself at the southwest corner of Fourth and West in 1879. It cost $3,000 and was designed in the Italianate style, which featured arched windows and decorative eaves supported by paired brackets.

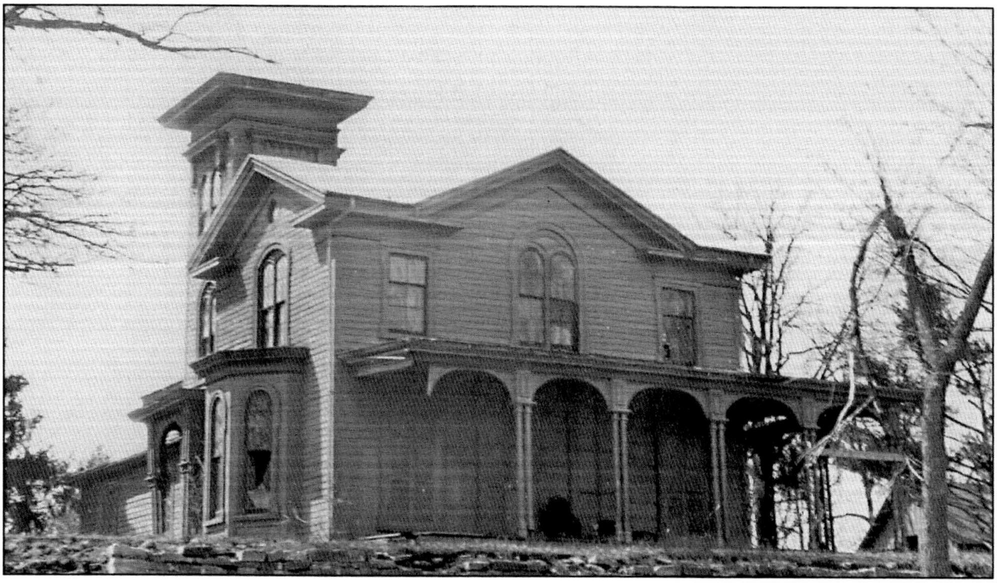

The Italianate style often incorporated the use of a tower, and on the Vittum house it reached a soaring three stories. The house was purchased by Civil War Colonel David S. Vittum in 1867 from Merril J. Drown, who most likely built it a few years earlier. The grounds encompassed an entire city block fronting on Seventh Avenue between Park and Summit. The house was split into two pieces in the early 1930s and made into two houses.

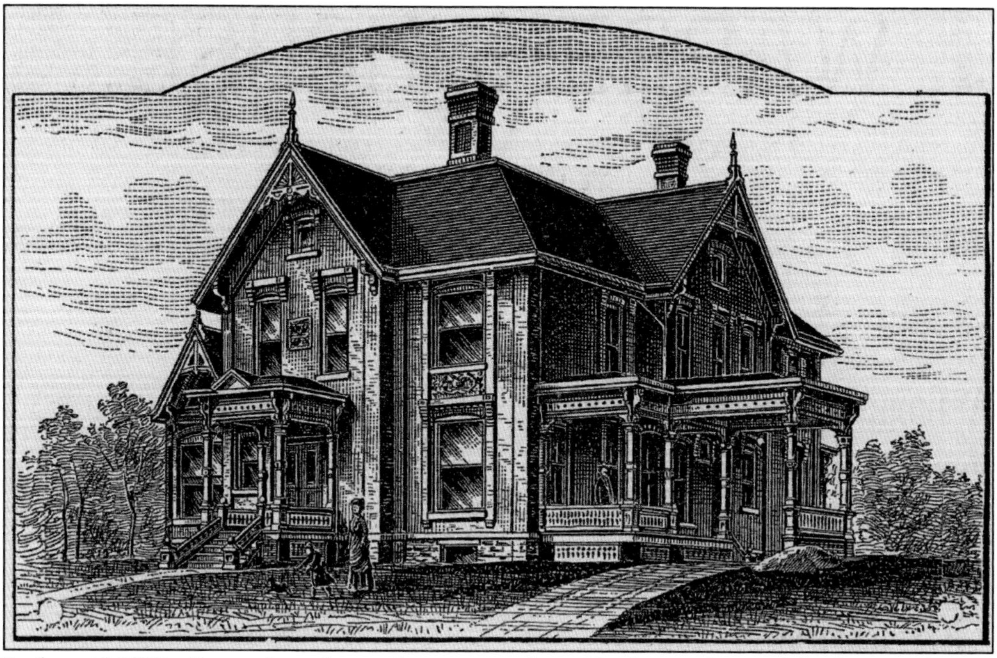

In the mid-1880s, Queen Anne homes became popular in Baraboo and one of the first was the F.T. Brewster home finished in 1887 at the southeast corner of Ash and Sixth. The home was redecorated in 1897 by society matriarch, Harriet Mackey, who christened the residence the "wigwam" and threw lavish parties there. In 1922, the home was purchased by Lou Ringling, widow of Al. Ringling—she lived there until her death in 1941. The home was razed in the 1960s.

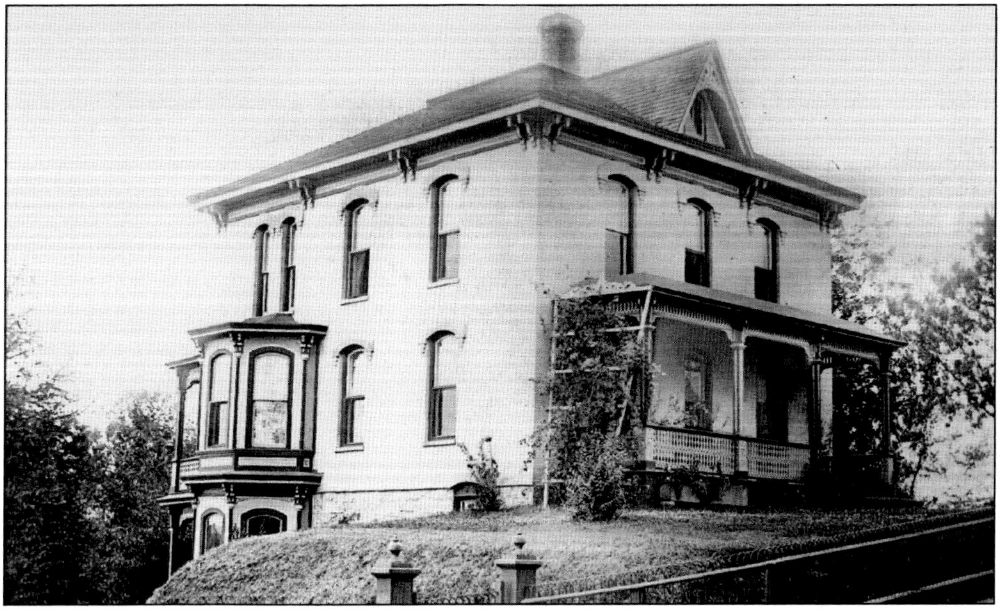

George M. Reul began construction on his own house in 1881 on First Street at the south end of Ash. The Italianate-style house was largely finished the following year, although porches were not added until after 1886. Reul, a German immigrant, owned a planing mill a few blocks away on Water Street, where he made windows, doors, and trim. His house was not only a residence, but an example of what could be made in his factory. The house had a two-story verandah on the south side and a two-story bay window on the east. The house was decorated with 115 scroll cut brackets of three sizes. Hundreds of scroll cut pickets made up the railings. Inside, the house featured arched doorways with sliding pocket doors and an oak staircase with elaborate newel post.

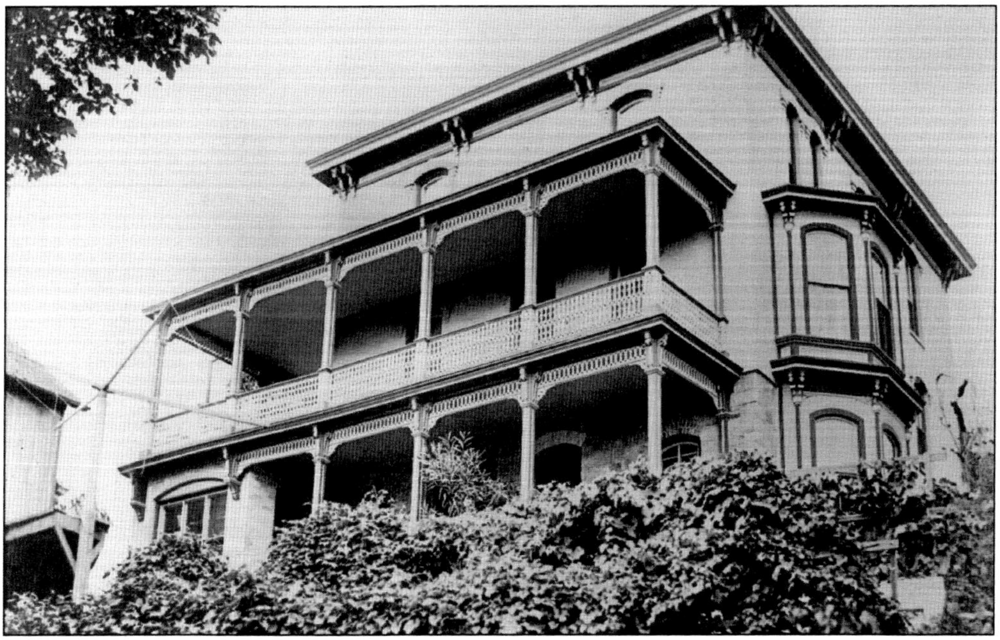

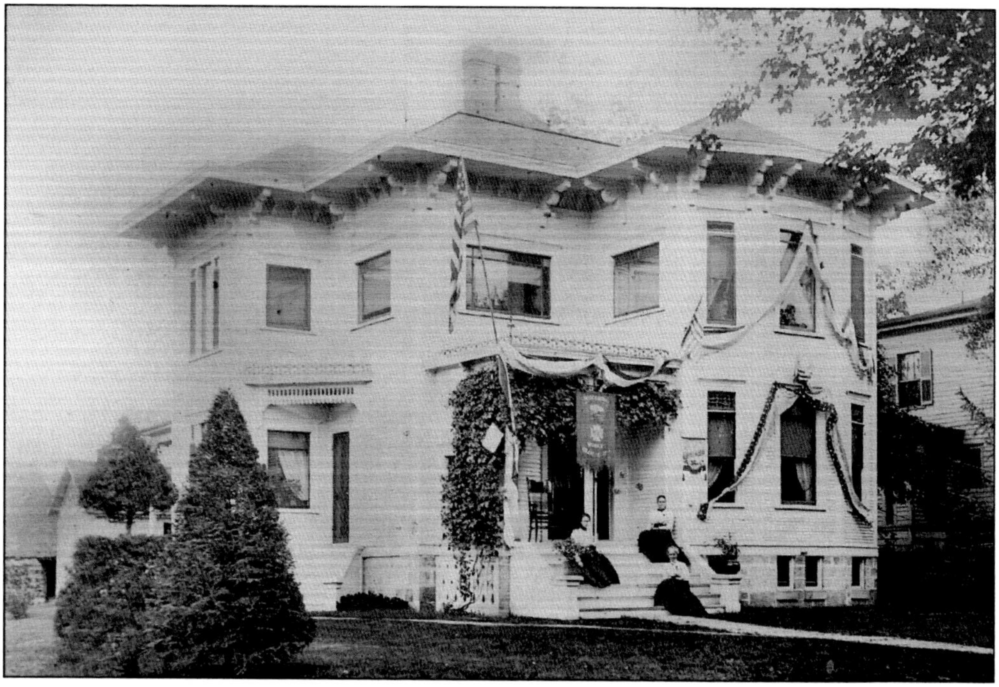

In 1884, Myron Shurtliff and H.P. Jones both had the same taste in houses. The two identical houses were built six blocks apart by the same builder. Shurtliff was a traveling salesman and had his house on East Street, above. Jones was owner of a men's clothing store in downtown Baraboo and lived on Third Avenue, below. Each home cost $3,000 and contained a parlor, sitting room, dining room, kitchen, bath, and bedrooms.

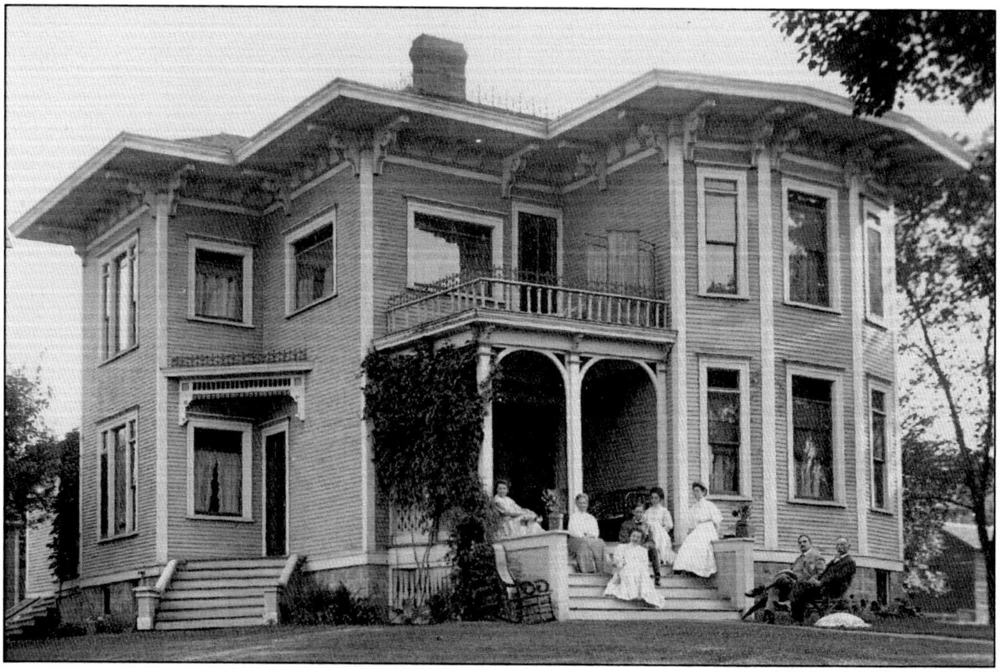

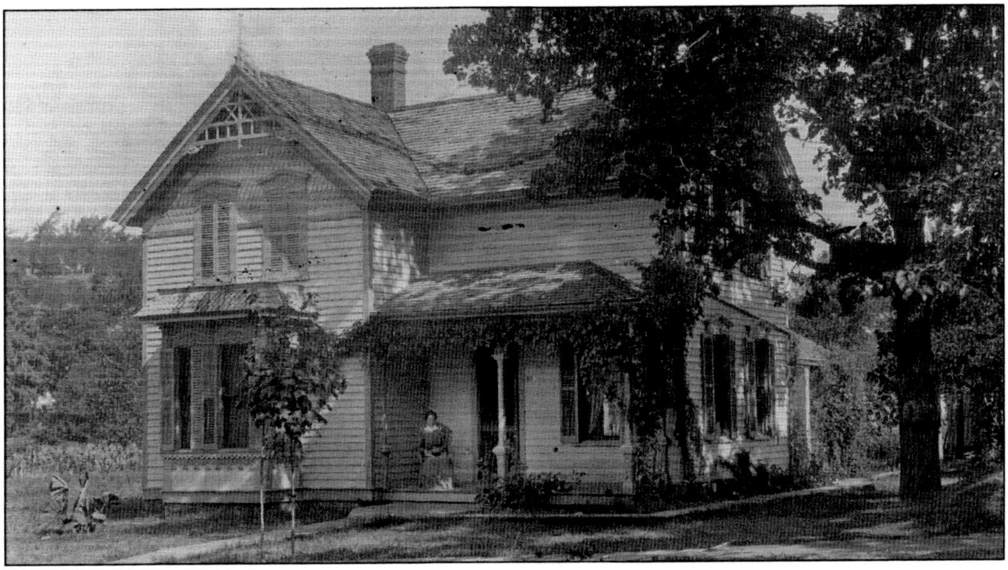

Harry Ellsworth Cole was an ambitious and energetic individual who moved to Baraboo in 1895 and purchased an interest in the Baraboo News, of which he was to be the editor for 33 years. In 1897, he was married in his native Indiana to Dorothy Matchette. One of the first homes they lived in was 129 Eighth Street, above, an older home with Queen Anne and Eastlake ornamentation. Later, they moved next door to 121 Eighth Street, below, a more modern home where on June 2, 1905, the Sauk County Historical Society was formed. Cole became the president of the society until his death in 1928, at which point Mrs. Cole took the helm. H.E. Cole also wrote an extensive county history printed in 1918.

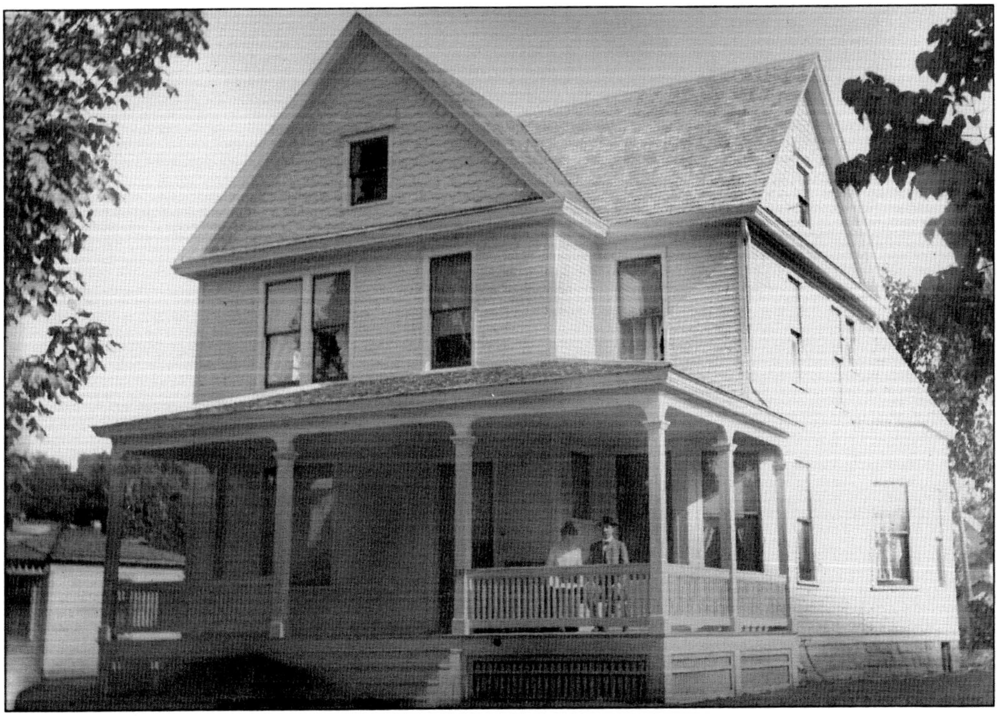

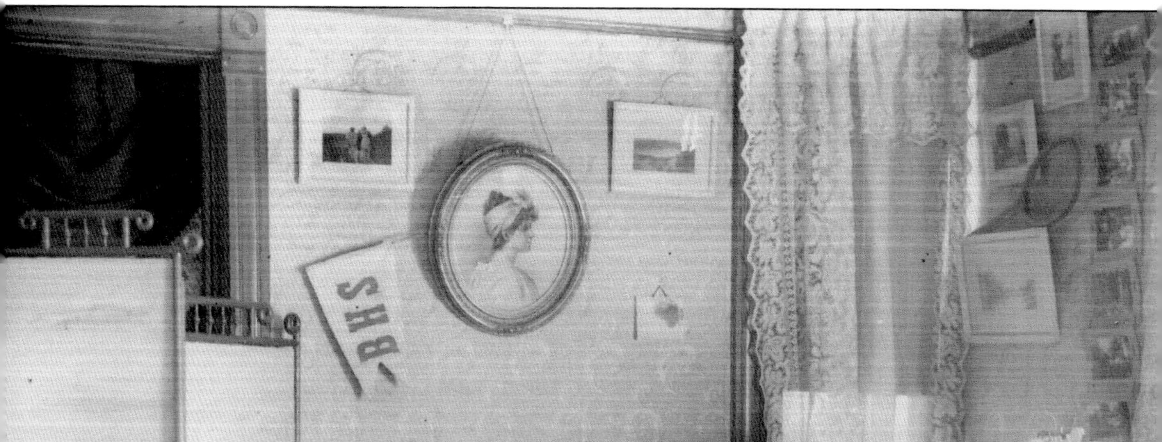

A turn-of-the-century interior is caught by a photographer. The carefully posed shot shows a cozy corner where one could read or play a game while sitting on a fringed chaise lounge. Photographs of area scenery including Devil's Doorway at Devil's Lake and Stand Rock at the Dells decorate the walls, as does a Baraboo High School pennant. Harper's Weekly magazine lays at the ready on the side table along with a crystal basket filled with fruit.

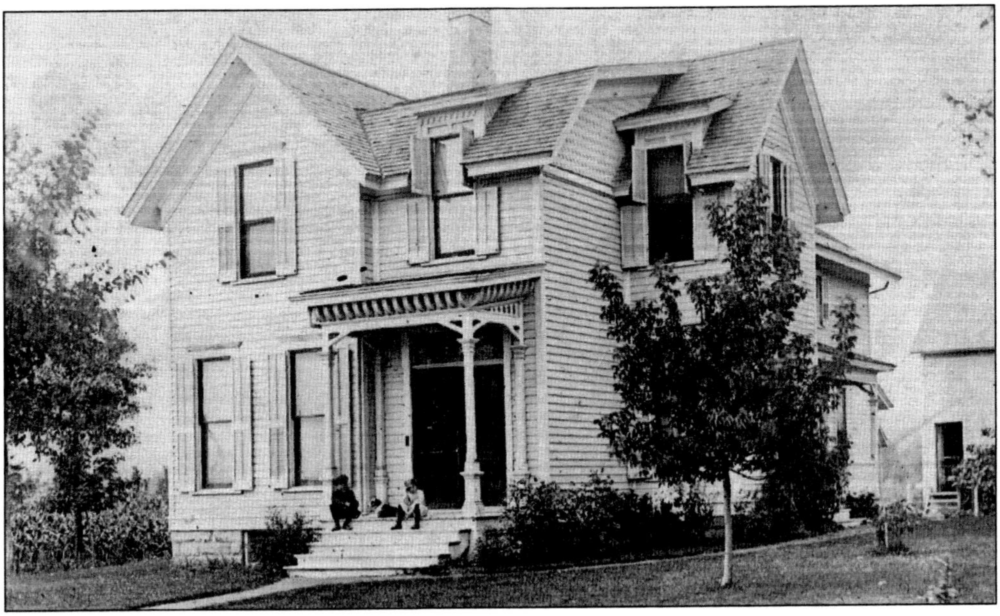

In 1879, banker Jacob Van Orden had a house built on Fourth Avenue by local builder, Thomas Thompson, above. The new house would be home to his widowed mother, his new bride Martha Atwood, and eventually their two children. By 1902, the house was outdated and was sold to Otto Schadde, who moved it across town where it stands today at Fifth and Wheeler. This cleared the site for a grand new house to be constructed, below. Finished in 1904, the new Tudor Revival house was designed by the Milwaukee firm of Ferry and Clas. Alfred Clas was born in Sauk City and had strong ties to his native county. The new house provided ample entertaining space for the Van Ordens, including a third floor ballroom where they celebrated their 25th wedding anniversary in 1905.

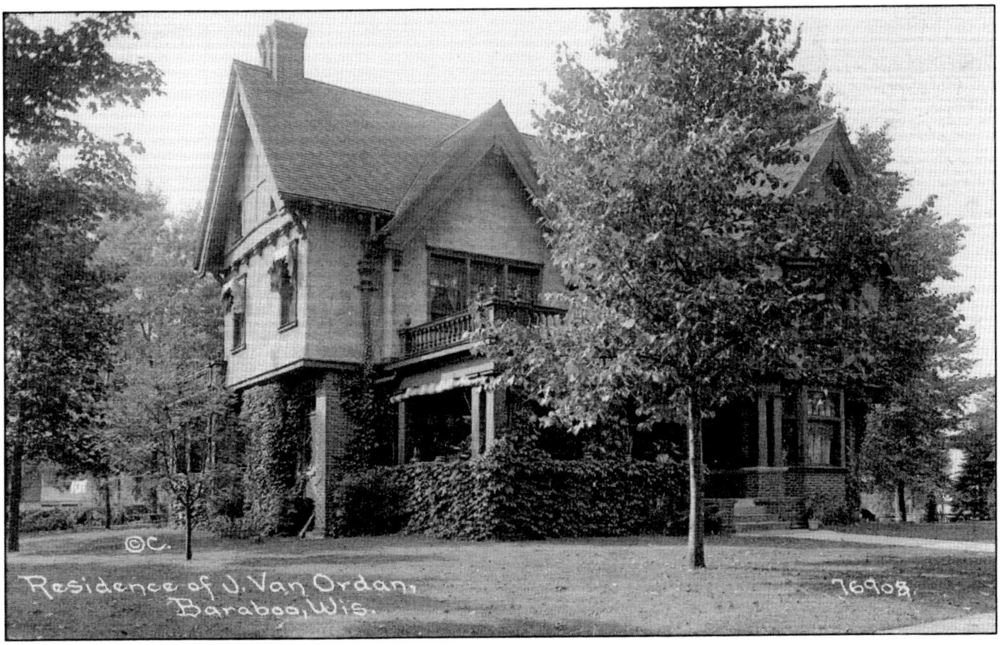

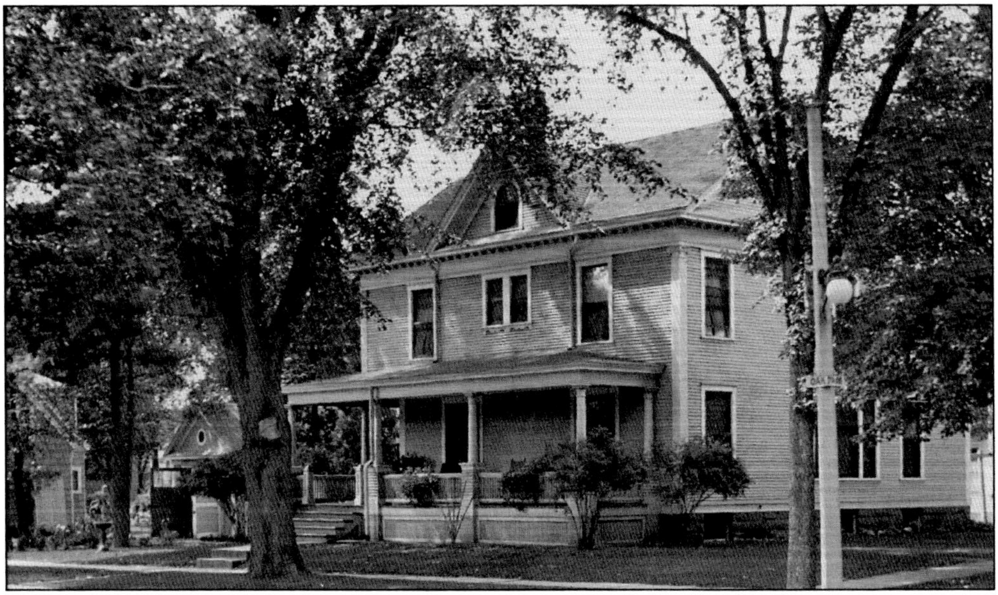

Salome Ringling, the mother of the famous Ringling brothers, probably never lived in a brand new home until she had one built in 1900 at the southwest corner of Seventh and Oak. The modest Queen Anne home was just big enough to have her large family home for Christmas. She died in the home in 1907 after a delayed Christmas get-together. The house was then lived in by Ida, her only daughter, and her family.

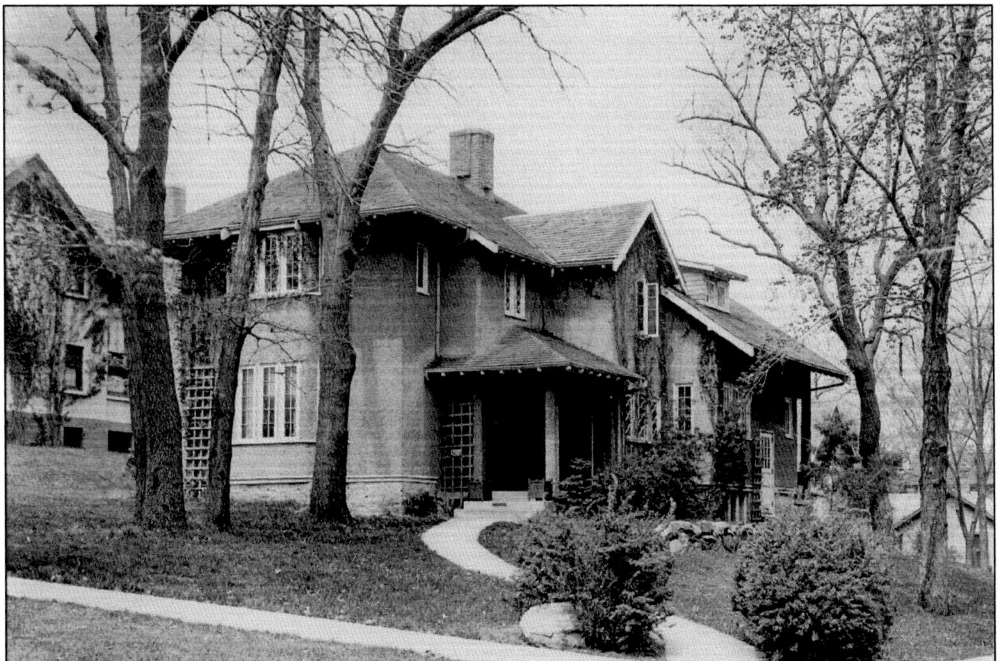

Something in the way of a modern house was built in 1910, at the northwest corner of Center and Fourth, for businessman William Schultz. The sum of about $4,000 purchased an English Arts and Crafts style home with maintenance free exterior stucco and quaint multi-paned windows.

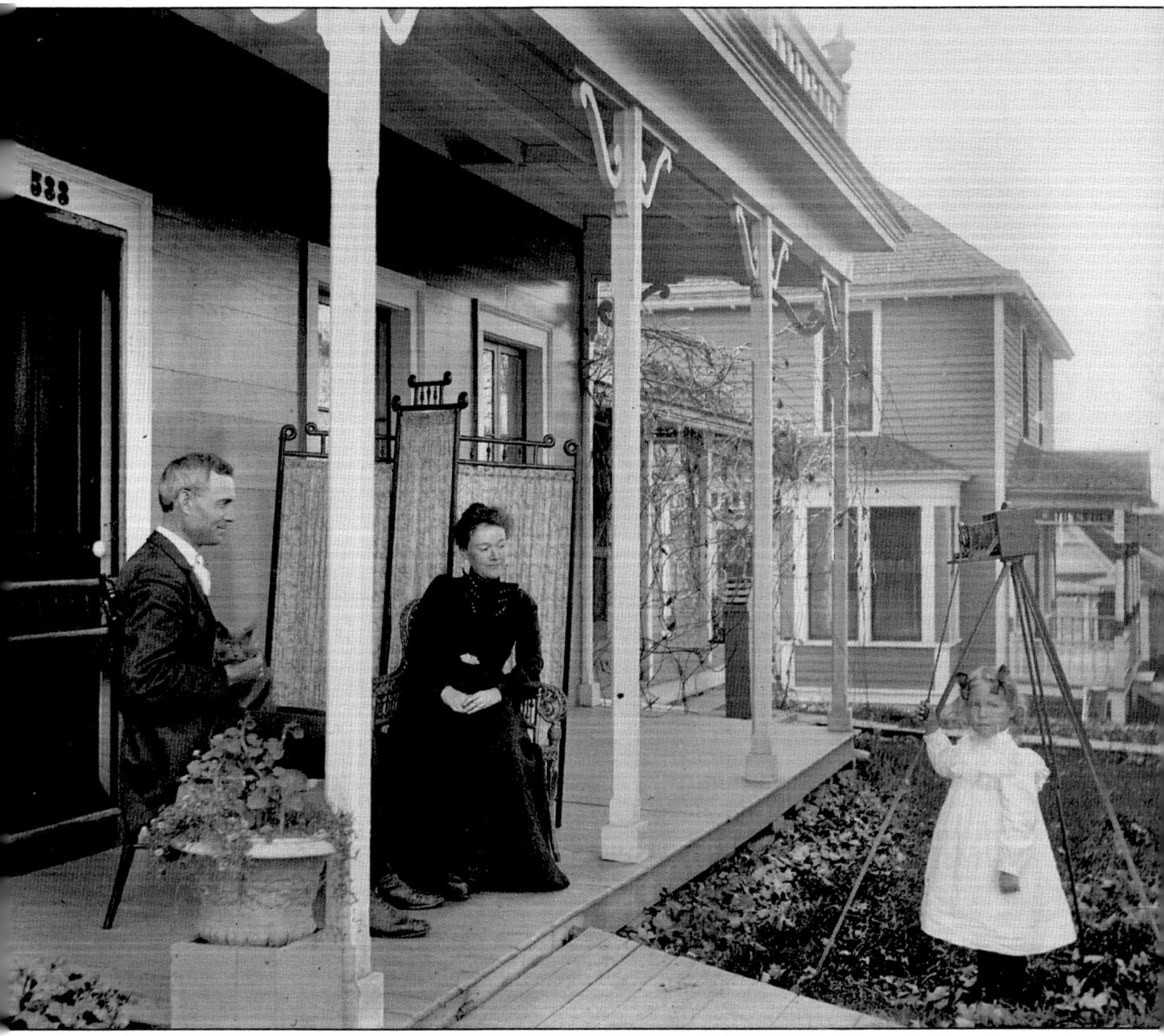

The camera of H.E. Cole captured his business partner, A.D. Dorsett; his wife Dorothy; and daughter, Addie, at their home at 533 Second Avenue about 1905. Cole, Dorsett, and J.F. Kartack were owners of the Baraboo News, a daily and weekly newspaper in Baraboo that later merged with the Baraboo Republic. The home, which was originally built in 1872, was extensively remodeled about 1917 with a new façade and a stucco exterior.

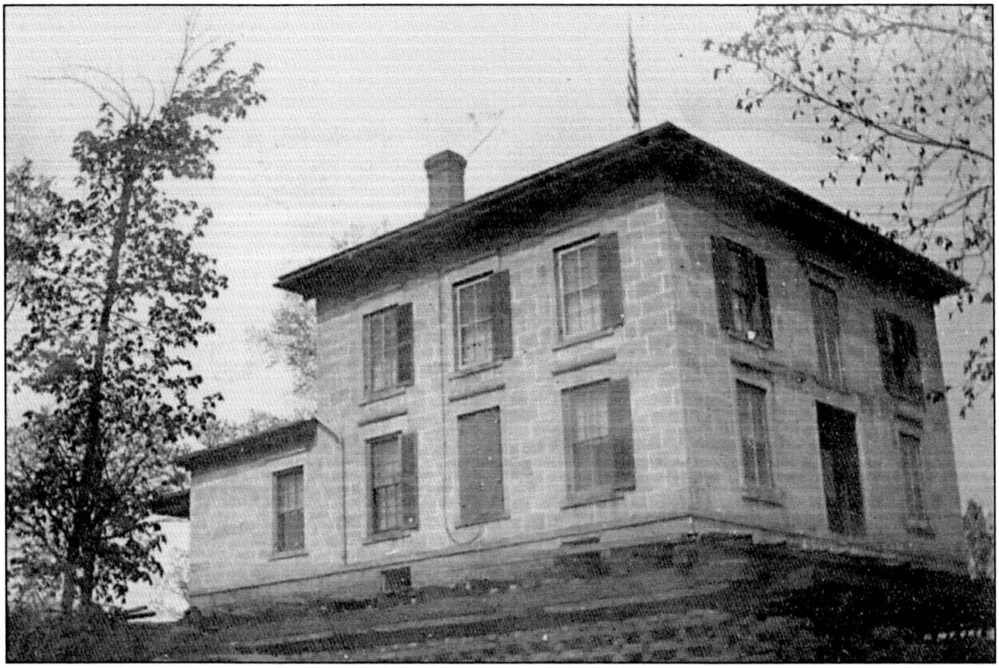

For many years, Ash Street did not extend north of Eighth Street, for at the head of the street was a large hill where, in the mid-1850s, a large stone villa was constructed for Nathaniel Powell. In 1898, five train-car loads of timber, jack screws, and rollers were brought to Baraboo to move and lower the 600 ton house, above, so that the hill could be removed and the lots sold. The first to buy one of the new lots was Charles Ringling, who had a palatial house built at the new northeast corner of Ash and Eighth. The photo below shows Ringling's new house with the stone villa in its new location to the right. In 1908, Charles Ringling purchased the stone villa and had it demolished for a bigger lawn.

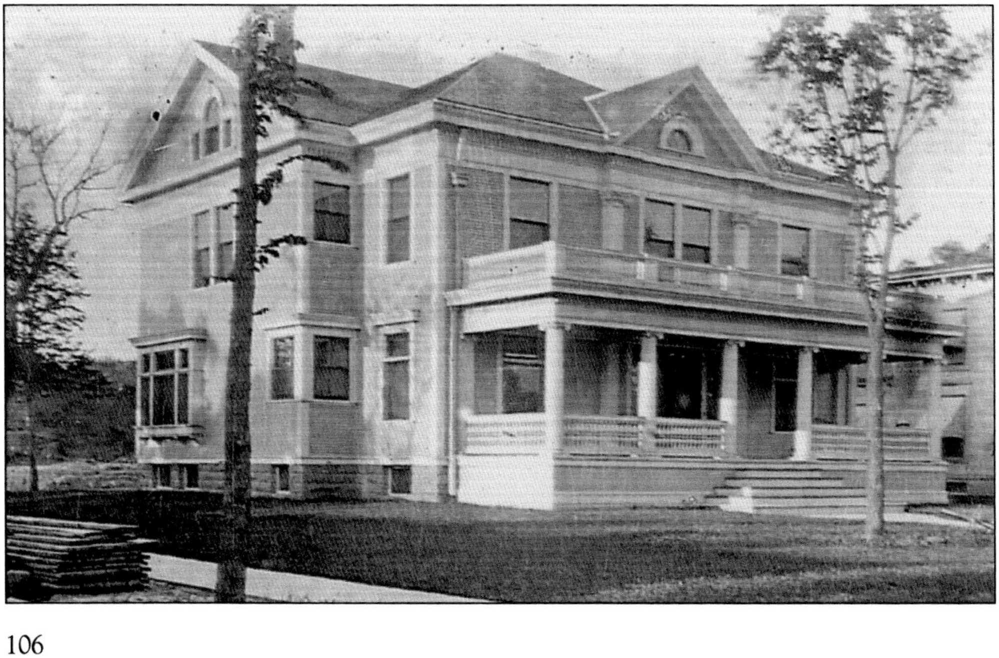

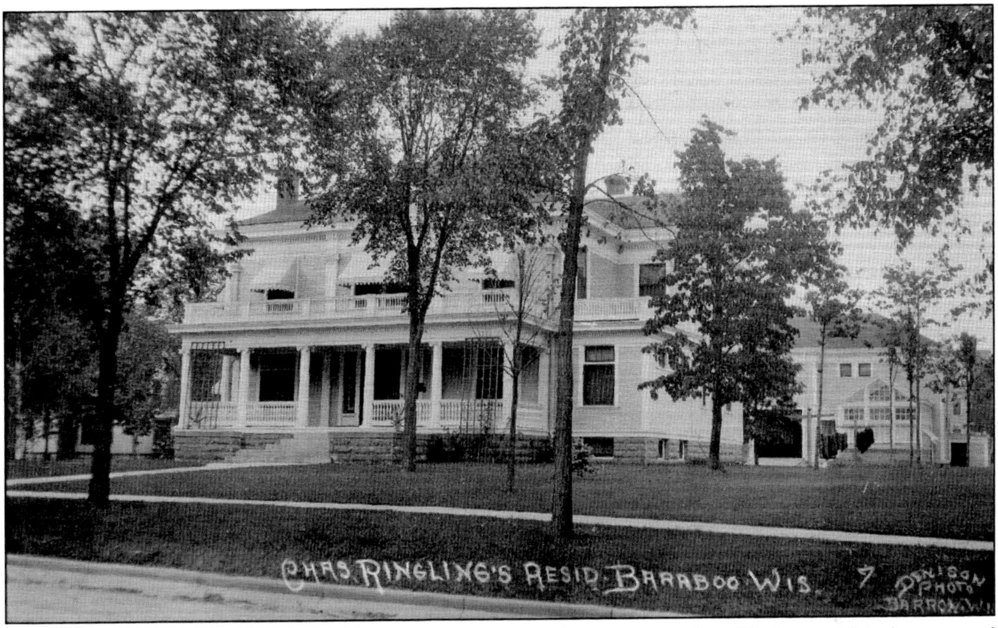

Charles Ringling's estate on Eighth Street continued to grow with additions to his house and new outbuildings, including a two-story carriage house with attached green house. A cottage for his mother-in-law was also built on the property. Ringling eventually left Baraboo but sold the home to his brother, Henry, whose family still owns the estate.

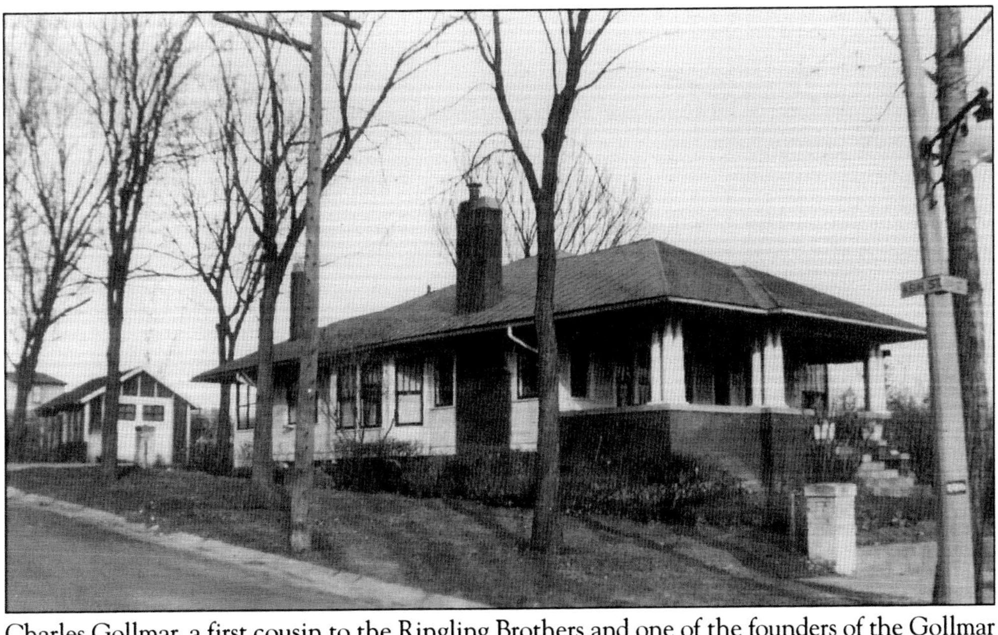

Charles Gollmar, a first cousin to the Ringling Brothers and one of the founders of the Gollmar Brothers Circus, had this residence built in 1915 at the northeast corner of Ash and Eleventh. It was mail ordered from Sears and Roebuck and delivered as a kit, including everything from the precut numbered lumber to the doorknobs.

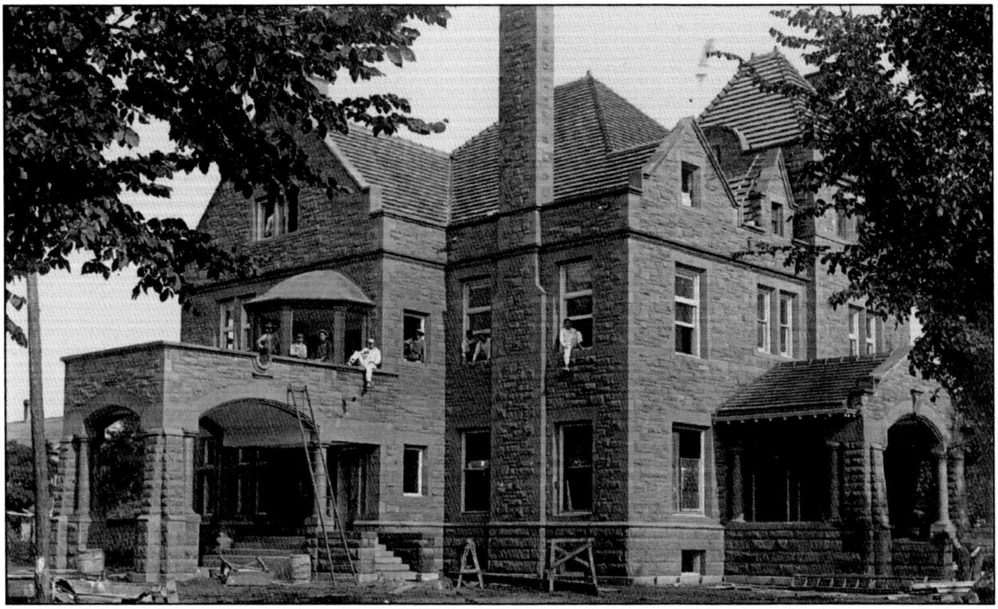

Baraboo's largest and grandest home was completed in 1906 for Al. and Lou Ringling at the southwest corner of Broadway and Fifth. The house was built on the site of the Ringling's former house, which was built in 1899 and moved around the corner. The new brown sandstone mansion was designed by Kees and Colburn of Minneapolis and was built by Baraboo's Isenberg Brothers, who labored for a year and a half on the building. The exterior was a mixture of English, French, and Gothic themes and included a porte cochere, or carriage porch, on the south side. The residence contained lavishly decorated rooms for entertaining, including a first-floor billiards room and a ballroom in the basement. Al. Ringling died here January 1, 1916, but not before he watched the construction of his new theatre from his bedroom windows. The house became the home of the Elks Club in 1936.

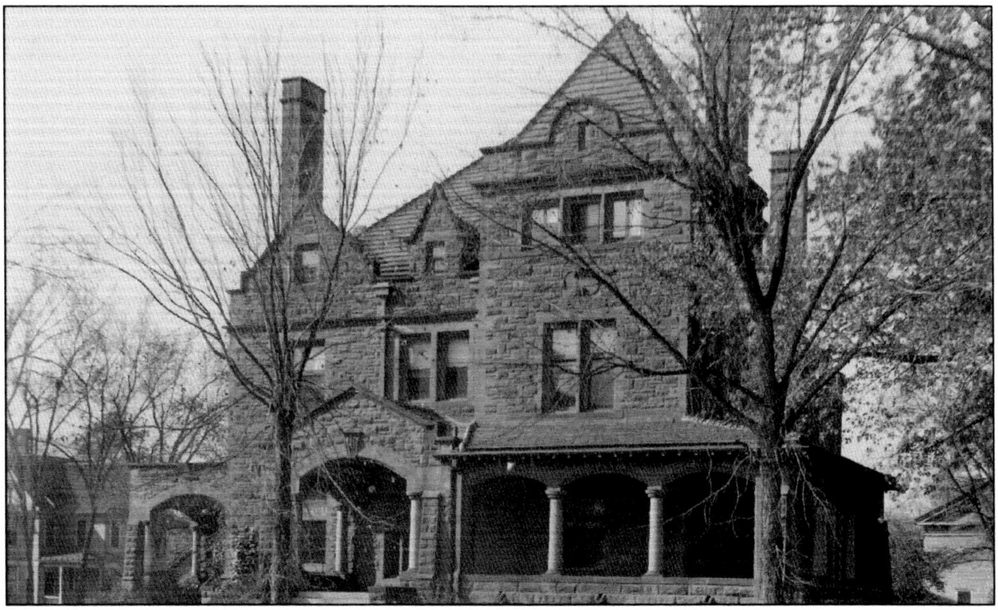

Nine

Churches and Schools

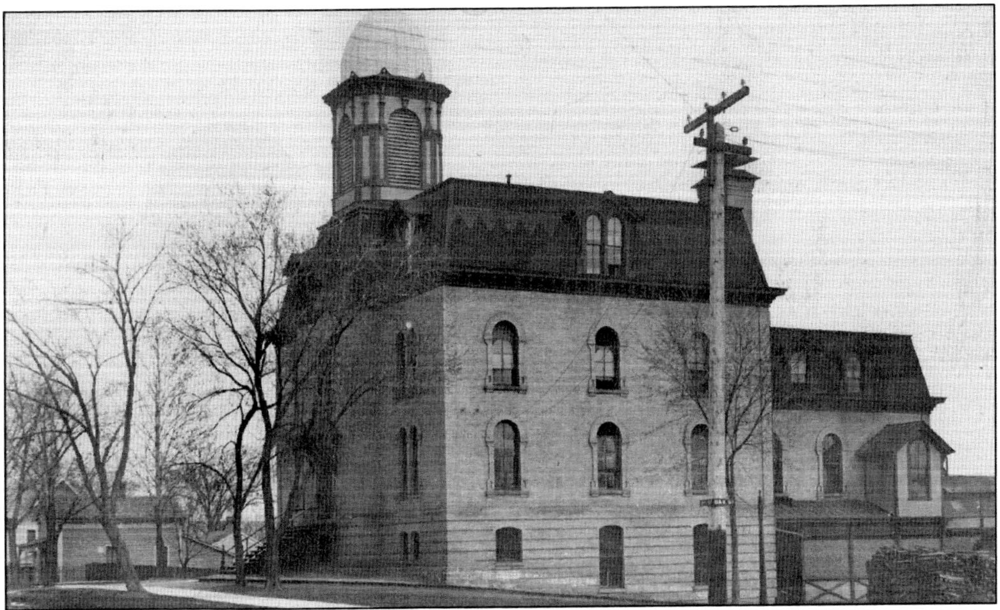

Schoolhouses and houses of worship were among some of the priorities of early settlers in the Baraboo valley, after their own shelters were secured. Only five years after the first permanent dwelling was erected in Baraboo the community put up its first log schoolhouse on Seventh Avenue, between Birch and West Streets. While it was only about 12 x 14 ft., it nonetheless served as a beginning to public education in the valley. By 1850, a new two-story building was built much closer to the square on Second Street between Oak and Ash Streets. Schools would continue to be built on this block for the next 77 years. When the village was eventually chartered in 1866, it was divided into three wards. Eventually, each of these wards would have a separate school building, while the upper grades would convene at a new schoolhouse completed on Second Street in 1870. When this building was consumed by fire in 1906, the city would again rise to the occasion with a bigger and better building. Churches were also some of the first buildings erected, although initially congregations met in houses or at the new courthouse, erected in 1848. In January 1850, the Methodists became the first to erect a chapel on the southeast corner of Broadway and Fifth. In the coming decades, other denominations would construct their own places of worship, many located around the square.

Finished in October 1870, the new Union School in Baraboo on Second Street, above, was the pride and joy of the city. The building cost $33,000 and was immediately filled with 600 pupils when it opened. It could hold an additional 270. By the turn of the century, it was deemed unsafe and old fashioned. Peoples' fears were realized when the building caught fire during a school day and was gutted.

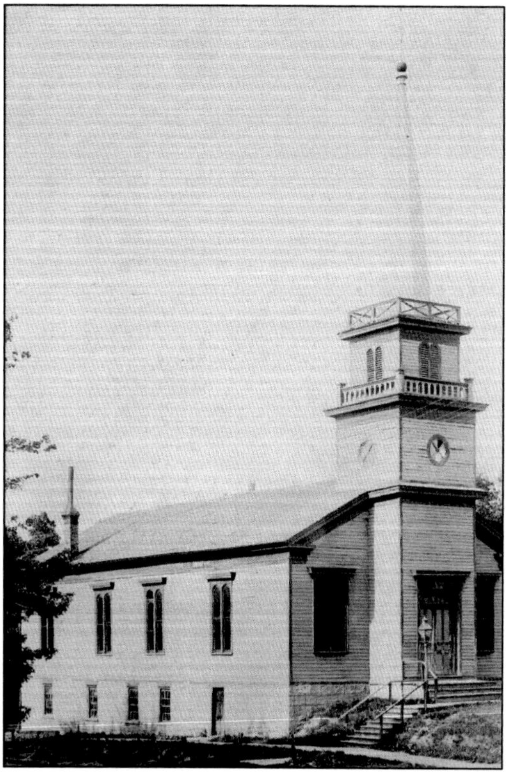

The Methodists were the first to build a church building in Baraboo in 1850. A chapel on the southeast corner of Broadway and Fifth was replaced with a church building finished in 1853. This was later enlarged and a tower added in 1866. The church was sold in 1898 after new quarters were built a block away. The building was ruined by fire on January 6, 1899.

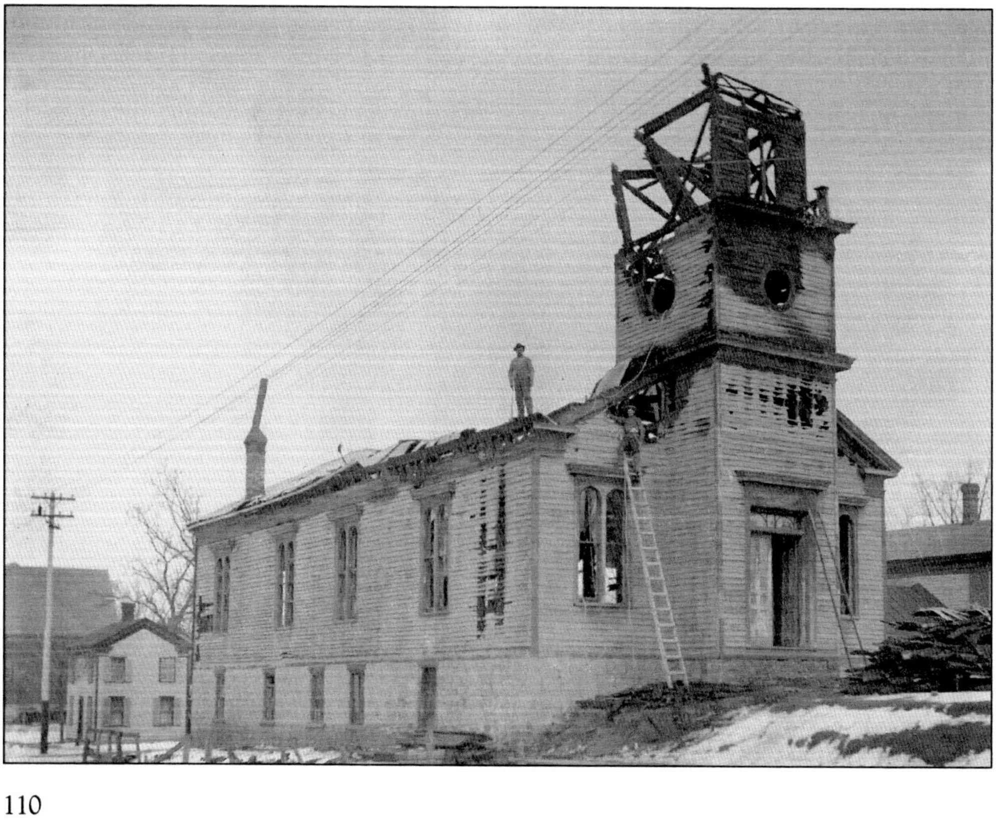

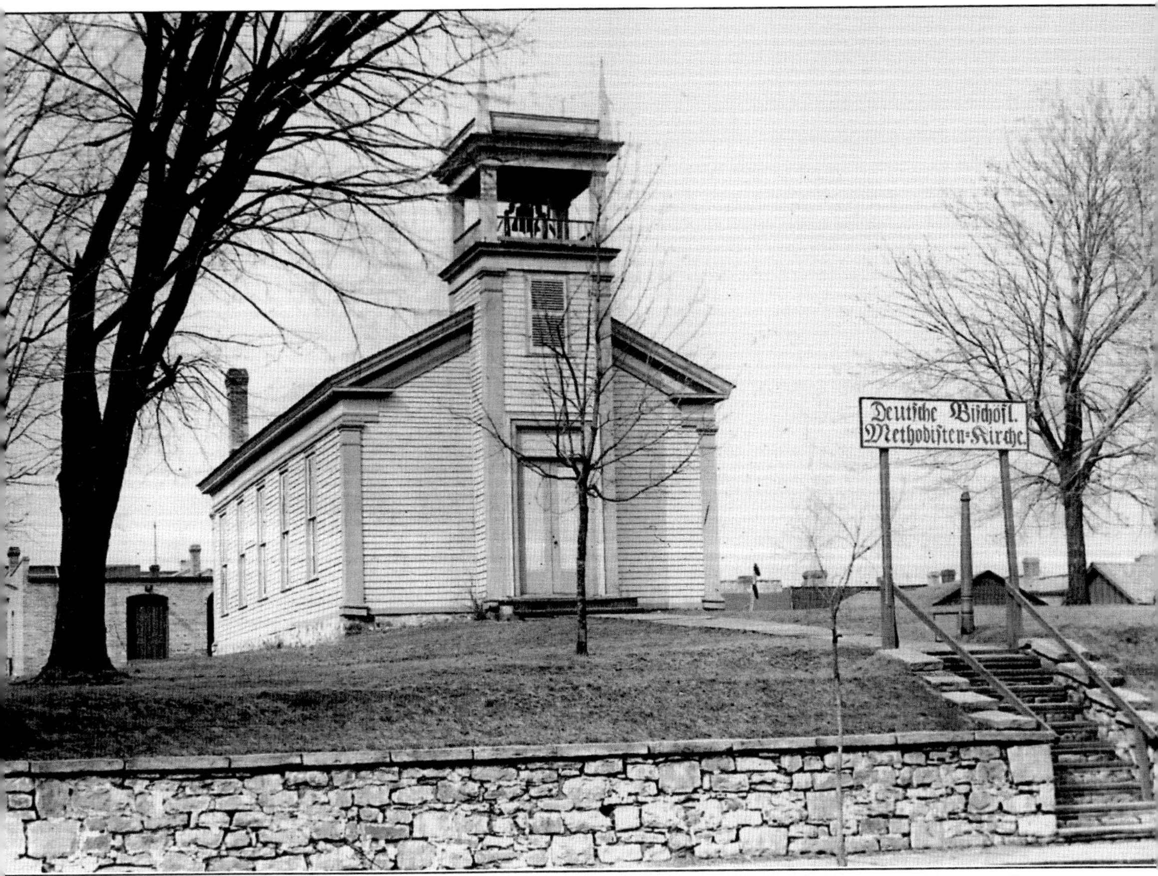

In 1851, a group of citizens met to form a Presbyterian Church and the same year work was started on a church building, which was finished in February 1852. The building stood on the north side of Second Street between Oak and Ash and was later enlarged in 1858. The congregation was the first in the valley to buy a bell, which was procured in time for the 1852 Fourth of July celebration where the bell was first rung. There was no belfry yet, so a framework was made to house the bell. The building was sold to the German Methodist congregation in 1873 after a new Presbyterian church was erected on Ash Street.

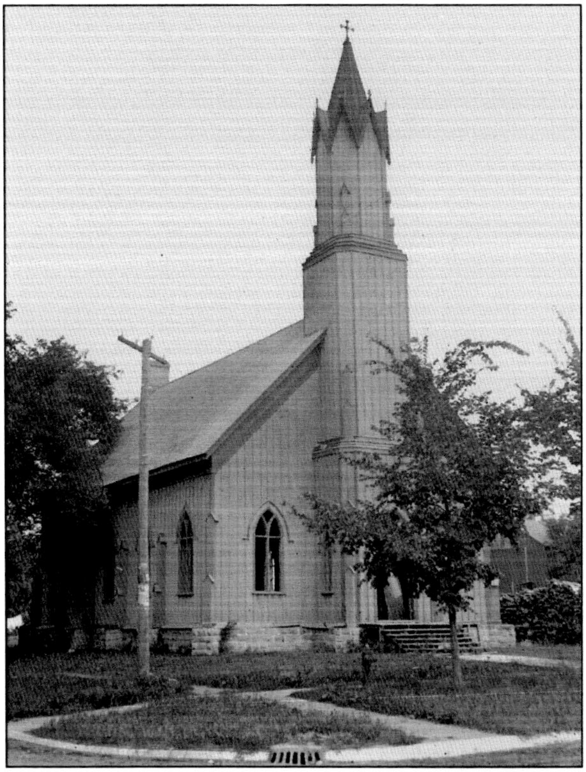

The Free Congregational Society was formed in February 1860 under the leadership of Rev. Ichabod Codding. In 1867, the congregation constructed a church building at the northeast corner of Birch and Fourth. The building was also used in later years for theatrical performances. The building was demolished in 1902 to make way for the new public library.

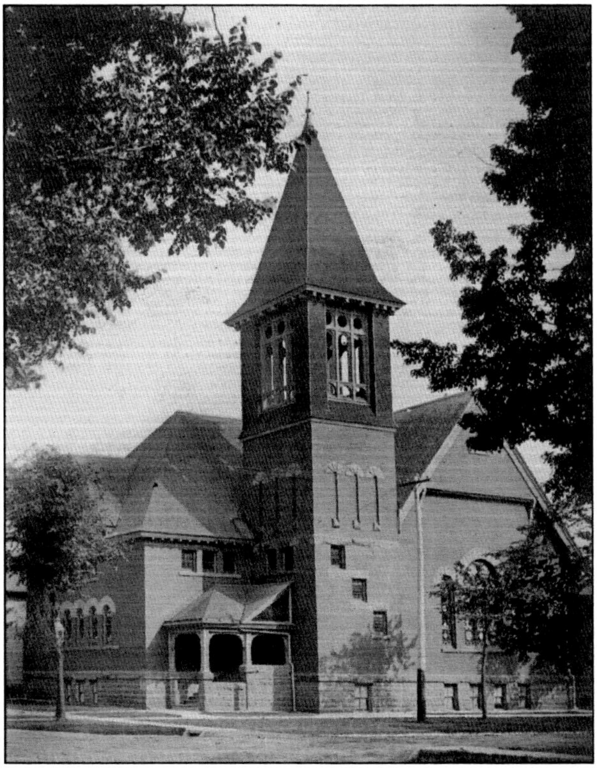

A new building for the First Congregational Church was dedicated in January 1895 at the southeast corner of Broadway and Sixth. The group had formed in the first log schoolhouse in Baraboo in 1847. The new brick church was the third building built by the group and was designed by Henry F. Starbuck of Milwaukee.

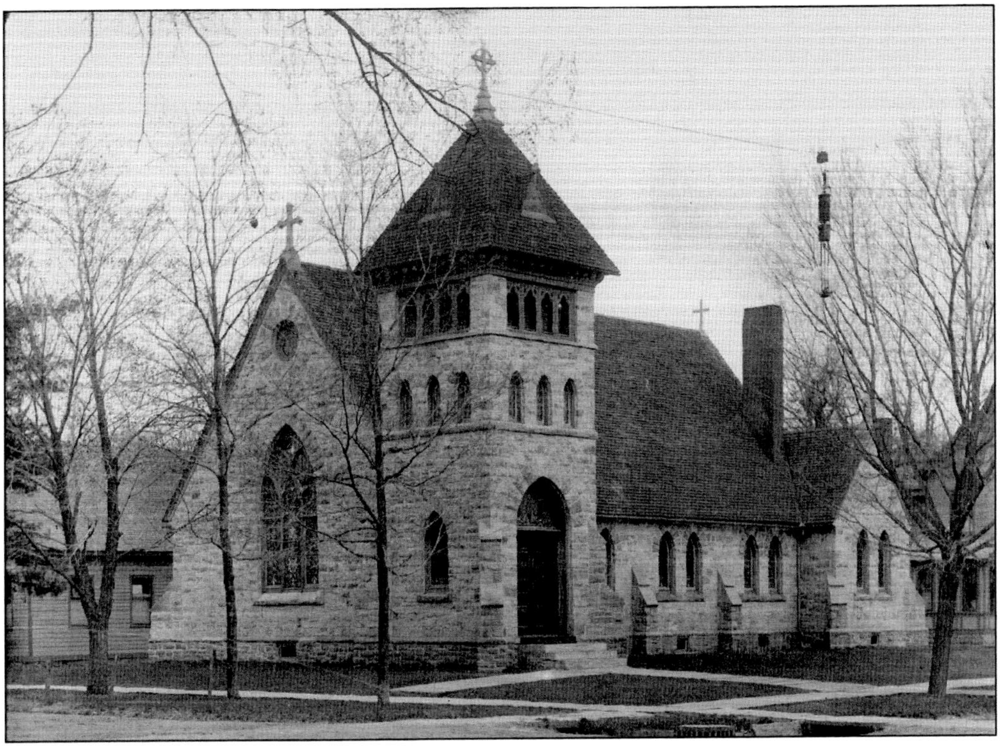

In 1891, a new stone church for the Trinity Episcopal congregation was constructed at the northeast corner of Oak and Sixth. The building was designed by C.R. Adams of Chicago and was enlarged at the east end in 1913. The congregation was formed in 1867 and purchased this corner in 1868. The interior was originally lit with beautiful gas chandeliers. Garlands of greens decorated the church for an Ephiphany Sunday service when this photo was taken.

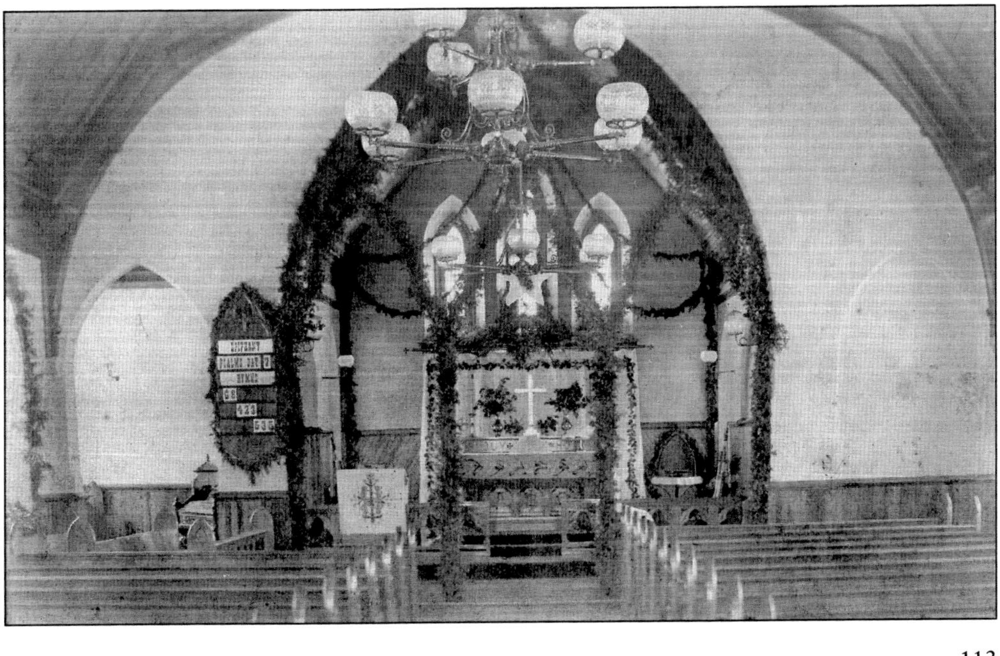

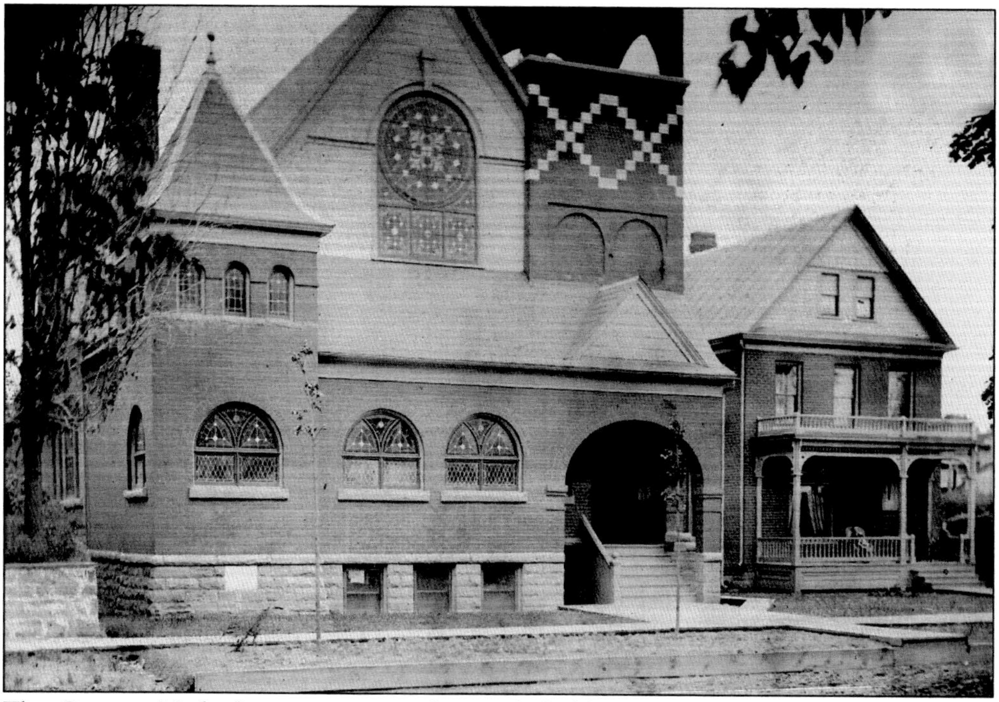

The German Methodist congregation first took hold in Baraboo in 1872, though other congregations existed in the townships of Freedom and Westfield. The group purchased the old Presbyterian church on Second Street in 1873 and later replaced it with a brick structure in 1896. The building still stands today and is used by the American Legion.

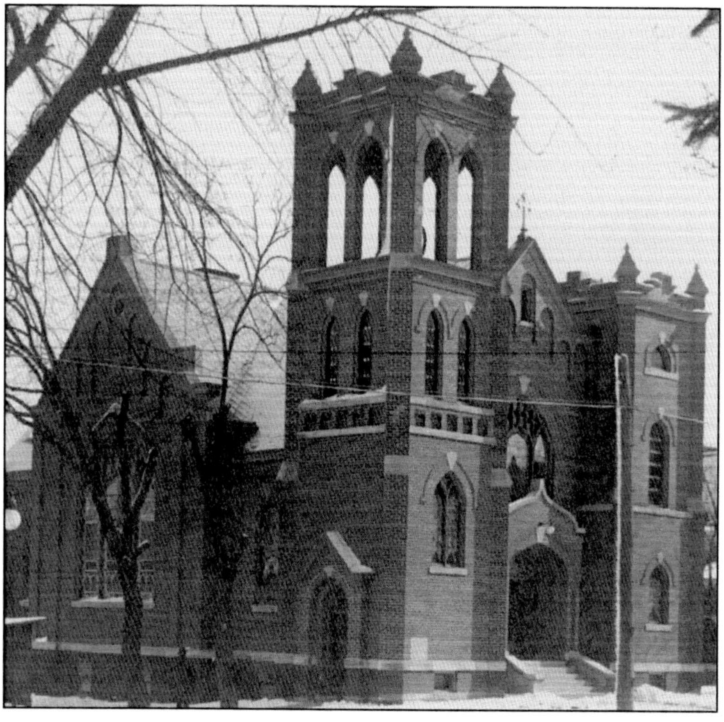

In 1914, a new red brick church building for the congregation of St. John's Lutheran Church was finished at the southeast corner of East and Fifth. It was designed by La Crosse architect Andrew Roth. The congregation was formed in 1873 and one of its founding members was August Ringling, father of the Ringling brothers. It was demolished in the early 1970s to make way for a more modern church building.

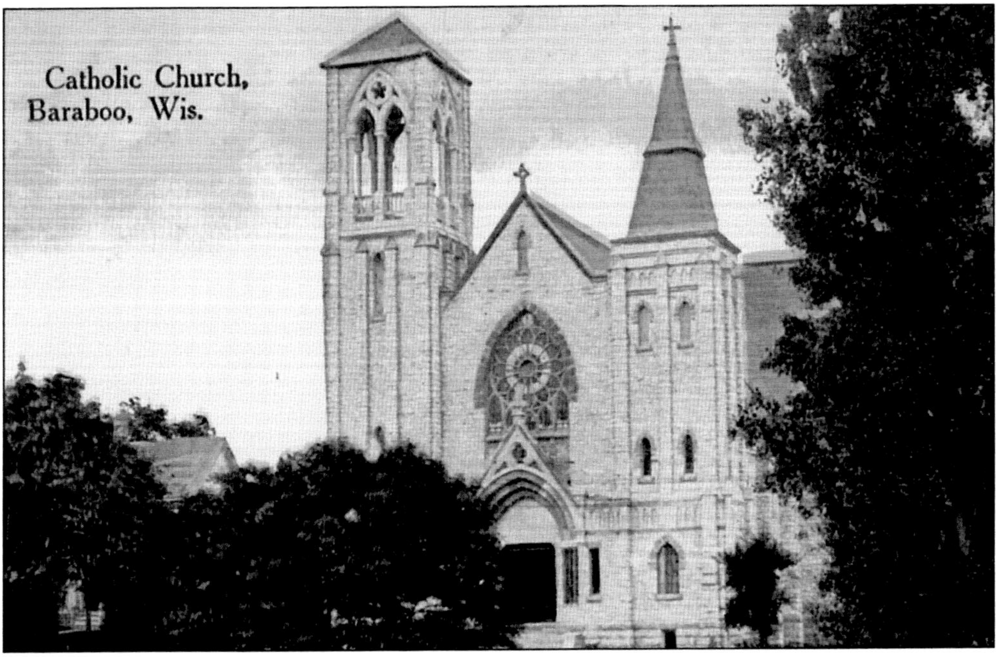

St. Joseph's Catholic Church built a grand new stone edifice on their site on East Street in 1904. The building was faced with native stone from Baraboo quarries and trimmed with red stone from Ableman. The project was brought about by the leadership of Father John T. Durward who also gave much direction for the plan of the building. The parish began in 1858 and first met in the Wisconsin House on the square.

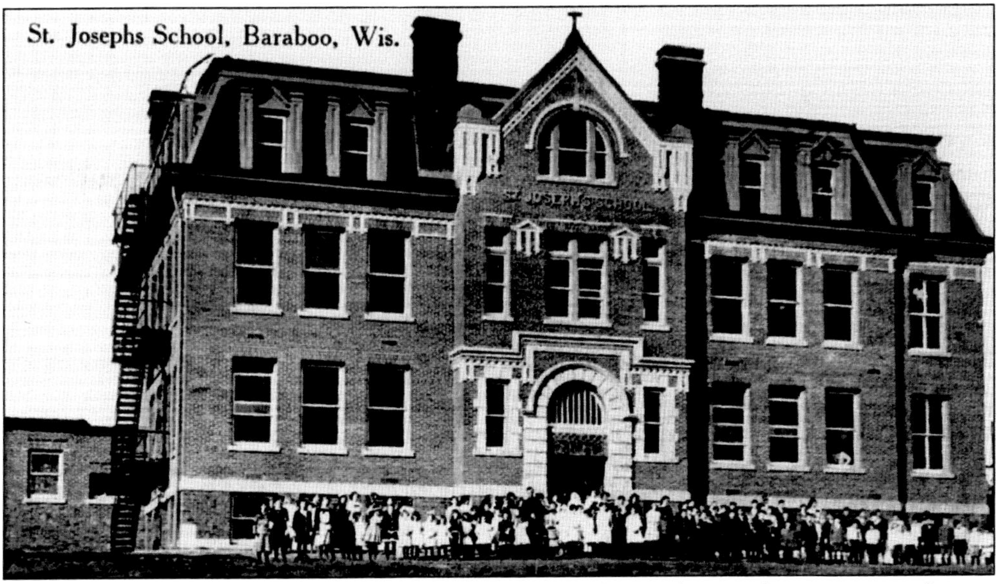

Seven years after the new Catholic church was finished, the parish started construction of a new parochial school building. The building site was just northeast of the church on a large ravine, which required 8,000 loads of dirt to fill, as well as the removal of tons of debris that people had thrown into it. The building was designed by Andrew Roth of La Crosse and contained a kitchen, hall, gymnasium, six class rooms, winter chapel, and auditorium. (Holt Collection.)

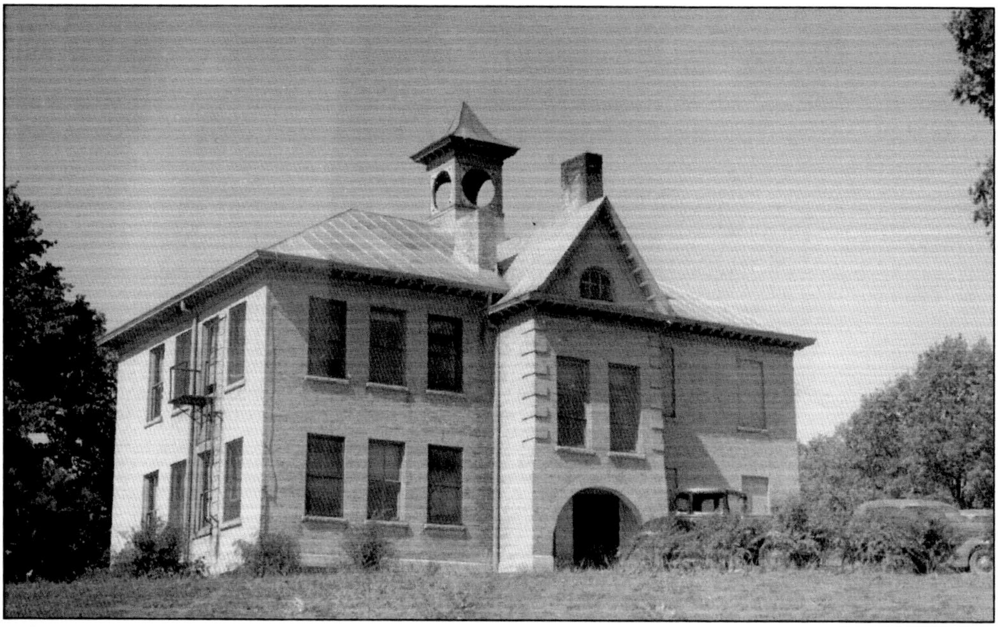

Schools were important in every community. In 1901, this large two-story brick schoolhouse was built in nearby Lyons (today West Baraboo). The old frame school was moved to Baraboo and eventually became part of Ochsner Park, where it still stands today as a storage building. The brick schoolhouse was demolished in 1981.

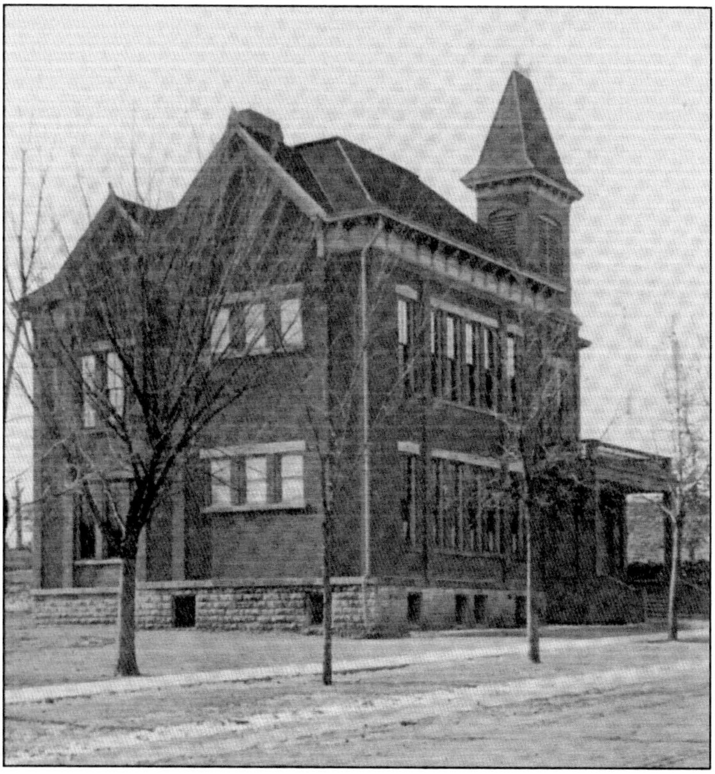

In 1882, Baraboo was incorporated as a city and divided into three wards. Each was to have a schoolhouse. The First Ward schoolhouse was built in 1885 at the southwest corner of Sixth and Summit at a cost of $8,000. It served until about 1950, when it was destroyed by a fire. It was replaced by the new West School. (Holt Collection.)

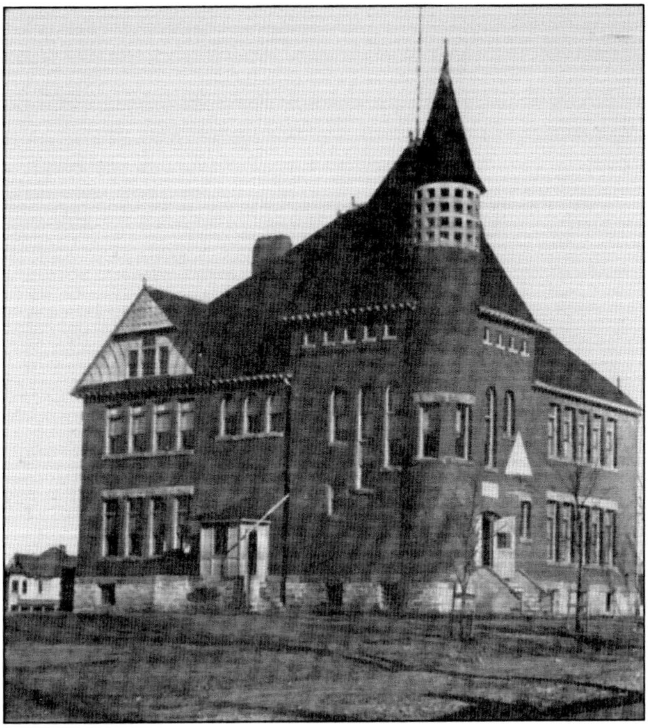

The Second Ward schoolhouse was built in 1889 and was designed by Conover and Porter of Madison. It was hailed as "one of the most perfect public school buildings in the state." It stood at the northeast corner of Fifth and Barker. The interior, below, was conveniently arranged and contained all of the necessary equipment for teaching. (Holt Collection.)

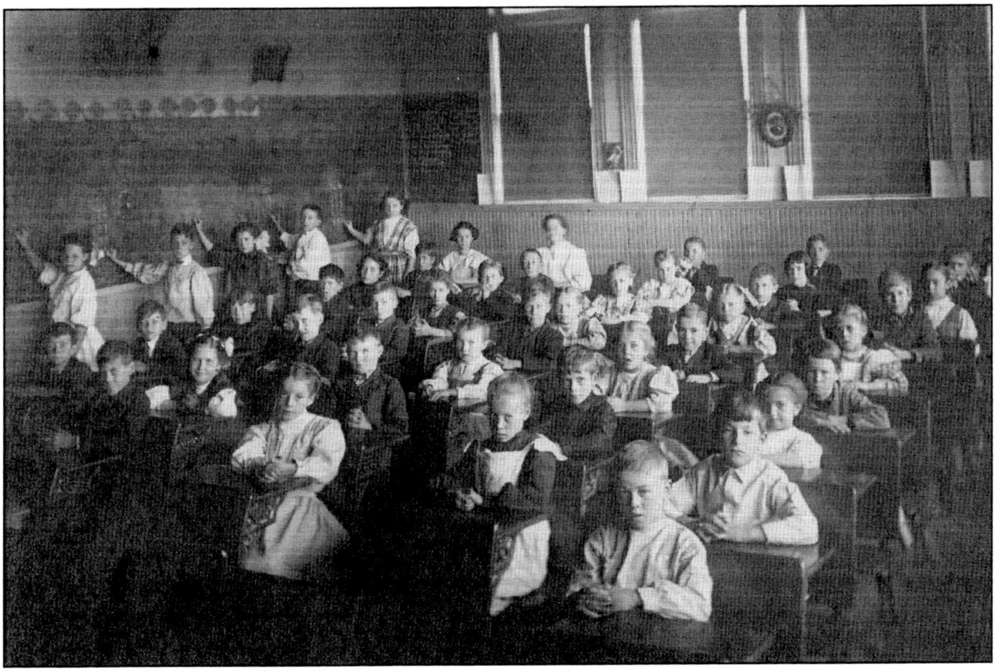

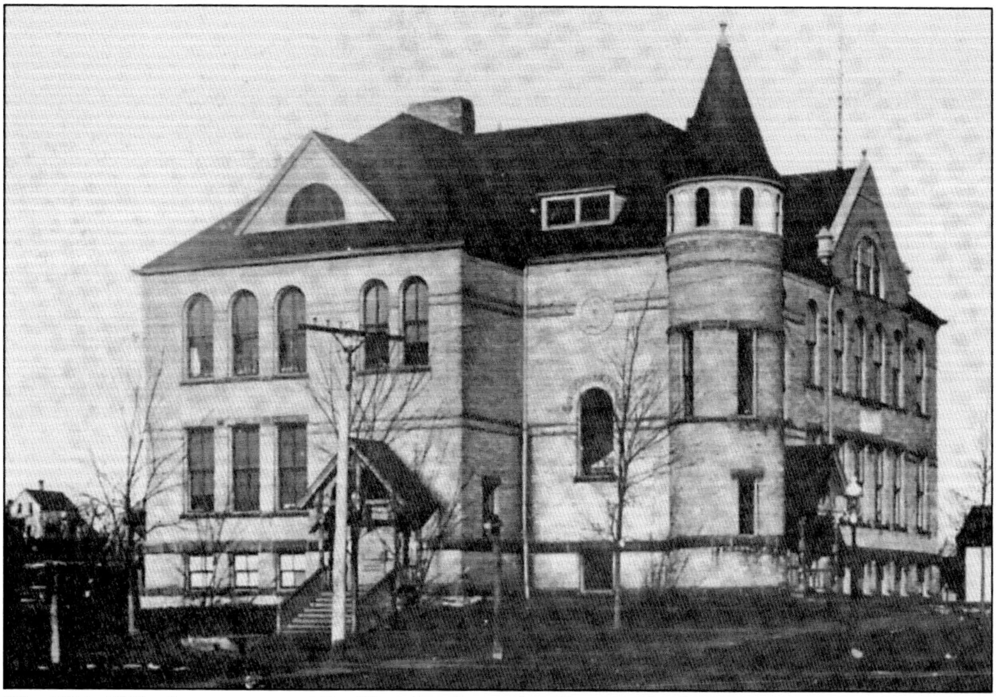

The Third Ward, comprising all of Baraboo's south side, was the last to receive a modern brick school building. Built in 1892, the building cost $12,000 and was located at Elm and Grove. (Holt Collection.)

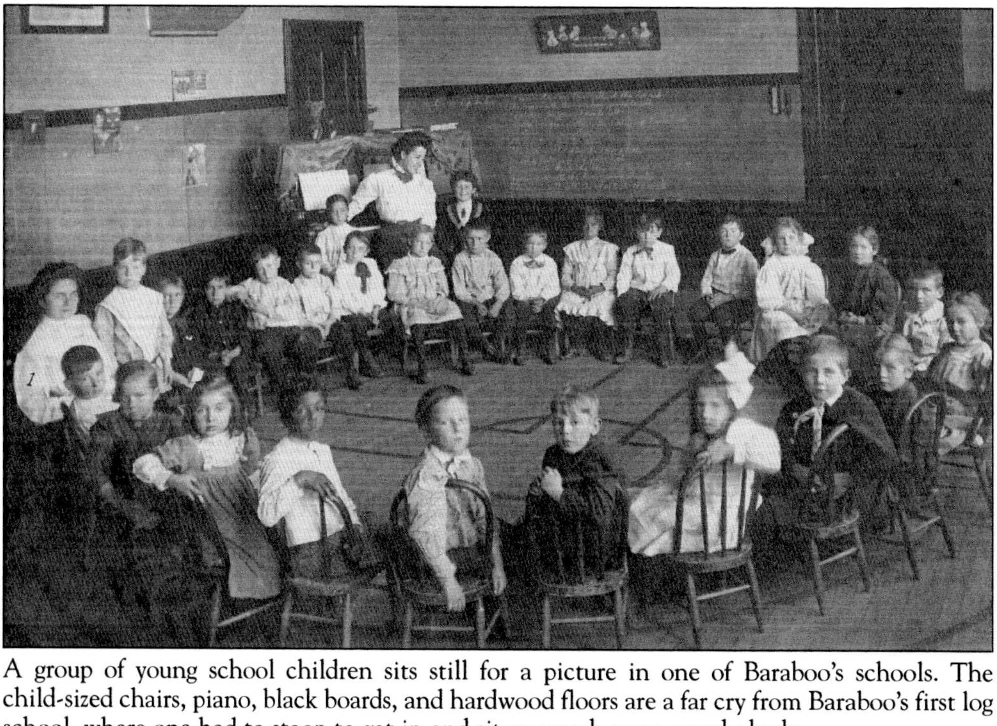

A group of young school children sits still for a picture in one of Baraboo's schools. The child-sized chairs, piano, black boards, and hardwood floors are a far cry from Baraboo's first log school, where one had to stoop to get in and sit on rough-sawn wood planks.

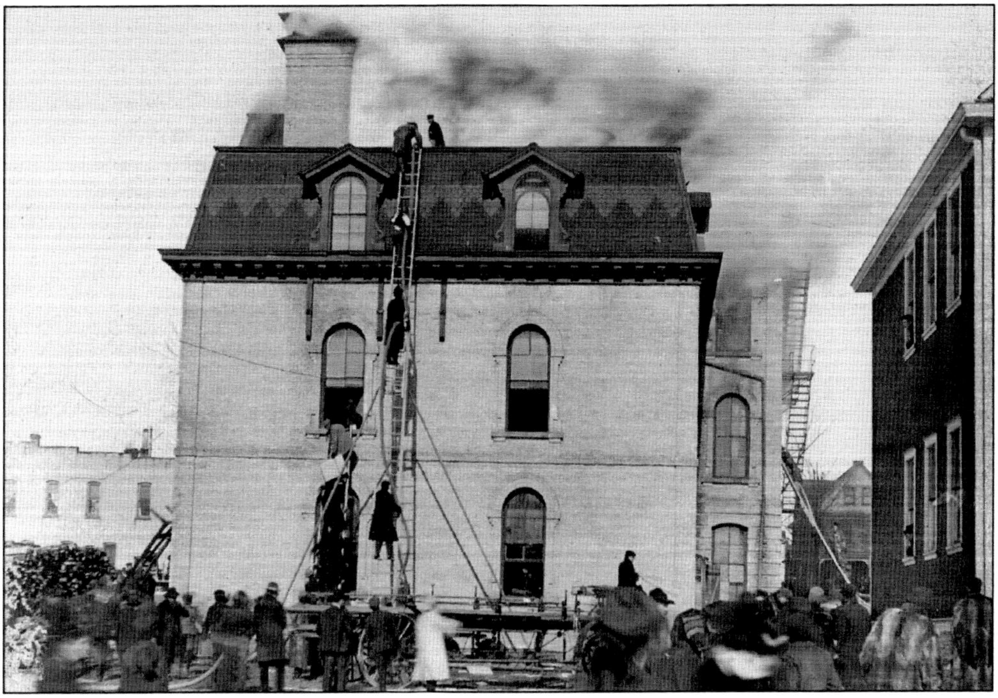

Shortly after 11 a.m. on the morning of February 9, 1906, it was discovered that the high school building was on fire. Students were safely evacuated as smoke started to pour into the classrooms from the registers. The fire spread quickly and firemen were forced to save nearby structures and let the school burn. Students and onlookers managed to get many of the records and books out of the building. By afternoon the building was a complete ruin. Any hopes of salvaging the building were further dashed when the west wall collapsed from wind. The building was completed in 1870 and had served for many years. Many were glad to see it go with hopes for a new school building.

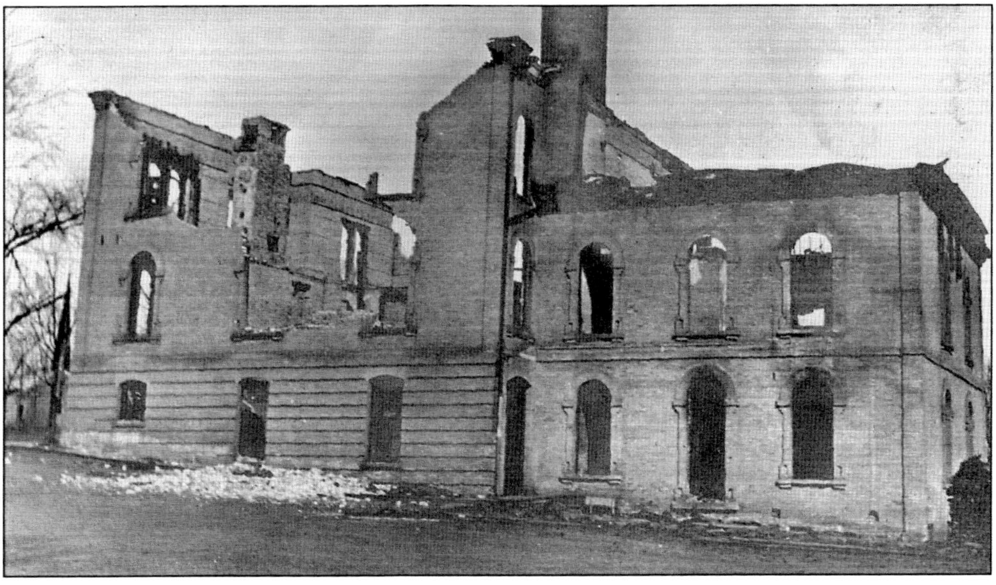

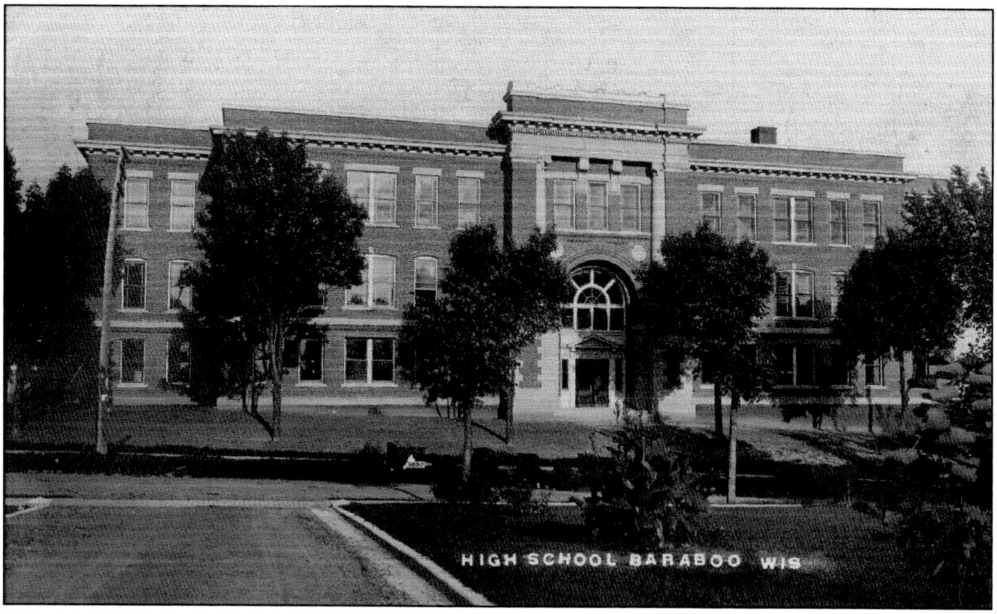

In 1906, work was begun on a new high school to replace the one that burned down. The new three-story red brick building was finished in time for the fall term of 1907. But new was not always better than the old. Three weeks after opening, the building was closed when new plaster ceilings began to fall, threatening the staff and students. The building was closed for several weeks as new plaster was put in. The building was eventually fixed and served the community until 1977, when it was razed.

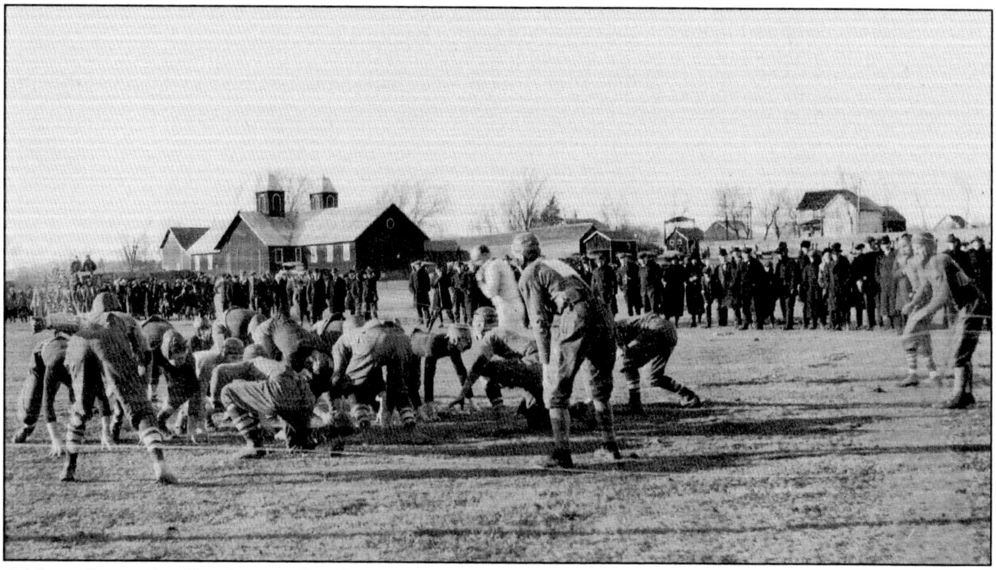

Although early Baraboo schools concentrated only on academics, by the 20th century extra-curricular activities like football became popular. In 1919, Baraboo's arch rival, Reedsburg, came to play a game at the Sauk County Fairgrounds, as captured on this postcard. The rivalry can be traced all the way back to the Saw Log War in 1851, when the upstream citizens of Reedsburg refused to let any more logs pass over their dam to go to Baraboo. A matter resolved by a U.S. marshal, who ordered the logs to be released.

Ten

DEVIL'S LAKE

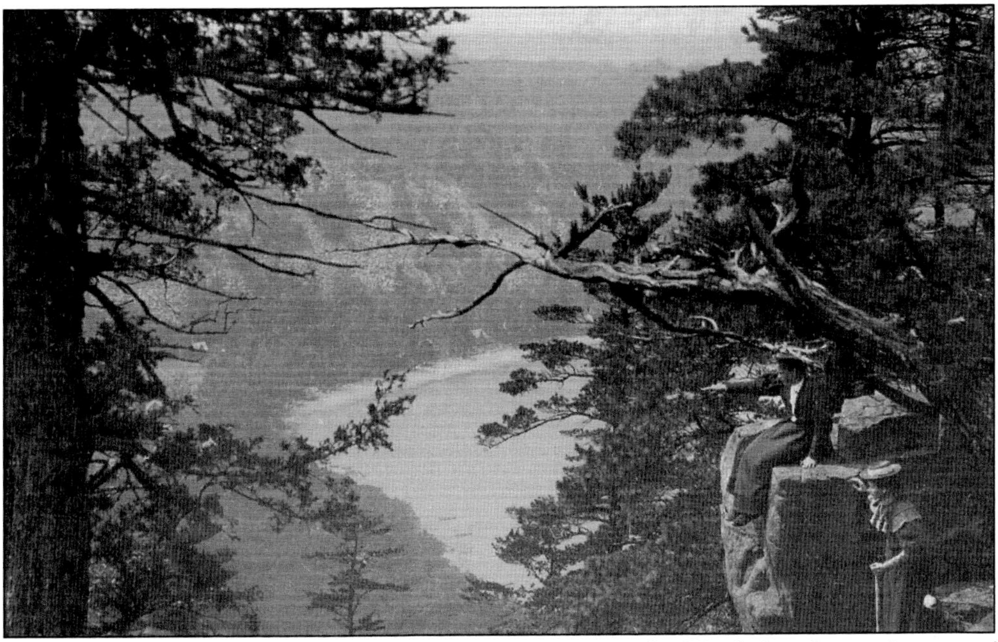

Devil's Lake is the crown jewel of the Baraboo area topography. Nestled in the south range of the bluffs and lying only three miles south of Baraboo, the lake captured the imagination of all who came across it. The Native Americans and the mound-building cultures before them held it as a sacred place, a lake where spirits live. This notion was somewhat crudely translated into the name that is still used today. The lake, with towering bluffs on three sides, some reaching 500 feet, was almost immediately seen as a natural wonder and a place that would bring visitors to the area. Even before the railroad connected Baraboo with the outside world, a hotel was being constructed on the north shore. It was followed by two more on the south shore, along with numerous cottages. The railroad era increased the exposure of Devil's Lake greatly, especially since the railroad line was put right through the gap in the bluffs where the lake lay. Unknowing passengers found themselves traveling right at water's edge with towering cliffs of quartzite on one side and a 360-acre lake on the other. By the turn of the 20th century, a movement had begun to preserve the lake and surroundings, and reverse the effects of private ownership, including quarrying operations. In 1911, the state legislature set aside Devil's Lake as the state's second park. Hotels and cottages were eventually bought out, removed, and replaced with public park structures.

Two Victorian era ladies have ascended the east bluff in full-length dresses, above, to enjoy the panoramic view of the south shore. Near the shore below them, the Kirkland and Lakeview Hotels provide accommodations for those choosing to take an extended stay at the lake.

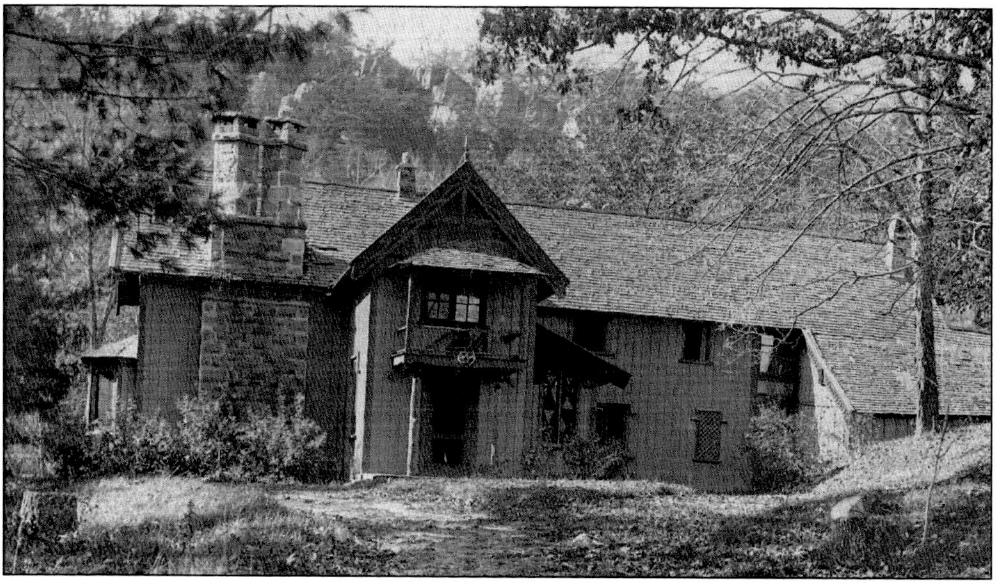

Louis J. Claude, an English immigrant, designed and built a spectacular house on the north shore of Devil's Lake for his wife and two children, Louis W. and Louise, in the 1850s. The house was designed in a mix of Tudor revival and English cottage style and was even more dramatic on the inside, below, where hand-carved fireplaces, faux-grained walls, and exotic furnishings inspired the imagination. The son, Louis W. Claude, went on to become an architect in Madison, joining forces with Edward Starck. The firm of Claude and Starck were regionally famous for their small-town library designs, of which they designed over 40. Baraboo's public library was their first such commission in 1903.

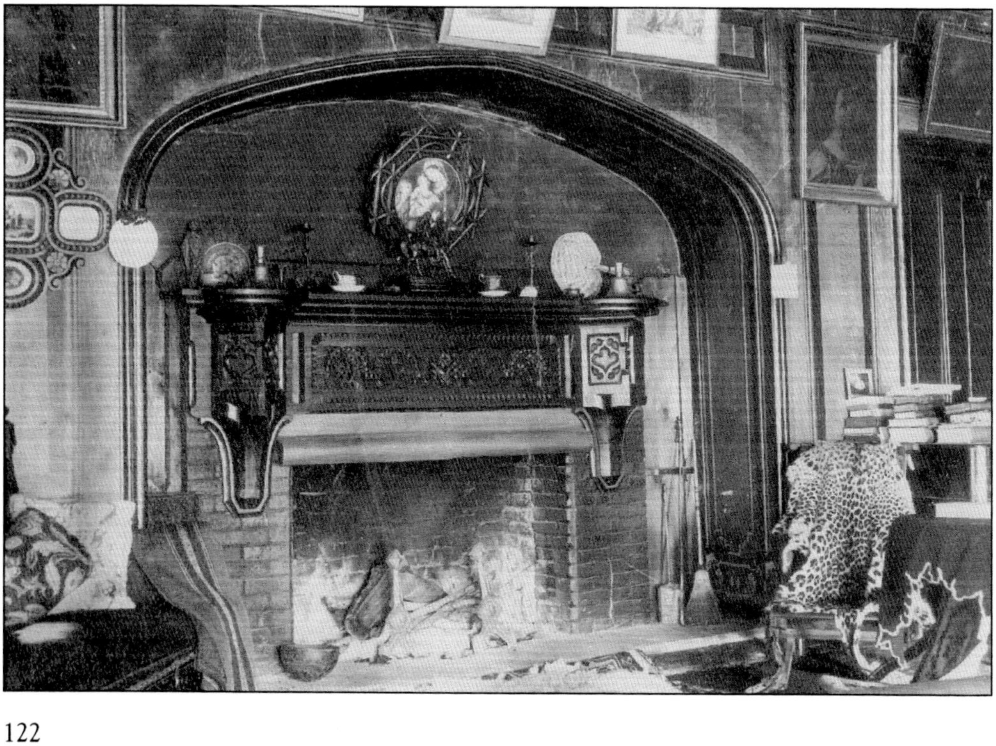

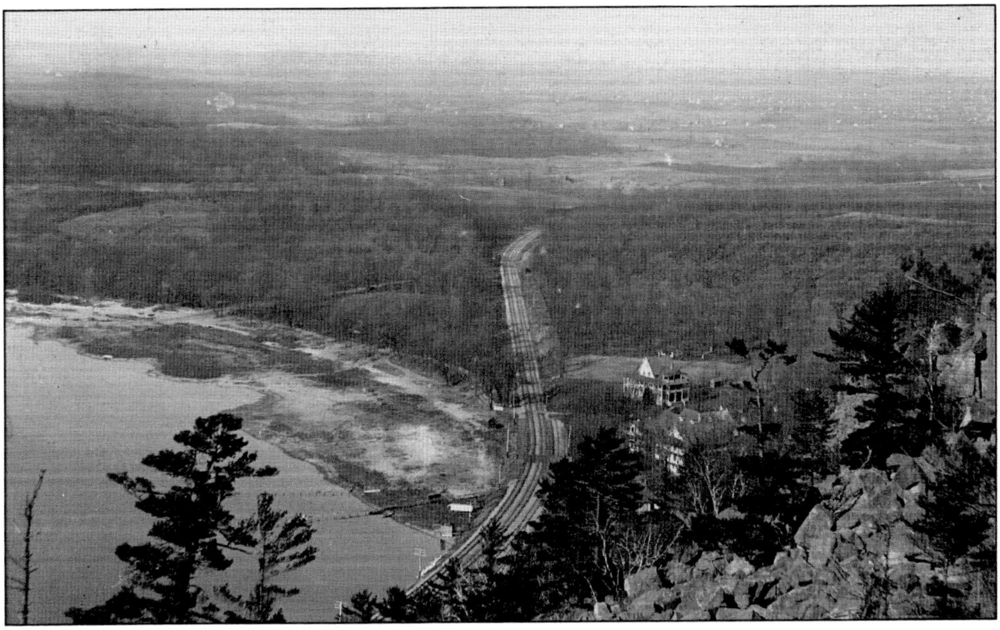

The resort era began at Devil's Lake in 1866 with the opening of the Minniwaukan House, a three-story hotel situated on the north shore at the base of the east bluff, above. Six years later, the railroad was laid through the gap at Devil's Lake and virtually at the doorstep of the hotel, which was greatly enlarged in 1872 and renamed the Cliff House. The plans were drawn by lake shore neighbor, Louis J. Claude, who designed the Swiss chalet style hotel, below, with three-story porches adorned with gingerbread. The Cliff House was very popular and in 1884 another building called "the Annex" was built to add guests, although it was not attached directly to the main hotel. By 1904, however, due to various reasons the Cliff House was not meeting expenses and was closed. It was demolished a few years later.

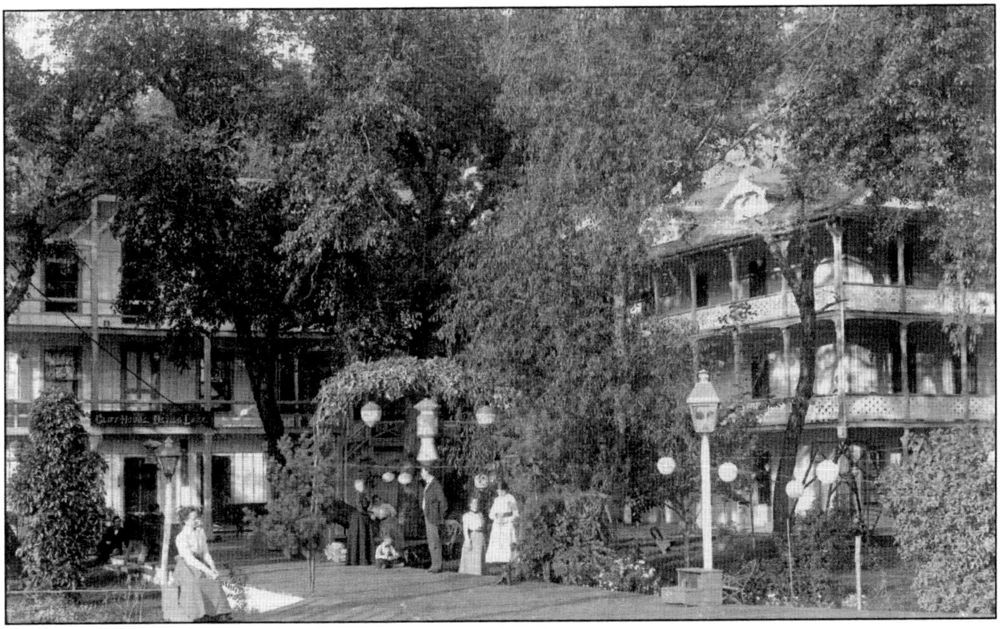

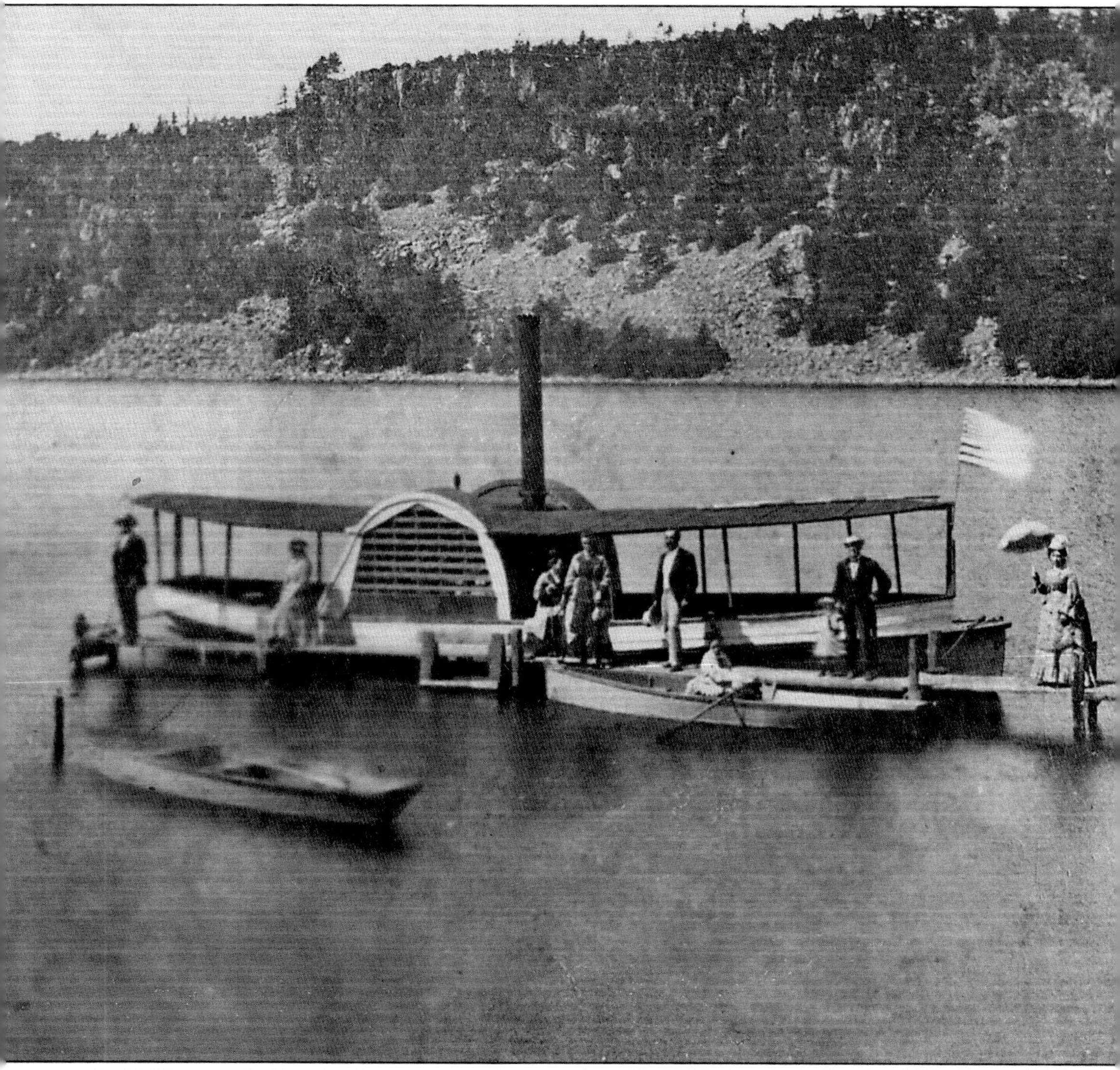

In 1869, a small side wheel steamer was launched on the lake, above, and named the Capitola, because it was purchased at the state capital. Its successor, the Minnewauken, was launched in 1874 and was even more popular with lake guests. Especially enchanting was when it was used for midnight concerts with the musicians playing from the middle of the lake. General Ulysses S. Grant was a passenger on the Minnewaukan on the morning of September 8, 1880, when he visited the lake with the owner of the Cliff House, Colonel William Vilas. The visit was short, but included a trip around the lake on the boat, which was decorated with flags, flowers, and a number of lion, leopard, and tiger skin rugs borrowed from the Claude home.

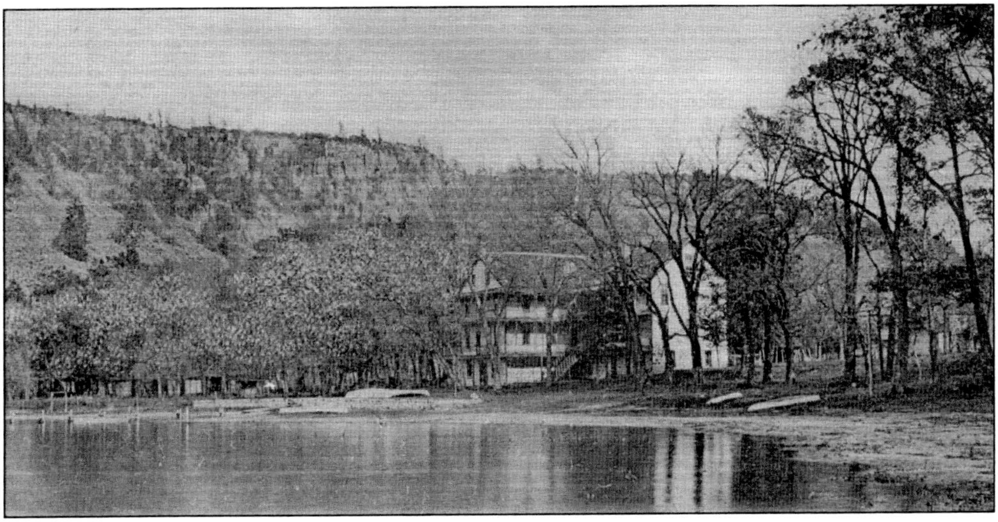

The south shore of Devil's Lake also had accommodations for guests, including the Lake View Hotel, above, and the Kirkland Hotel.

Activities at Devil's Lake could include climbing the bluffs or spending time on the water on a sailboat or steamship. The west bluff forms the backdrop for this photo at the north shore.

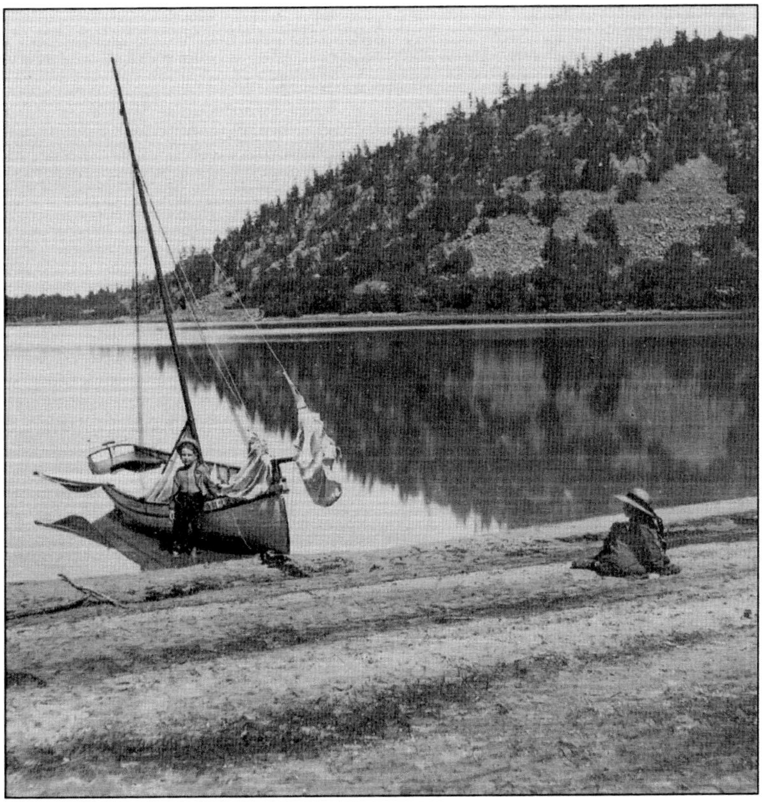

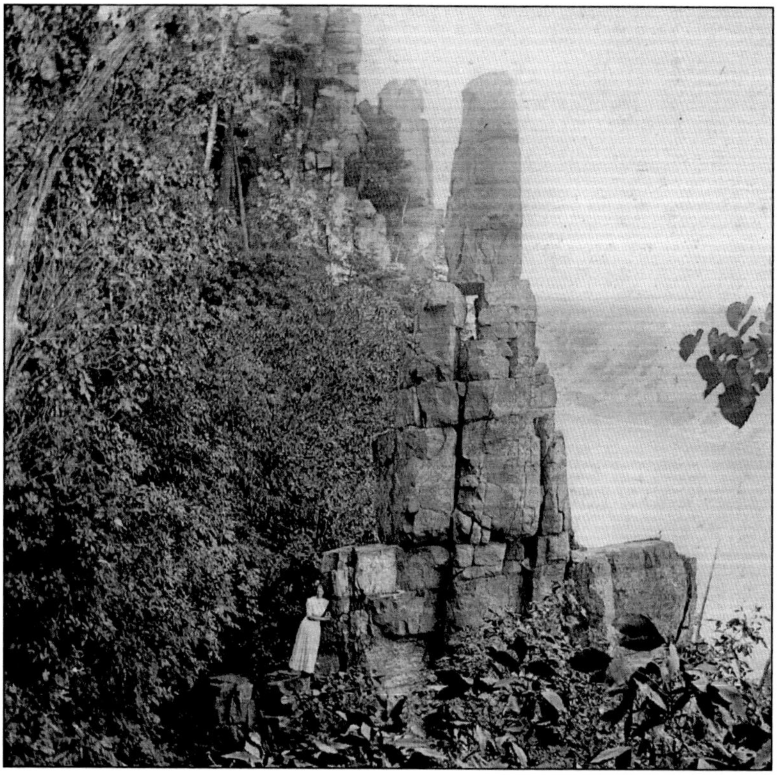

The rock formations on the bluffs at Devil's Lake were natural wonders that were given fanciful names due to their unusual shapes. Cleopatra's Needle on the west bluff, left, was apparently named for its resemblance to a needle and an obelisk from the time of the great Egyptian queen. Below, elephant rock, at the north end of the east bluff, was often the scene of an amusing photo.

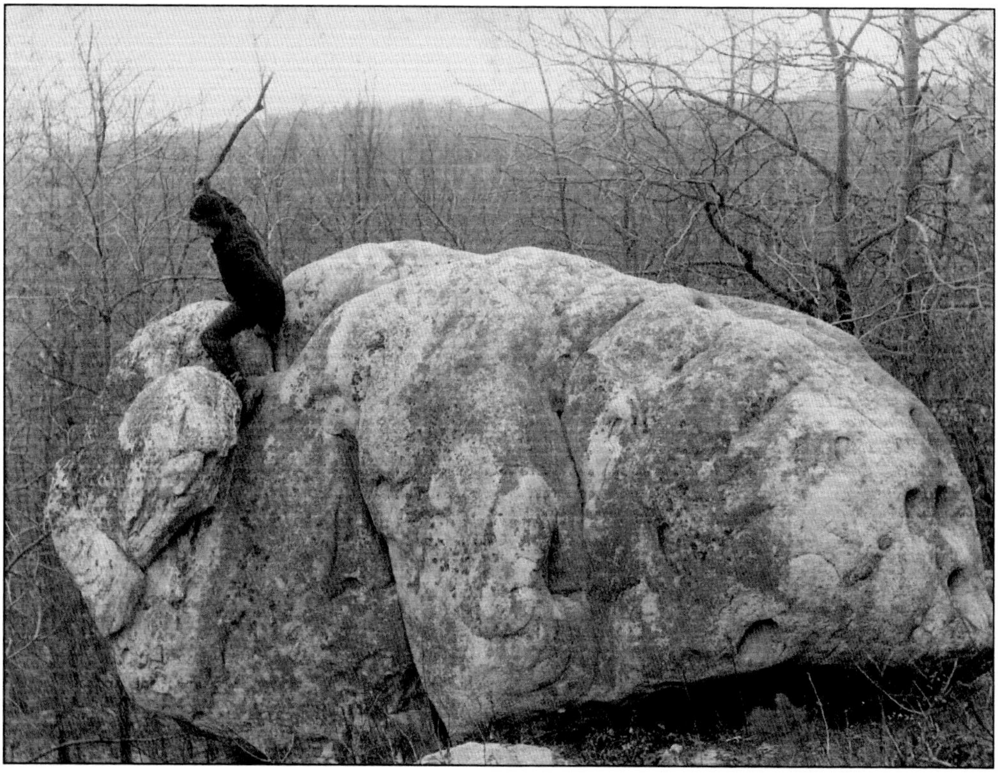

Devil's Doorway on the south end of the east bluff, is perhaps the signature rock formation of Devil's Lake. It was a good place to take a photo at the turn of the 20th century, as well as to leave some mark that you were there, above. By the time Devil's Lake became a state park, graffiti was a serious problem that would take some time to erase.

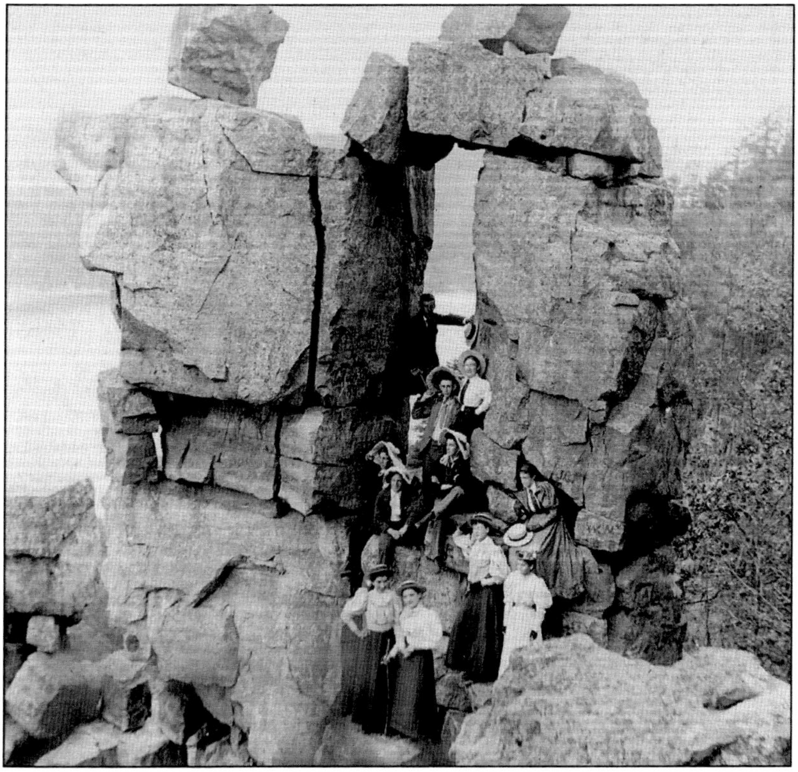

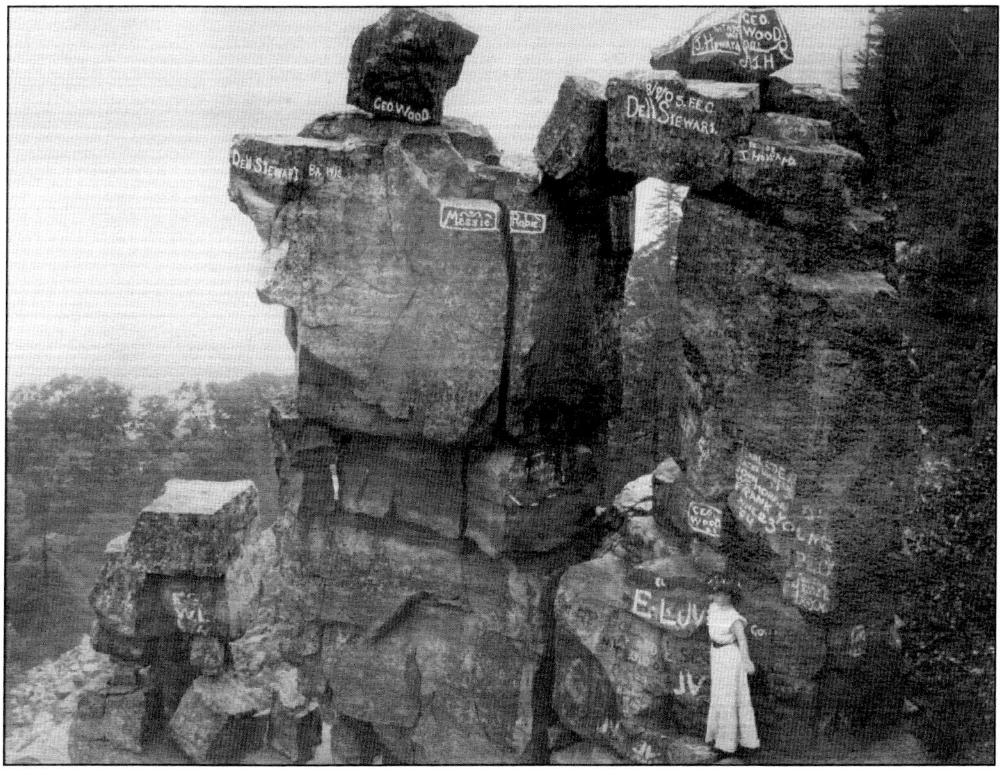

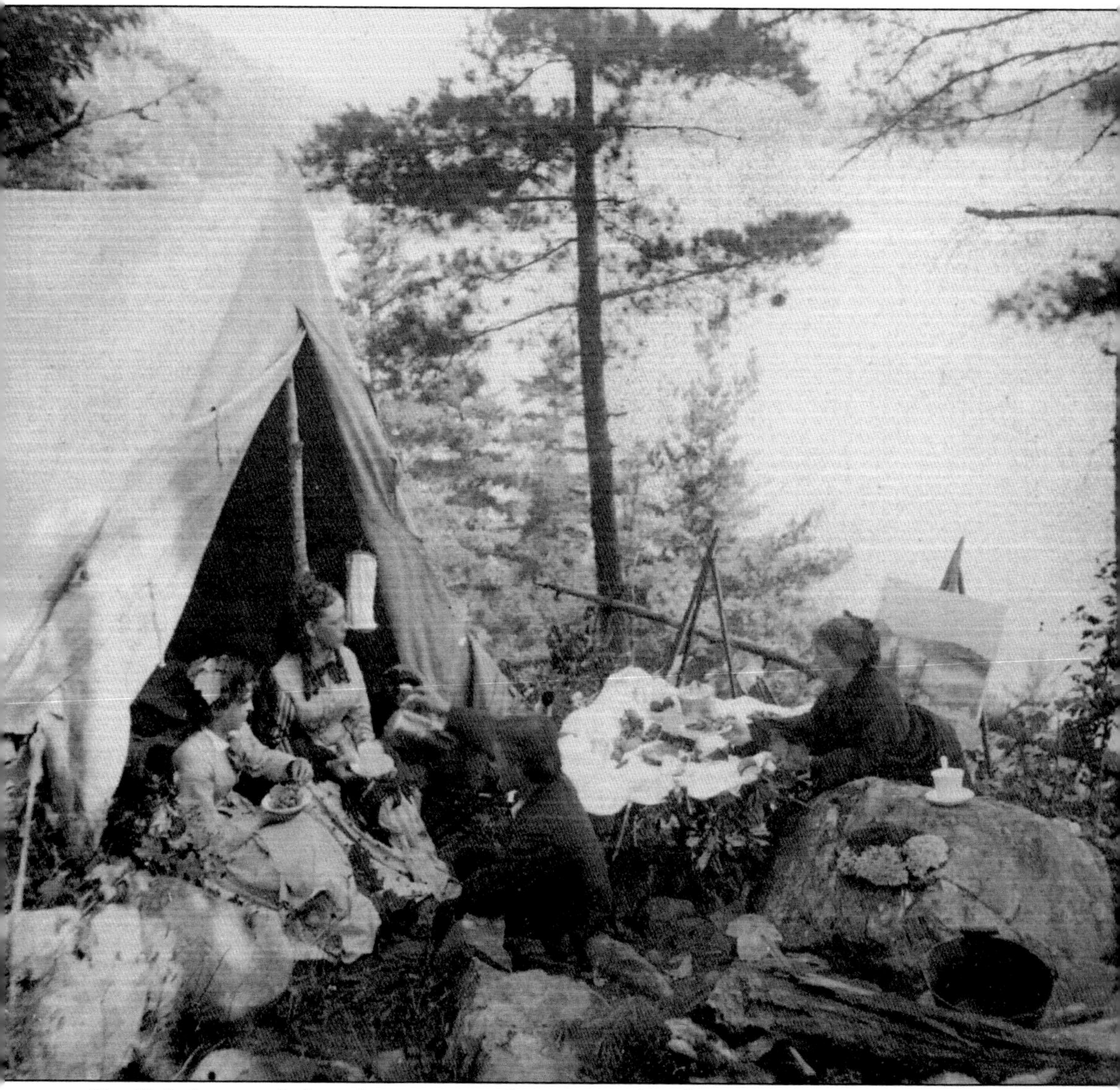

Devil's Lake provided ample inspiration for artists and nothing compared to painting the lake from atop one of the 500 foot bluffs. Even artists had to eat and sleep however, which could be done in style if one brought furniture, china, and food up the winding trails to the campsite. This image from a stereograph card dates from the 1870s.